1920

ALSO BY ERIC BURNS

⊸◈⊶

Broadcast Blues: Dispatches from the Twenty-Year War
Between a Television Reporter and His Medium
1993

The Joy of Books: Confessions of a Lifelong Reader
1995

The Autograph: A Modern Fable of a Father and a Daughter
1997

The Spirits of America: A Social History of Alcohol
2003

Infamous Scribblers: The Founding Fathers and the
Rowdy Beginnings of American Journalism
2006

The Smoke of the Gods: A Social History of Tobacco
2007

Virtue, Valor and Vanity: The Founding Fathers and the Pursuit of Fame
2007

All the News Unfit to Print: How Things Were . . .
and How They Were Reported
2009

Invasion of the Mind Snatchers: Television's Conquest
of America in the Fifties
2010

1920

THE YEAR THAT MADE
THE DECADE ROAR

ERIC BURNS

PEGASUS BOOKS
NEW YORK LONDON

1920

Pegasus Books LLC
80 Broad Street, 5th Floor
New York, NY 10004

Copyright © 2015 by Eric Burns

First Pegasus Books cloth edition May 2015

Interior design by Maria Fernandez

Library of Congress Cataloging-in-Publication Data is available.

ISBN: 978-1-60598-772-9

10 9 8 7 6 5 4 3 2 1

Printed in the United States of America
Distributed by W. W. Norton & Company

THIS BOOK IS DEDICATED, WITH ENVY, TO

Michael and Jan,

Mitchel and Kim,

Mark and Melissa

who, knowing the meaning of life,
will forever be together,
as was intended by the vows at the outset

CONTENTS

1920

1920

INTRODUCTION

I T WAS THE FIRST FULL year after the Treaty of Versailles had officially
ended the Great War, and Americans were not as relieved as they had
hoped to be. They were joyful, of course, but at other times saddened;
optimistic, but no less confused; enthusiastic, yet unable to escape a certain sense of dread. It is neither easy nor usual to hold such conflicting
emotions at the same time; then again, the year was neither easy nor usual.

Americans were joyful, naturally, that the fighting in Europe was over
and their troops were back home; but their sadness that the troops had
ever had to depart in the first place still lingered, as did an even deeper
sadness that so many young men had *not* returned. Americans were optimistic that the twentieth century could at last begin without interference,
and that its remaining eighty years would be the most productive and
profitable ever for the nation. But they were not productive and profitable
now, as, in the words of one historian, "a punishing postwar recession"
had settled like a cloud of mustard gas over manufacturing and industry
and would not fully disperse for another two years.

They were enthusiastic, though, about something else in the air, the
beat of distant music, music that had never been heard before, making
those who felt it celebratory, eager to twist their bodies into contortions

new and lascivious, unable to sit still. And, in some cases, unable to behave conventionally any longer. Some women began to smoke cigarettes in public. Some joined men in sipping cocktails to the point of giddiness, cocktails that had not even existed before the war and could be as dangerous to the imbiber's health as the war's weaponry.

Other Americans were also enthusiastic about more substantive matters: the League of Nations, which would never come to be, but which President Woodrow Wilson had assured them would bring everlasting peace to the world; and advances in transportation, education, and factory output.

Even so, they were fearful, a chill running through them as they wondered whether the treaty agreed upon last year in Paris could hold, would keep them safe. Might future conflicts break out regardless of the present accord, conflicts even more brutal than those they had just known?

Might those conflicts even be fought on their own soil? Might the armaments be more powerful? In the wake of the Great War, the French composer Claude Debussy lamented to a friend, "When will hate be exhausted?" He did not expect an answer.

Many men and women, soldiers and civilians alike, especially those between the ages of twenty and thirty, were, in the phrase uttered by Gertrude Stein but popularized by Ernest Hemingway, a "lost generation," unable to find their moorings, to regain their belief in the visions of political leaders who kept speaking at them. In the wake of the fighting and devastation abroad, they found themselves living in a world they thought was "shallow, corrupt, and depraved." They were suffering, as Thornton Wilder said about his older brother, who had served in France, from "some kind of radical depletion, made up of battle fatigue, sleeplessness, and nervous strain."

On the one hand, Americans were hopeful that the worst was behind them and ahead lay homes and employment for all, as well as families to raise and children to be watched as they grew benignly into adults never to know war, living as beneficiaries of the ease that technology would inevitably bring.

Yet, on the other hand, it might have been true that, in the words of historian Paul Fussell, "Neither race had won, nor could win, the War. The War had won, and would go on winning."

Nineteen twenty, and the nine years to follow, make up the only such period in the country's history to have its own clear identity, a widely applied nickname: the Roaring Twenties. But although the year that is the subject of this book was a preview of a decade, it turned out to be more than that: it would be a preview of the entire century and even the beginning of the century to follow, the one in which we live today. The year was like the trailer for a movie, and the movie was an epic beyond the scope of a director even as skilled as D. W. Griffith, a film of such sweeping proportions that it seemed there would never be a last reel. The birth of an even *greater* nation. But it did not start out that way. Nineteen twenty was not the happy-go-lucky year of popular myth.

It was then, for instance, that the United States pretended the Constitution was a high school term paper and, ignoring it, conducted raids on suspected terrorists, battering down the doors of men whom government agents believed had sent bombs through the mail to prominent state and local officials. Later in the year, terrorism on a much greater scale struck Americans for the first time, and among the reactions were calls for homeland security, although the term was not used back then.

But just as there were pleas to close the borders, so were there arguments to keep them open. The issue was an incendiary one, and disagreements, heated and sometimes irrational, broke out both in legislative chambers and private settings that housed family, friends, and co-workers. Were those who wanted the borders closed xenophobic, those who wanted them open unrealistic? Or were the former self-protective and the latter self-destructive? Was closing the borders even possible? The "perimeter" of the United States, a much more difficult calculation than it seems, one dependent upon definition as much as pure measurement, is somewhere between 19,857 miles and 54,670 miles; could such an area be sealed so tightly that an organism as slight as a single man or woman, a small family, could not get through? And, perhaps most important, did a nation of immigrants really want to do something like that?

It was in 1920 that the increasing power of American women first became legally recognized with passage of the Nineteenth Amendment to the Constitution, exactly 365 years after the first American woman had insisted on voting in the New World, demanding a voice in her government and being told she was not entitled.

Coincidentally, as the Nineteenth Amendment became law, one woman was already running the entire nation, although no one had marked her name on a ballot and few people even knew of her power. Many who *did* know resented it and found the circumstances surrounding her ascension intolerable. This could not be allowed to happen again. For the time being, however, there seemed no alternative.

Another woman, much less influential as 1920 began, would soon begin to touch the lives of millions, becoming much more powerful in the long run than the lady "president." Imprisoned a few years earlier, she had by now been free long enough to plan and begin to create the institution that would forever change the meaning of intimacy between men and women. She was, at present, simply looking for a place to set up her headquarters.

Yet 1920 was the only year in American history, post–Bill of Rights, in which two constitutional amendments were passed, and the second became the most openly ignored regulation in American history. Even by those who were normally law-abiding citizens. Even, in many cases, by those whose occupation it was to enforce the law. It had its heart in the right place, one might have said of the Eighteenth Amendment, but its brain was severely defective. Not only did the Amendment fail to be heeded; it often failed to be acknowledged with a straight face. Vaudeville comedians began to work it into their acts, and it always brought painful laughs of recognition.

"Prohibition is better than no liquor at all," said the humorist Will Rogers, consoling those who were victims of the inferior product so common in the twenties. Then, summing up the Eighteenth Amendment shortly after its repeal, Rogers asked a question: "Why don't they pass a constitutional amendment prohibiting anybody from learning anything?" he wanted to know. "If it works as well as prohibition did, in five years Americans would be the smartest race of people on Earth."

It was in 1920 that corruption in public and private affairs began their ascent to levels that were unprecedented up to that time. There had long been misdeeds in government at all levels; but when the presidential election that autumn brought to the White House the so-called "Ohio

Gang," all barriers of decency were crossed. The Gang started small, but eventually worked its way up to the greatest scandal that American politics had seen up to that time. As for the president, most people thought him innocent of wrongdoing, a bit thick-headed perhaps, but appalled at the behavior of his supposed friends. His regrets did not kill him, of course, but something about the timing of his death, so unexpected, made the citizenry wonder about the real cause of Warren Gamaliel Harding's premature passing. Was it, in fact, as stated? Why were so many possibilities being suggested?

It was in 1920, with the country prospering more than ever following the Great War, that many Americans, especially the most recent arrivals, began to look for the streets of gold that had been their dream in the old country. Most did not find them, not even a glimmer; in most cases, they found streets not even paved. And so America's ever-swelling number of immigrants lost all hope, however unrealistic those hopes might have been in the first place, and became cogs in the machinery that allowed the chosen few, the so-called robber barons, to make their own golden thoroughfares a reality, amassing fortunes beyond the power of the immigrants even to imagine. As far back as 1913, for example, John D. Rockefeller is said to have had almost a billion dollars in his toy chest, "or 2 percent of the U.S. gross national product; a comparable share today would give Rockefeller a net worth of $190 billion, or more than triple that of the richest man in the contemporary world, Bill Gates."

Actually, it was even worse than that for the human cogs. Machinery is maintained and repaired when necessary; the men who operated it were simply pushed until they dropped and then replaced by others. None of them had health insurance; workman's compensation (it would not be called "worker's" compensation for many years yet) was harder to get than it is today. The robber barons disdained it, called it socialism, fought it in capitalism's courts—which, for all practical purposes, they owned.

A few Americans, though, achieved wealth either by working hard or by demonstrating extraordinary vision, or both. A few others had parents who brought their own money with them from abroad. And a very few others, not having inherited a vast sum and too impatient to spend a lifetime accumulating it, figured out ways to stockpile a fortune in a different manner, and so easy did it seem that they wondered why others had not devised similar deceits. One man in particular would become legendary for his scam, a brilliant notion that started out legally but quickly went south, the result of which was that his name lived on, and continues to live, in ignominy. Long after he had been stripped of his millions and started running from the law, he died not only in poverty but in eternal night, thousands of miles from either his American or Italian home.

It was in 1920 that radical expressions in the arts revealed themselves to be what they really were: a rebellion in politics, culture, and the very premises upon which the *Main Street* type of society, a much more realistic version of the American dream, had been erected. In fact, Sinclair Lewis's volume was first published in 1920. But in painting, film, and music, as well as literature, there appeared goals and techniques that had never been seen or heard before; new genres were created and, refusing to settle for merely telling stories or rendering placid landscapes or other kinds of diversion, determined not to divert at all, but to demand. They would look beyond life's exteriors, into the soul not only of society but of the people who populated it; they would seek the most profound meanings, answer the most vexing of questions. They were aspirations that did not sound as naïve then as they do now.

There was a countervailing force at work, though, and in retrospect one sees it as the most important and enduring event of 1920: the invention of the American mass media. It began with radio, whose allies quickly became the newspapers with their tabloid value systems—and, in massing, the two media would form the most persuasive and pervasive of all American industries, as they went about making far too much of matters ever less consequential, the private lives of actors and singers, musicians and authors, comedians and athletes, heirs and heiresses, perpetrators and victims, millionaires and billionaires, and, later, disgraced public officials, pitchmen and anchormen, radio and TV talkers, sitcom stars, drama stars, game-show hosts, chefs, bloggers, Internet jesters, and even carefully chosen nonentities, some of whom would headline their own sublimely unrealistic "reality" shows.

Further, they would report murders, robberies, fires, automobile accidents—these and more aberrations as if they were common occurrences. The mass media would make so much of them all that eventually a tidal wave of irrelevance would wash over the United States, and by late in the twentieth century the entire American lifestyle, the entire code of behavior and range of ambitions, would be unrecognizable from what it had been in the nineteenth. The country would have achieved the un-achievable—the dumbing-down of its audiences as they sank into vapidity with gleeful abandon, as delighted with their plight as if they were riding the newest attraction in an amusement park. American communications—radio and television, movies and newspapers, and eventually the so-called social media, provided by computers and their offspring—would transform the most powerful country on earth in its military and manufacturing might to a third-world nation in its tastes and values. So it is today; so it gives every sign of remaining.

Many of the names that were well known in 1920 are still well known at present. In other cases, the historical record no longer seems to have room for them, but the deeds for which they were responsible still resound in either impact or interest or both. Among the former are Woodrow Wilson, Warren Harding, J. Edgar Hoover, Andrew Carnegie, J. P. Morgan, John D. Rockefeller, Charles Ponzi, Thomas Edison, George Westinghouse, Louis Armstrong, Duke Ellington, F. Scott Fitzgerald, Ernest Hemingway, Sinclair Lewis, Eugene O'Neill, and T. S. Eliot.

Included in the latter group are A. Mitchell Palmer, the attorney general whose raids on radicals resulted in more laws broken than terrorists captured, but who, much too late, might have solved the year's most vexing mystery; Luigi Galleani, a terrorist with powerful anti-American biases who was waved in through Ellis Island as if he were a visiting dignitary; Wayne Wheeler, the most powerful and deceptive teetotaler the country has ever known; Carter G. Woodson, whom most of the country did not know at all, a virtually anonymous African-American who accomplished more for his people than anyone until Martin Luther King, Jr.; Marcus Garvey, Woodson's antithesis, flashy in manner and attire, a highly educated African-American leader who undermined himself with self-defeating bravado and unrealistic goals; Margaret Sanger, who, without ever using the phrase "women's liberation," did more to bring it about than any other woman in the land; Edith Wilson, a housewife of sorts who suddenly found herself in control of the most important house in the nation; Edwin P. Fisher, who wore three sets of clothes at once so that he didn't have to carry a suitcase, and predicted the events of 1920's most onerous day with eerie precision; and thousands of anonymous but over-publicized "flappers," the young, un-lady-like ladies with their short, bobbed hair; their short, often pleated skirts; and their whirling legs, dancing to that distant music once it finally came close enough to move them. We can still close our eyes and see these girls, all a-flutter, a zumba class for its time; those of us who are old enough can still bring the tunes to mind.

Ev'ry mornin', ev'ry evening', ain't we got fun?
Not much money, oh, but honey, ain't we got fun?
The rent's unpaid, dear, we haven't a bus,
But smiles were made dear for people like us.

Such a soundtrack, such a cast of characters, such an accumulation of deeds, admirable and otherwise. Such a time to be alive!

It was in 1920 that the Roaring Twenties first began to roar.

But it was not the year that people think it was. The roar might have been a sound of pain as much as power, frenzy as much as affirmation. For during the uniquely hectic twelve months in which the United States first solidified itself as a world colossus, it did so despite increasing internal turmoil. Big government versus anarchy, conventional values versus unholy new doctrines, labor versus management, "wets" versus "drys," the lost generation versus the Jazz Age, wealth versus poverty, restraint versus hedonism—perhaps *this* was the continuing warfare so many had dreaded, struggles that took place between neighbors rather than nations.

It is an irony little short of breathtaking that the United States could grow and thrive and in fact enrich itself exponentially while engaged in such internecine struggles, some of them actually shedding blood. It was, at times, as if we were two different nations, opposites in temperament, yet forced by geography to exist side by side.

No less an irony is it that 1920 foretold the years to come so accurately. Foretold them, in fact, with such precision that there is an eeriness about it, a rattling of chains in the night. The story of the first full year of peace after the Treaty of Versailles seems on occasion as if it were as current as an e-mail alert, a beep that one hears within seconds of the message's arrival.

PART ONE

CHAPTER ONE

"Two Sheets of Flame"

ABOUT TEN MINUTES BEFORE NOON, on Thursday, September 16, 1920, a horse clomped slowly westward on Wall Street, tugging a cart behind it, struggling with a heavy load. It pulled over in front of a mighty granite building with a glass dome on top. The driver steadied the horse, looped the reins around the handle inside the cart, then stepped down from his perch and disappeared forever. Some people thought they saw him, but not well. A quick glimpse, a bad angle, a flash of sunlight obscuring the view. So later, when they told policemen what the driver looked like, they provided a variety of descriptions. There were, however, a few similarities, some features that kept being mentioned. The man "was very short and stocky." Of this, all were certain.

As for the horse and cart, even fewer people seemed to pay attention, and none of them were law enforcers. In this relatively new age of labor unrest, which almost always meant violence, a disproportionate number of men in blue had been assigned from Lower Manhattan to Brooklyn, where transit workers had begun to strike. Very few policemen were patrolling Wall Street at midday.

The animal tapped a hoof on the Wall Street cobblestones a few times, but otherwise did not move and did not seem impatient. Around it were buildings that represented the glories of America's past and its hopes for the present: the Trinity Church, symbol of the former, had occupied its current location since the end of the seventeenth century, before Benjamin Franklin was even born, and, after several renovations, continues to display its splendors to the present. Symbolizing the latter, and a few doors away from Trinity, the New York Stock Exchange was already planning to expand to another structure nearby with more offices and a larger trading floor. Next to the church was the United States Sub-Treasury and the Assay Office; and across the street, in all of its architectural grandeur, rose the J. P. Morgan Bank, with its granite walls, the peculiar dome atop them, and the horse and cart in front.

At the time, the Morgan boasted assets of $200 million, more than two billion in today's money. Numerous other financial institutions, in New York and elsewhere, were also thriving, if not as much as Morgan's. Retail concerns, manufacturing, the import-export trade, various service providers such as life insurance and financial counseling—most of these were profiting too, which is to say that, virtually, so was the entire American economy. The exceptions were few and did not cause alarm.

In the aftermath of the Great War, with much of Europe having been destroyed, the United States flourished almost by default; it was rich and on the verge of growing richer than any other nation in history, a nation being led by the robber barons, to whom we may refer as a second generation of Founding Fathers—no less brilliant, if in too many cases more brutal and uncaring, than the first. They were men who had re-invented the mechanics of industry, the intricacies of investment, the very definition of progress. And venality.

They began their remaking of the American economy after the Civil War, with the building of railroads. Several lines had existed before the war, of course; but now, with the country at peace again, the pace of track-laying became frantic, one company racing to cover more of America with iron strips than any of its competitors. This was especially true in the South, much of which had been damaged or destroyed by Union troops; as Reconstruction began, Southerners wanted their railroads reconstructed as much as anything else. They pleaded for federal subsidies to "lay down railroad tracks from somewhere, anywhere in the South to the Pacific Coast. In short, they wanted an infrastructure that would allow them to join the commercial-industrial revolution that was convulsing the rest of the country."

The South got its rails, and quickly. The North also got its rails and began to employ them with almost equal speed. The "technology of haste," historian Daniel Boorstin called it—and the result was that lines were laid in seemingly helter-skelter fashion, slapped onto the ground and hammered in, metallic trails now running from major city to major city, from village to mining encampment, from some place to no place. In 1900, 193,000 miles of rail were crisscrossing the United States; by the start of 1920, the total was a quarter of a million, and it would be 265,000 before the year was out. The hubs and outposts of the United States were being joined, woven together, in a manner no one had ever previously envisioned.

But the technology of haste, Boorstin cautioned, was also the technology of carelessness, "with little regard to safety, comfort, or durability."

MEANWHILE, AS TRAIN TRAFFIC SHUTTLED back and forth across the country and the railroads became the first great American monopoly, automobile production started and experienced its own rapid growth. Motorists were exhilarated when their cars were running well, frustrated when something broke down or even fell off as they bumped along a mud-rutted road, a frequent occurrence. "You'll scare the horses!" farmers yelled as the new-fangled machines puttered noisily past them on country roads. Drivers waved back as if they had just heard friendly greetings rather than cries for a more recognizable world.

In 1900, there were a mere 13,824 automobiles in the United States. Horses had little to worry about. But by 1910 the number had risen to half a million, and in 1919 it had climbed fifteen times more, to 7,558,843. In the following year, American automakers, most of them small operators who would soon be out of business, began to produce almost 2.3 million cars annually.

Unfortunately, the roads on which they traveled were "a national disgrace," nine tenths of them "made of dirt and in a generally appalling condition—with miles of chassis-deep mud the consistency of horse glue."

As for air travel, it was uncommon and erratic in 1920. Many airlines had three or four vehicles in service, but it didn't help. A small airline would go into business and then out again a few weeks or perhaps months later, to be followed by another that would suffer the same fate, and then another. None of the companies lasted, none offered dependable or safe service. Airports, as well as control towers, were nonexistent. In lieu of runways, there were farm fields; big, empty, and bumpy, with a line of passengers waiting for the next plane to arrive. Often, these passengers stood against a row of cornstalks, their fists wrapped around a handful of dollar bills—this despite the fact that each plane could seat but one or two passengers. Boarding and departing from the aircraft were not lengthy procedures; getting to the front of the line, however, could take most of a day. Those awaiting a plane, needless to say, were delighted to see one coming in for a landing, but if automobiles frightened the horses, airplanes positively terrified the crows.

BUT AMERICA'S MIGHT WAS VISIBLE in other ways too. As historian Philip McFarland writes about Cuba,

> By the final decade of the nineteenth century, Spain had installed over 100,000 troops on the island, charged with supporting a regime that had grown increasingly corrupt and arbitrary. Against so massive a force native resistance was reduced to guerilla warfare: burning crops, blowing up train tracks, striking hit-and-run at isolated detachments of soldiers.

In 1898, though, the United States entered the fray on the side of the rebels. The struggle became known as the Spanish-American War—and the Americans proved victorious, with a mere three months having passed from the start of the U.S. offensive at San Juan on May 12 to the signing of a Protocol of Peace in Washington on August 12. With those strokes of the pen, Americans removed the Spanish presence not just from Cuba but from the Philippines, where war had also been waging, and both countries now found themselves either "free" or under American imperialistic rule, depending on your political views.

As quickly as that, then, the United States had established itself, for the first time, as a military power with global reach. It was a new role for the country, which, in some ways, it seemed not to want, at least initially. There was no flexing of muscles after the war, no pounding of the chest—except for Theodore Roosevelt, hero of the San Juan Hills, who was always pounding his chest about something or other; rather, President William McKinley, soon to be the victim of an assassin's bullet and to be succeeded by Roosevelt, ordered the shrinkage of the U.S. military. In short time, it became "a small 'mobilization army,' focusing much of its time and energy on planning and preparing for future expansion to meet contingencies."

But, apparently, the planning and preparing were enough, at least for the time being. It was America's entrance into the Great War that finally brought the struggle to a close, just as it was America's insistence on punitive measures in the Treaty of Versailles that would lay the foundation for the next great war. President Wilson, remarkably short-sighted for a man of his intellectual gifts, had insisted on these measures, directed primarily at the Germans, perhaps seeking revenge for having been drawn into a conflict of which he swore his nation would never be a part. The Germans had made a liar out of the Chief Executive who, among all who held that office in the twentieth century, sought peace fervidly.

THE RAILROADS, AUTOMOBILE AND AIRPLANE manufacturers, and military forces needed steel, never-ending shipments of it, millions of tons. Only one nation could have met a demand so immense. Met it, in fact, with barely an increase in normal production quotas. In 1901, the Carnegie Steel Company, the largest venture of its kind in the country, had merged with the National Steel Company to form United States Steel, the world's first billion-dollar corporation. Capitalized at slightly more than that, $1.4 billion, which is forty billion in today's dollars, the new entity was, in the main, the doing of J. P. Morgan. His chief partner in joining the two firms, attorney Elbert Gary, was also an eminent fellow, giving his name to an Indiana city that would become an official entity in 1906 and would produce smoky, sooty, filthy wealth for the fortunate few until the American steel industry started dying its slow death more than half a century ago.

As for Carnegie, in selling himself out of America's bedrock industry, he made $6,098,351,361, give or take, in present currency, but he did not believe he had been overpaid. Neither did Morgan nor Gary—and neither had, for United States Steel now *was* United States steel, and its output had become staggering, its profits even more so. The railroads were satisfied. The automobile industry was satisfied. The military was satisfied. As for investors, some of the larger ones were beginning to believe in streets of gold after all.

Carnegie was satisfied too, even more than just that. The enormous sum he had been paid for his steel company, in addition to the hundreds of millions he had previously made in the business, was more than enough to fund his second career as a philanthropist, and until the Gates Foundation came along, he was the greatest dispenser of cash for good causes that America has ever known. For one thing, he provided money for the astonishing total of 1,696 public libraries, most of them in the Midwest, 164 in Indiana alone, and another 142 in California.

The philanthropist was one side of the man, and his nobility in this role cannot be overstated. But there was also another side to Carnegie, a side that made his philanthropy seem less an act of charity than an attempt at penance. Before Carnegie could give his money away, he had had to make it—and his methods of achieving the latter were the gruel of existence for virtually all who spent their days and lives in his smoldering mills.

NINETEEN FOURTEEN WAS THE YEAR in which the Great War began. It was also the year when construction of the Panama Canal ended. More than three decades after the French had started to build the waterway, the United States, still manifesting its destiny, completed the job. The $365 million, 51-mile-long feat of engineering was the most important sea lane ever created for shipping, and the first oceanic path of any sort to link America's two shores, important not only for shipping but for defense in the event of attack from abroad. "For millions of people after 1914," writes canal chronicler David McCullough,

> the crossing at Panama would be one of life's memorable experiences. The complete transit required about twelve hours, and except for the locks and an occasional community along the shore, the entire route was bordered by the same kind of wilderness that had confronted the first surveyors for the railroad. . . . This was a military rather than an aesthetic decision . . . the jungle . . . was the surest possible defense against ground attack.

MEANWHILE, BACK IN LOWER MANHATTAN on that mid-September day in 1920, six years after the Panama Canal had opened, passersby might have noticed something unusual about the horse in front of the Morgan Bank, and not just that he was old, tired, and sagging: he was also extraordinarily calm despite the din around him. "Wall Street seemed to be one great construction site," Yale University's Beverly Gage reports in her definitive study of the day's tragic occurence, *The Day Wall Street Exploded.* "Blasting and hammering echoed through the district's canyons, and shipments of marble, wood and machinery blocked the already congested streets." The new buildings would not just be plentiful, then; they would be elegant, made of the finest materials and designed by the finest architects in the world.

It was more good economic news, of course. In fact, as the *Wall Street Journal* had reported the previous year, and as was still true, "Sales and re-sales of property in the Wall Street district are greater than ever before."

The horse, however, oblivious to real estate values, also seemed oblivious to the commotion around him, remaining still in its midst.

As for the cart, the more it remained in place, the more it seemed out of place. The paint on the sides was peeling, the sideboards were warped, and the wheels were slightly misshapen, no longer perfect circles. The cart might have been red; it might not have been. It might have had a sign on the side; it might not have. The sign might have advertised one of the great companies in all of American industry; it might have named a one-wagon firm. Few people would agree on details when it was time to ask about them.

Regardless, the cart was not the kind of vehicle to be parked, however briefly, in front of a place like the Morgan Bank. There was something wrong with this picture. If only someone had noticed in time.

As the morning's end approached, there was no sign of rain, which the morning papers had predicted. The sky was clear, and the temperature, sixty-nine degrees at midday, also defied predictions; it was not supposed to be this warm. Humidity was virtually non-existent, almost perfect end-of-summer weather.

Suddenly, the Trinity Church bells added to the noise, beginning to ring twelve times, as they did every day at noon. It was the signal for employees of the various financial institutions surrounding the church to begin their mad rush out of the buildings, hundreds of men and women on their way to eat and drink their lunches. Journalist Mark Sullivan writes that "the sidewalks were as usual thronged with stock-exchange traders, brokers, clerks, bank messengers, stenographers—all . . . jostling each other as they sought to make headway."

Some of them ran. The rest walked quickly, heels clicking on the sidewalks making a clatter so constant, it was like the sound of marimbas shaking. Most of the people had only a half-hour break, and by the time they got outside, the bells had almost finished striking; close to a minute of meal time was already gone.

AS FOR THE FUEL THAT was needed to power America's extraordinary growth, quantities seemed inexhaustible. When the nineteenth century came to a close, Philip McFarland points out, Thomas Edison's "aggregation of ingenuity, imagination, and wealth adopted the corporate name General Electric," properly suggestive of the company's stature. McFarland also wrote that at the World's Columbian Exposition of 1893, Edison's competitor, Westinghouse Electric, had "powered the unprecedented display of 92,000 incandescent lamps all simultaneously and safely alight, along with an electric sidewalk in motion and the first modern electric kitchen."

By 1920, the United States was able to electrify a family's entire home: thirty-five percent of American homes, in fact. Ten years later, the figure had almost doubled. Similar growth was visible in the workplace, where industrial innovation became a commonplace, factory production increased, and stores and shops were able to stay open later and make more money—their merchandise, thanks to electricity, now brightly lit and the ambience cheerful and welcoming even after hours. The entire nation hummed with an energy that had never existed before.

BUT THE ENERGY WOULD NOT have been possible without coal either, which was being dug out of the ground in record amounts. In 1910, Americans excavated 500,000,000 so-called "short tons" from its burial places; a decade later, the number had climbed to 657,000,000. At first, it was more tonnage than could be efficiently transported, which caused such an increase in demand for railroad cars that even United States Steel struggled at times to meet it.

And, as if that weren't enough to solidify U.S. manufacturing dominance, the biggest oil deposits in the world outside of Texas would be found in Alaska in 1920. "While in Juneau Tuesday," the *New York Times* reported, several "Cabinet officers were informed of the discovery of oil in Southern and Southwestern Alaska and the *Juneau Daily Empire* said that 35,000 acres had been filed upon by prospectors." So far. More would be filed upon soon. Nineteen twenty was to oil in the United States what 1849 had been to gold.

By the end of the twenties, the stock market had climbed an astonishing 400 per cent. But the gross domestic product had risen only 60 percent, and as historian Bill Bryson points out, there was "little correspondence" between the two figures: the "inflated rises [of the market] had nothing to do with any underlying productivity; all that kept them so giddily buoyant was the willingness of fresh buyers to bid the prices even higher." The giddiness, as it would turn out, was a form of manic-depression; before the decade ended, the latter of the two hyphenated traits would be settling in to devastate the thirties.

There were, in fact, hints of the crisis to come well before it arrived, the faintest of scents in America's continuing gusts of optimism. In the year that is this book's subject, the November 13 issue of *The Magazine of Wall Street* provided one of them. "Fluctuations in sugar during 1920," it reported,

> were probably more violent than in any other commodity. Prices ranged from 4⅝ cents to 24½ cents for duty paid raw sugar and from 7½ cents to 27½ cents refiners' list price for refined sugar. To give an accurate understanding of the violence of these fluctuations the American Sugar Refining Co. points out in its annual report that an investigation of the prices of one hundred years, including the years of the Mexican and Civil Wars, failed to reveal a change in any one year one-half so great as the fluctuation of 19.875 cents per pound of [1920].

It should never have happened.

Neither should the wild swings in bond prices that were also a subject of the same issue of *The Magazine of Wall Street*. The bond market, after all, was known for stability, even more then than it is today. Was there something unsettling under the country's surface?

Meanwhile, as the United States was making its transition from rural to urban, from a nation primarily agricultural to one dependent on industry, lands devoted to farming began a startling and economically unsettling drop.

In New York, for example, in a trend beginning in 1920 and continuing for the next thirty-two years, crops were grown on a total, after those three decades-plus, of 4,600,000 fewer acres, about 13 percent of the total area of the state.

But 1920 provided only the first few signs of decline, and even if more people had spotted them, it is unlikely that they would have recognized them for what they were. *The Magazine of Wall Street*, after all, was hardly the *Saturday Evening Post*. As for the vast majority of Americans, they were willing to let the streamers fly and the confetti drop with complete confidence.

AS SOON AS TRINITY'S FINAL bell of the noon hour struck on Wall Street on the day of the horse and cart's presence, so did the bomb. Journalist John Brooks wrote that the "explosion darkened the area for several minutes with a huge cloud of greenish smoke, set fire to awnings twelve stories above the street, broke virtually every window in the immediate vicinity and some as much as a half-mile away. It bent the heavy bars protecting the Assay Office. . . . It shook to the foundations, but by miracle or chance did not materially damage, Wall Street's own church, Trinity."

People who worked nearby were horrified. "That was the loudest noise I ever heard in my life," said a long-time Morgan clerk, Andrew Dunn. "It was enough to knock you out by itself." Another Morgan employee, Walter Dickinson, who headed the credit department and was not going out for lunch that day, said, "I was sitting at my desk under the glass dome when I heard an explosion just like the sound of a Gatling gun." A man in the import-export trade reported that, at the moment of impact, he "was at the southeast corner of Wall and William Streets, walking east, when the terrible roar caused me to turn. I saw two sheets of flame that seemed to envelop the whole width of Wall Street and as high as the tenth story of the tall buildings." His reaction was to get away, far away, as quickly as he could. He did, but only after shaking off the spell of the impossible sight behind him. Two sheets of flame that looked like solid objects to him had somehow risen from the ground, hotter than perdition. The man in the import-export trade started running, but the heat seemed to be gaining on him even as he fled. In fact, the injuries of numerous blast victims were compounded by severe burns.

Joseph P. Kennedy, who would eventually be the patriarch of America's first family of politics, was a 32-year-old financier on the make when "'he felt a concussion' on exiting the subway 'and found himself on the ground. He got up in a dazed and stupefied condition and ran back to Wall St. where he saw clouds of glass flying and men and women there with heads split and blood streaming down their faces. Numbers were crying in agony and fear.'"

And a fifteen-year-old messenger boy, having just delivered a package, claimed that he "was lifted completely off the ground."

"Survivors on the street," wrote Brooks, "first fled the scene in wild confusion, filling the air with their screams and stumbling over the bodies of the dead and injured; then, in a matter of minutes, their curiosity overcame their fear of a second explosion and they surged tidally forward, joined by thousands of others pouring out of the surrounding buildings. Within five minutes there were ten thousand persons milling around the area. Underfoot, the injured cried out for self-protection if not for first aid."

Thirty-eight persons were killed in the blast and another four hundred-plus injured, fifty-seven seriously enough to be hospitalized. Among the latter were a few others who would be dead within the month. George Lacina, an injured survivor, worked for the Equitable Life Assurance Society and, having gotten an early start on his noontime break, was hurled down the steps of Fred Eberlin's New Street Restaurant. His face hit one of the steps, and the world melted into a soft red. The spiked railing snagged his shoulder and one of his lapels. . . . He later noticed that his coat buttons had popped off and his watch was ten minutes slow. "I picked myself up somehow," he told the [New York] World, "and said to a fellow who was also at the bottom of the steps: 'What the hell has hit New York?'"

Damage to property was estimated at somewhere between half a million and two and a half million dollars. "For several blocks," writes Mark Sullivan, "plate glass windows in stores were shattered and the façades of buildings were badly pitted. Several fine hand-wrought bronze doors were warped and broken." Further, it was reported, "A nearby automobile flipped 20 feet into the air."

The Morgan Bank, more than just a symbol of American finance, was in fact its very embodiment. And on this day, it might have been of special interest to terrorists, "as nine-tenths of a billion dollars in gold, in the form of small bars each weighing about twenty-five pounds and neatly packed in a wooden box, were being moved under armed guard from their old repository in the Sub-Treasury Building to a new one in the Assay Office next door. The workmen were carrying the gold along a wooden ramp across the narrow alleyway between the two buildings, and the spot in the street where the explosion occurred was almost directly opposite this alleyway."

Fortunately for the workmen, they had left the site early for lunch that day, before the blast occurred.

As for the horse, it lay on its side in the street, almost exactly where it had been when standing. Two of its hooves, it seems, had been torn off, but the number varies in different reports. The cart was blown to splinters; a later investigation would determine that it had contained the equivalent of one hundred pounds of dynamite and five hundred pounds of cast-iron sash weights, which acted, in effect, like shrapnel. A timing device had been set to ignite the explosives when they would do the most harm. It had worked to perfection.

Some could not remember their initial reactions to the explosion. They had been stunned by their proximity to it, so much so that they would never recall exactly what had happened.

Others, however, reacted quickly, emotionally, and erroneously. The Great War had not really ended, was their thought, and now for some ghastly reason a new front had opened, actually *inside* the United States. But why? Who were our enemies? What did they want? Was the despair of the past few years now to be replaced by a sudden dread of those to come? Could the American psyche, battered as it had been in Flanders, Verdun, and the Somme, withstand yet more violence?

The President of the United States took no action. He made no speech, issued no statement, did not reassure the American people that this was an isolated incident, unrelated to international affairs. In all likelihood, the president did not even realize that a bomb had exploded in New York. In all likelihood, his wife had not told him; she was his only link to the outside world these days, and she would not have wanted to upset him. He cried so easily now—something he had never done before, at which, in fact, he would have scoffed. If for some reason she *had* revealed the horror to him, Woodrow Wilson would not have known what to do anyhow. For the past year, his title notwithstanding, he had not even known how to be president. It had been a difficult time for Mrs. Edith Galt Bolling Wilson, who had never expected to be the wife of an invalid nominally in charge of a nation bursting at its seams with prosperity.

WHAT HAPPENED ON WALL STREET during the noon hour on September 16, 1920 was the first terrorist attack ever to occur in the United States, and it would be the most destructive until the bombing of the Murrah Federal Building in Oklahoma City by Timothy McVeigh in 1995, when 168 people lost their lives and more than 600 others were injured.

CHAPTER TWO

Homeland Security

I N RESPONSE TO THE FIREBALL in front of the Morgan Bank, both police and federal troops arrived *en masse*, as soon as they could, from every station and garrison in New York and surrounding precincts, some of them in other states: Connecticut, Pennsylvania, New Jersey. By the time the church bells chimed mid-afternoon, the crime scene was swarming with men in dark coats and ties, others in blue uniforms with badges winking on and off in the sunlight.

But that was the problem. So *many* people had descended on Wall Street from so many places that no one had any idea who was in charge or what to do. Or even, with any kind of reliability, what had happened. Eyewitnesses were plentiful, and eager to tell their stories, but they were also of limited assistance, for most eyes had witnessed something different from what other eyes had witnessed. Everyone agreed that there had been an explosion, but no one was certain *what* had exploded: a building, a construction site, a statue, a package left on a doorstep . . . a horse and cart?

In a situation as chaotic as this, it was inevitable that the cops and feds would do little more than add to the confusion, which they did by fighting for jurisdiction, by literally bumping into one another as they traipsed through the debris like visitors to a museum of grotesqueries, and finally by asking the same people the same questions several times over and comparing responses to no advantage. None of them had ever seen anything like this before; none knew where to begin looking for clues. And, as they would later learn, they had themselves greatly reduced the odds of discovering clues: they had perhaps even consigned them to the bottom of the sea.

FINALLY, AN ORDER: THE FEDERAL government assumed command of the scene and officials decided that the area around Wall Street should be immediately sealed off. The mission was accomplished, with blockades set up at key intersections and at the ends of principal streets—but it was busywork, nothing more. The man who had carried out the order, and probably even those responsible for the planning, knew that—to make an unintended pun that at the same time summarizes their actions—they were closing the barn door after the horse had already escaped. As for the man who had carried out the equine's suicide mission, he had surely departed several hours earlier, stepping down from the wagon after he had deposited his deadly cargo, then blending into the crowds or being swallowed up by them. In fact, although it would never be proven, what he had probably done was walked or taken a trolley to the docks and then boarded the first ship bound for Naples.

As evening approached, with authorities in Washington having been consulted and some already making their way to New York, a chain of command had been established. The federal Bureau of Investigation, or BOI, now took over. In a few years, the BOI would become the Federal Bureau of Investigation under the leadership of a youthful zealot named J. Edgar Hoover.

The BOI was issuing more orders almost before it hit the ground running. Among others, this batch included increased vigilance at all points of entry to or departure from the United States—but, once again, the immediate purpose seemed more a matter of busywork than crime-solving.

There was no reason to believe that the perpetrator remained in the United States. More likely, he had crossed the Canadian border or set sail for a destination from which he would never return to the scene of the crime.

But the perpetrator surely had not acted alone; and those who supported his deed, even those responsible for planning it, determined the BOI, might well have been Russians. In 1917, that country's revolution had overthrown the tsar and replaced autocrats with communists and socialists. The distinction between the latter two was minor and muddled, but together they were a major new force loosed upon the world, proud and ruthless followers of Karl Marx, who claimed to believe that all men were not just created equal: they *remained* equal for the entirety of their lives, and were therefore entitled to equal shares of their nation's bounty. Any nation, anywhere. The communists' vision was a grand one, even grandiose, taking in the entire world, the party's success in Russia having given it confidence that similar success awaited it wherever it chose to attack next. Which it certainly would.

From the communist point of view, America represented everything that was most despicable about the notion of government, which is to say that it was inevitably ruled by plutocracy, men of great and unearned wealth who had purchased the legislative process and found it the best investment they had ever made. America was not, as it claimed to be, a democracy, but rather the whip of the capitalists over the backs of the masses, resulting in the unequal distribution of wealth and labor, status and leisure.

Actually, it proved a fair assessment in all too many cases, and an argument will be made for that viewpoint a few chapters from now.

As far as the United States was concerned, however, Russian revolutionaries posed the most extreme threat possible to the nation's way of life, a disregard of the very pillars upon which a just and decent society was built. There were numerous reports of communists heading for the United States, flowing through Ellis Island, America's main port of entry, and from there into the nation's bloodstream. Even worse, there were reports of communists already here, working in dank, dark basements; choosing targets and assembling bombs. And worse yet, some of the bombs had begun to explode before even September 16, 1920.

At first, communists were known as Bolsheviks, a Russian word that, literally translated, means "those in the majority." The prefix "bolshe," put most simply, is "more." Less respectfully, especially in the United States, the new conquerors of Russia were known as Bolshies. Their uprising was the subject of a book by an American so sympathetic to the Bolshie cause that, when he died in 1920, he became the only non-Russian to be buried within the Kremlin walls, and remains so to this day. John Reed concluded his volume by quoting the following resolution from several factions of Bolsheviks after their victory. The first group to which the resolution refers is, in English, a mouthful known as the All-Russian Central Executive Committee of the Soviets of Workers' and Soldiers' Deputies:

> The joint session of the Tsay-ee-kah and the Peasants' Congress express its firm conviction that the union of workers, soldiers, and peasants, this fraternal union of all the workers and all the exploited, will consolidate the power conquered by them, that it will take all revolutionary measures to hasten the passing of the power into the hands of the working class in other countries, and that it will assure in this manner the lasting accomplishment of a just peace and the victory of Socialism.

Reed called his book *Ten Days That Shook the World*. It was too modest a claim. The West was shaken for much longer than that—for seventy-two years, to be precise, all the way through World War II, the haunting illogicality of the Cold War, and up to 1989, when the Berlin Wall came crashing down. Only then could the West relax from the threat of communism, for it was not just the polar opposite of American ideals philosophically; it was a form of government, albeit one that never worked as planned, which advocated and proudly accomplished acts of violence.

It might have been Bolsheviks who set off the bomb.

AMERICANS WERE ALSO WARY OF anarchists, especially Italians like the shoemaker Nicola Sacco and the fishmonger Bartolomeo Vanzetti. On April 15, 1920, two men—one armed and one not—were murdered in an attempted robbery in the Boston suburb of South Braintree. Each of the men was carrying a metal box for delivery to the main factory of the Slater and Morrill Shoe Company. Inside the boxes was a total of more than $15,000 for the company's latest payroll.

Sacco and Vanzetti, two men whose names are yoked historically, did not live close to each other and did not know each other very well. In part for this reason, they were not the only initial suspects. Ferruccio Coacci, who owned the house closest to where the getaway car had been abandoned, became, ipso facto, the leading candidate for the crime. But for only the briefest of times. Unfortunately for law-enforcement officials, Coacci was living in Italy when the shoe company was victimized.

For the time being, he had turned over his dwelling to a friend named Mario Buda. When police first encountered him, Buda was in the company of two friends, Sacco and Vanzetti, and all were thought to have been involved in a failed payroll heist the previous Christmas Eve in the nearby town of Bridgewater. But even under the lax standards for punishing foreigners at the time, especially foreigners who believed that the United States had been oversold to them, Buda could not be tied to either the unsuccessful crime on Christmas Eve or the bloody Slater and Morrill theft four months later.

When authorities searched Sacco and Vanzetti, on the other hand, they "were found to be carrying loaded pistols and a good deal of ammunition, some of it for guns other than the kinds they carried. They also possessed an anarchist literature." Still, "neither man had been arrested for anything before and though [Bridgewater, Massachusetts Police Chief Michael E.] Stewart had no evidence to suggest that either had been anywhere near South Braintree at the time of the murders, he had them charged." Not for the crime that wasn't, but for the one that was, and therefore carried with it the death penalty.

In May, Sacco and Vanzetti were formally charged with murdering two payroll guards and stealing $15,776.51 from them. Eventually, they were tied by strong circumstantial evidence, eyewitness accounts almost as conflicting as those about the Wall Street explosion, and their firmly held and often-expressed anarchist views. The two men pleaded innocent and would never waver, not even on the day of their execution.

The eventual verdict of historians would be that Sacco was probably guilty, Vanzetti probably not. That decision, however tentative though it is, would await the passage of many years; and in the first of those years, few people paid attention to the South Braintree murders. They were just one more crime, two more killings, and even more charges against anarchists in a country revered for granting freedom of speech. In 1921, Sacco and Vanzetti were sentenced to death for the shootings, and in the six years of life behind bars that remained to them they gradually but surely became the greatest martyrs in the history of American anarchy, supported by an ever-growing number of celebrities and government officials in this country and abroad. On the other hand, they were reviled by the judge who presided over their case, the thoroughly reprehensible, "Dago"-hating Webster Thayer, who spoke about the trial in the locker room of his country club as coarsely and prejudicially as a less-educated man might speak of it in a low-rent speakeasy.

But having already been incarcerated, Sacco and Vanzetti could have had nothing to do with the explosion outside the Morgan Bank. Or could they? Later on, in a strange twist of fate, the two men would be integrally, if indirectly, tied to the violence, a few more strands in the year's menacing web of events.

FOR THE TIME BEING, THE Bureau of Investigation turned its attention to other Italians, among them the notorious Luigi Galleani, of whom Sacco and Vanzetti were among hundreds, maybe thousands, of dedicated American disciples. Attorney General A. Mitchell Palmer was not alone in believing Galleani to be "one of the most notorious anarchists in the United States." He might have been alone, however, in his risibly rococo oratory about Galleani's influence on the flames of anti-Americanism "licking the altars of the churches, leaping into the belfry of the school bell, crawling into the sacred corners of American homes, seeking to replace marriage vows with libertine laws, burning up the foundations of society."

Having grown up in the small town of Vercelli in northern Italy's Piedmont, Galleani was the son of a lawyer, expected to follow in his father's footsteps. In fact, when he was accepted by the law school at the University of Turin, his future seemed assured. But while studying law, he determined that it was not the occupation it seemed; it was, in fact, not an occupation at all, but a means of indoctrination, his textbooks being really instruction manuals in servitude to unjust masters and their equally unjust principles. It was the role of revolution, Galleani concluded before long, to put law in its place. He dropped out of school and began a career of what he believed to be morally justified violence against everything for which the University of Turin stood.

Galleani arrived in America, which he had grown to revile from afar, in 1901. He was forty years old, eager to put his hatred into action. "With his neatly trimmed beard," writes Susan Gage, "and balding pate, Galleani looked less like the stereotype of the wild-eyed anarchist than like the lawyer he had once intended to be. Appearances were deceiving." They were also revealing. To look at photos of Galleani is to see a man who is not staring into the camera but through it, a man with a cold, lethal intentness about him. According to Paul Avrich, in his study *Anarchist Portraits*, Galleani was a zealot with a "hatred of capitalism and government [that] would burn with undiminished intensity for the rest of his life."

Like those who shared his beliefs, Galleani swore by the "propaganda of the deed"—and if anarchists had ever had such a thing as a slogan, that would have been it, another way of saying that one should express his beliefs not by talking, but by acting. And that those actions should be made memorable, emblazoned into headlines, should become lessons for all who could not see the anarchical way: kill the tyrants who occupy the offices of government and industry, burn their structures to the ground, and overthrow the institutions that supported them. The world must be reformed, and if, paradoxically, mass destruction was the first step in the process of spiritual generosity and the desire to enrich those less fortunate, so be it. The shortcut to heaven, in the anarchist creed, is the enactment of hell.

Despite his reputation for terrorism in Italy, where he had served time in jail for organizing anti-government demonstrations, and despite anti-American sentiments both spoken and written and repeated ad infinitum from various forums, Galleani had no trouble gaining admission to the United States. No one at Ellis Island stopped him or even questioned him.

The Justice Department's William J. Flynn, head of the BOI, was baffled by the ease with which Galleani had been allowed to immigrate. Flynn not only shared Palmer's fear of him, but despised him above all others of his kind. His eloquence, the persuasiveness of his speeches, of which he gave many, made him a figure of magnetic appeal, Flynn believed. He regarded Galleani as "[o]ne of the most difficult individuals the United States secret service has ever had to deal with, because he was the brainiest."

Soon after landing in America, Galleani began confirming Flynn's opinion of him, becoming a hero to all who shared his views. To name a few: Alexander Berkman, who would later try to murder industrialist Henry Clay Frick during the riots caused by a strike at the Homestead, Pennsylvania works of Carnegie Steel; Emma Goldman, who came to the United States from present-day Lithuania at the age of sixteen and, as the leading female anarchist of the time, as well as Berkman's occasional lover, helped him plan the Frick assassination attempt; and "Big Bill" Haywood, the chief of the country's largest pro-communist union, the International Workers of the World, or IWW, referred to by many as the "Wobblies." All listened to Galleani's speeches, all read his writings, saw the truth of his vision.

It might have been anarchists who set off the bomb.

LOWER ON THE LIST OF suspects, but important to an understanding of the unrest that plagued the United States in 1920 as it struggled to maintain its growth spurt and newly earned position of world prominence, was the Ku Klux Klan. Although founded in the post–Civil War era, a resurgence of the group, or, more properly, its third incarnation, was already engaging in its own perverse brand of vigilantism in 1920.

The KKK seemed on the surface a comical lot, as some of its original members, in the immediate post–Civil War era, went to bizarre lengths to seek a distinctive look for themselves. They raided a "Mrs. Martin's linen closet, draped themselves with sheets, pulled pillow cases over their heads and went out riding and caterwauling through the town [Pulaski, Tennessee] to the immense satisfaction of themselves and to the consider-able curiosity of the locals." Like children at play, they had passwords, secret handshakes, and nightmarish rumors swirling about them, which they delightedly encouraged. The Klan meetings were supposedly held "in caves in the bowels of the earth, where they were surrounded by . . . rows of skulls, coffins and their furniture, human skeletons, ominous pictures copied from the darkest passages of the *Inferno* or *Paradise Lost.*"

The group's ruling elite, over the years, included such absurdly alliterative titles as Klokard, Kleagle, King Kleagle, Grand Dragon, Grand Goblin, Grand Cyclops, and Exalted Cyclops. In local units, the Klaliff might be the vice president, the Klokard the lecturer, the Kligrapp the secretary, the Klabee the treasurer, and the Kludd the chaplain. It is hard to imagine a young divinity student wanting to grow up to one day become a Kludd, but such apparently was the case.

When several of the local groups met, or when they joined one another in a national assembly, the gathering was, naturally, a Konklave.

In reality, though, the Klan was not in the least comical. Its various reigns of terror, spaced widely in time and place, may be loosely compared to latter-day outbreaks of the Inquisition—with one of the differences being that Klansmen hated more widely than did the religious zealots who began their reign of torment in the twelfth century. The Inquisition's target was heretical Roman Catholics. The Klan, meanwhile, hated not only Catholics, but Jews, Asians, African-Americans, and Europeans who were not from the non-Nordic countries of the north.

But like Bolshies and anarchists, they believed in the propaganda of the deed. They would ride across the countryside in the middle of the night and, stopping at the home of someone who had angered them, perhaps by nothing more than his very existence, perform the demonic act that had become their trademark, the burning of a cross on the lawn. Perhaps they would do no more for the time being; perhaps, though, they would go further, entering the house and shooting their foes or dragging them into the woods for lynching or the administering of other forms of torture that would have made Torquemada proud. Perhaps the torture would precede or be combined with the shooting or lynching. The Klan was an assortment of genocidal maniacs operating on a scale almost too small to be noticed and certainly too small to be effective in its grand aims. But it was large enough, in some parts of the country, to qualify as an association of mass murderers.

The Klan were considered possible suspects in the Wall Street eruption because, by 1920, they thought the United States had opened its doors too wide and indiscriminately to immigrants. They wanted the doors closed, bolted, chained, and were angry when legislators did not heed their demands. The explosion, then, according to this theory, was a message from Klansmen to the Establishment to keep America for Americans, and to define Americans only as the Klan did.

Federal officials didn't really believe that an incendiary device was something the Klan would employ, certainly not one set off in Manhattan; the group's modus operandi was to act against individuals, not to take on large institutions, and to wreak their terror in small towns or sparsely populated farm country, not major American cities. But all possibilities had to be considered; the group, then, was among those scrutinized by the BOI, however superficially.

It might have been the Klan that set off the bomb.

BUT THE ATTORNEY GENERAL OF the United States didn't think so. Palmer believed the explosion was the work of the first two groups, which he tended to lump together into a single perilous mass; anarchists, he thought, were simply communists who had slid a step further down the scale of humanity, their methods more violent than those of communists and their beliefs similar—their membership rolls, in fact, probably including some of the same people. Further, Palmer had concluded that under the influence, if not the direct orders, of the dreaded Galleani, a batch of aliens had been responsible for a wave of bombings the previous year, a frightful introductory act.

In April 1919, a bomb sent through the mail exploded at the home of the mayor of Cleveland. Another device, similar in nature and also delivered by mail, damaged the residence of a Massachusetts state legislator. Attempts were made to kill judges in Pittsburgh, Boston, and New York, where the vestibule of the jurist's home was shattered. Neither he nor his family was injured; it is not even certain that anyone was at home. But such was the force of the blast that a young man approaching the house, apparently having after-hours business with the judge, was killed on the sidewalk. The only other injury in the series of April bombings was suffered by a maid, who, in trying to open a package, had both of her hands blown off.

The United States, Palmer continued to insist, was under siege. A "blaze of revolution" was sweeping the country "like a prairie fire," he stated, not toning down his language. He asked for $500,000 to investigate and combat radicals; Congress voted him the money as quickly as the ayes could be uttered. Further, writes Clifton Daniel, Palmer "announced that a plot existed to kill high officials and force recognition of the Soviet Union. Then, almost as if to prove it, a bomb blasted the front of [Palmer's] house on R Street in Washington." It sounded "as if something had been thrown against the front door," Palmer would later say; and it detonated, late at night, just as Theodore Roosevelt's married daughter, who lived across the street, was coming home from one of her nightly revels.

> Alice [Roosevelt] Longworth in her capacity as ever present historian witnessed the midnight scene: "The pavement in front of the [Palmer] house was marred with glass and leaves—the front wall looked as if it might fetch loose at any moment," she recalled. "Fortunately just before the explosion, the Palmers had gone to bed in the back part of the house. We went in to see Franklin and Eleanor, who lived just opposite. A leg lay in the path to the house next to theirs, another leg farther up the street. A head was on the roof of yet another house. As we walked across it was difficult to avoid stepping on bloody hunks of human being. The man had been torn apart, fairly blown to butcher's meat."

No one ever knew who the man was, or what he was doing in such an upscale neighborhood so late at night. Some people guessed, not improbably, that he was the bomber, and an amateur in the role.

Two months later, with the Palmers again at home, another bomb exploded, once again on their porch. It was shortly after eleven on the night of June 2, 1919, almost bedtime, when, according to historian Robert K. Murray, "a terrific explosion demolished the front of his residence at

2132 R Street N.W. Windows in homes surrounding that of the attorney general's were blown in and startled neighbors rushed into the street to determine the cause. . . .

"Upon examination, it was discovered that the attorney general and his family were badly frightened but not harmed, and that the explosion had probably been premature. The bomb thrower evidently had stumbled on the stone steps leading up to the front door and had blown himself to bits with his own missile. Only fragments of his body and clothing were found, but enough to indicate that the bomb thrower was an Italian alien from Philadelphia."

The clothing was a polka-dotted necktie, which enabled the man to be identified as Carlo Valdinoci. "This was a big loss to the anarchist movement," Bill Bryson believes. "Though just twenty-four, Valdinoci had become a legend in the underground. Federal agents had recently tracked him to a house in West Virginia, but he had escaped just ahead of them, adding to his reputation for cunning and invincibility." He would escape, however, no more.

Two bombs had now been directed at Palmer's house in two months. He, his wife, and their daughter were unharmed; still, the attorney general could be forgiven for wanting revenge.

But he didn't, having been brought up to rein in such impulses. He came from a family, in fact, that belonged to the Society of Friends, or Quakers, for which pacifism is a principal tenet. He and his wife and children frequently attended meeting, sometimes speaking up, sometimes just listening and reflecting, as is the way of such services. But however they responded, their devoutness was unquestioned.

It was for this reason that, in 1913, when Palmer was distinguishing himself as he served the third of three consecutive terms in Congress, he had turned down the position of secretary of war. "The more I think of it, the more impossible it becomes. I am a Quaker. As a Quaker war secretary," he said, "I should consider myself a living illustration of a horrible incongruity."

Nonetheless, Palmer was not a man to be bullied, nor to yield to opposition he deemed unjust, a threat to deeply held beliefs. He was known to his supporters as the Fighting Quaker. To his detractors, however, who held his religion against him and believed it made him timid in times of crisis, he was the Quaking Fighter.

He looked more like the former. Palmer was a tall man, handsome, a little over six feet tall and capable of filling out his three-piece suits with an easy ruggedness. At this stage of life, his hair was beginning to gray; he wore it brushed neatly to the side in two modest waves. Photographs seem to show that he was more comfortable with a stern expression on his face than a grin, but friends described him as congenial, if almost always distracted, during these days of great tribulation.

FINALLY, PALMER DECIDED HE *would* seek revenge, not just for the attacks on his house, but, more important, for what seemed a growing challenge to his country and its leading citizens. Thoughts of the vexing incongruity between his faith and his duties continued to plague him but could no longer dictate his actions; he had taken an oath, and his first responsibility was to fulfill it, to serve and protect the United States as best he could. In this case, that meant taking the offensive.

Choosing the second anniversary of Russia's Bolshevik revolution, late in November 1919, as his date for striking, he "initiated the first of his major deportation raids," Susan Gage tells us, "arresting more than a thousand members of the little-known Union of Russian Workers, an anarchist organization composed mainly of Russian immigrants. He justified the arrests as an antiterrorist measure . . . and a model for future action to contain the dynamite threat."

Palmer hoped to be the Republican candidate for president in 1920. His attack on radicals would be all the talking points he needed, but he also required a slogan. Whether it was his idea or someone else's is not clear, but henceforth Palmer proclaimed that he was waging war on "the Great Red Scare." It seemed to catch the public fancy.

The future action, the second of the two so-called "Palmer Raids," came on January 2, 1920. With many Americans still feeling the high spirits, full stomachs, and pulsing headaches that followed New Year's hijinks, Palmer ordered the "most spectacular" of his forays yet against perceived enemies of the state, resulting in the most spectacular of headlines. According to one New York paper, the *World,*

2,000 REDS ARRESTED IN 56 CITIES THROUGHOUT NATION IN
GREATEST SIMULTANEOUS FEDERAL RAIDS OF HISTORY

VAST WORKING PLOT TO OVERTHROW GOVERNMENT FEARED

The *New York Times* added these details:

> Meetings wide open to the general public were roughly broken
> up. All persons present—citizens and aliens alike without
> discrimination—were arbitrarily taken into custody and
> searched as if they were burglars caught in the criminal act.
> Without warrants of arrest men were carried off to police
> stations and other temporary prisons, subjected there to the
> "third degree," their statements written categorically into
> mimeographed question blanks, and they [were] required to
> swear to them regardless of their accuracy.

Many of those who wrote statements did not want to, refusing to confess
guilt when they knew they were innocent. In that case, they were beaten
until they changed their minds. When officials denied the beatings,
Palmer's assistant, the young, pudgy, and ambitious J. Edgar Hoover,
was asked to investigate. "I was sent up to New York later by Assistant
Attorney-General Garvan," Hoover said, "and reported back that there
had been clear cases of brutality in the raids."

The truth, however, at least according to some claims, was something
far different. Bill Bryson reports that "some six thousand to ten thousand
people (accounts vary widely) were arrested in at least seventy-eight cities
in twenty-three states. Again, there was much needless destruction of
property, arrests without warrants, and beating of innocent people. The
Great Red Scare proved not to be so scary after all. In total, the authorities seized just three pistols and no explosives."

Regardless of the truth, and there was a wide range of possibilities
in which it could have resided, neither series of Palmer raids uncovered
a criminal mastermind, a plot of coast-to-coast proportions, an arsenal
of weaponry, or a massing army of anarchists preparing to strike. The

Palmer raids, which had started out so promisingly for their namesake, would in time prove the end of his presidential aspirations.

NONETHELESS, THE *WASHINGTON POST* WAS among several newspapers that supported Palmer's beliefs and actions. "There is no time to waste on hair-splitting over infringements of liberty," it proclaimed. And, according to Robert K. Murray's assessment of popular opinion, neither was there time to waste on anything else concerning Palmer's second wave of assaults.

> The January raids dazzled the public. The mass of Americans cheered the hunters from the sidelines while Attorney General Palmer once again was hailed as the savior of the nation. In view of the obvious abridgement of civil liberties which the raids entailed, such support can only be explained on the basis that the public mind was under the influence of a tremendous social delirium—a colossal fear which condoned monstrous procedures and acts. Against a background of three major fall strikes, the Centralia murders [a conflict between socialists and American Legion members in Centralia, Washington, on the first anniversary of Armistice Day], and exaggerated press and official claims, that fear seemed so real it was positively overpowering. Said the Washington *Evening Star,* "This is no mere scare, no phantom of heated imagination—it is cold, hard, plain fact."

Palmer was not a vain man. Still, he could not help but agree with claims that his raids "halted the advance of 'red radicalism' in the United States."

HIS QUAKER FAITH NOTWITHSTANDING, PALMER WAS right in seeking reprisal for the package bombs, the threat that they posed, the deaths and injuries they caused. But he was far too cruel and indiscriminate in his methods. So believed a man named Louis Freeland Post, and it was Post, as Assistant Secretary of the Department of Labor, whose responsibility it was to rule on the warrants issued against the aliens. It did not take him long. He promptly found two thirds of the warrants to be illegal. He glanced at them, scoffed at them, dismissed them—that quickly was Palmer's work undone. There are different versions of what happened to the radicals who were not found guilty of criminal activity or thought by Freeland. According to Ellis Island historian Vincent J. Cannato, "only 762 were ordered deported and only 271 were actually deported. . . . In the year after May 1920, an additional 510 aliens were deported."

Whatever the correct numbers were, and they will never be known or even closely estimated, Palmer was livid about them, and no less livid about the cavalier attitude with which Post had seemed to act. He took a minimum of solace from the House Rules Committee's decision to begin impeachment hearings against Post in May 1920. He immediately began planning his testimony, intending to make of the hearings a last stand for the Republican presidential nomination, a final showcase for his beliefs that America was a far more imperiled nation than most of its citizens were willing to admit.

But the Fighting Quaker was not to have his day. It was already too late. "By then," Cannato writes of late April 1920, "the Red Scare had petered out almost as quickly as it had begun. When Palmer's dire warnings of a May Day revolution failed to come true, the public lost interest in the crusade. Congress quietly dropped its proceedings against Post."

Cannato is right, but the canceled hearings are a puzzling phenomenon despite the lack of May Day fireworks. One possible reason, Robert K. Murray speculates, is that "many domestic radicals had been so scared by the aggressive action of those like Palmer that they had lapsed into a sort of pinkishness which made them less conspicuous to a Red-conscious public." In other words, despite the excesses and illegalities of the Palmer raids, despite their inability to rid the nation of the prescribed number of aliens, they were successful, to a degree, in discouraging similar behavior in the future.

IRONICALLY, YET ANOTHER VICTIM OF the Palmer Raids was Palmer himself. In the aftermath of the first raids late in 1919, planning began for the second front, the following January. For the attorney general, however, it proved too much. He is thought to have suffered "a complete collapse," although his private secretary, Robert Scott, denied that his boss had been so seriously stricken. "The Attorney-General has been working under heavy pressure during the last three or four years," Scott told reporters, "and his doctor has advised him that it would be the part of wisdom for Mr. Palmer to lay off for about a week for rest and recuperation."

It turned out to be mid-December before Palmer could return to work, a month rather than a week; and when he did, it was in an obviously weakened condition. Meanwhile, most of the planning for the second series of raids, those of January 1920, had been carried out by his assistants. Their boss, though, had seen and approved them all.

But despite Post's determination that the raids had been largely illegal, Palmer was not dissuaded. Having returned to the office now and regained at least some of his lost energy, the Attorney General was more certain than ever that some combination of unsavory foreigners had been responsible for the mail bombs and would certainly resort to more deadly devices in the future. As a result, after January 2, he and Hoover made an even further hash of American jurisprudence.

Even before the new assortment of regulations had taken effect, Ellis Island had been one of the most inefficient bureaucracies in all the federal government, made even worse by an East Coast version of the Keystone Kops playing border guards; they were, said the *New York World*, a band of "one-legged, one-armed or decrepit old men," who were as inept at understanding the rules and procedures of immigration as were the men and women from abroad to whom they were supposed to be providing assistance. Ellis Island, the *World* continued, was on the verge of becoming "a perpetual joke."

But if attempts to comprehend the rules of entry to the United States were difficult before Palmer and Hoover intruded themselves, the results afterward were impossible, leading to the most massive traffic jams in the history of the country's grand portal. At times, prospective Americans were backed up so far outside the Immigrant Inspection Station that it appeared that they were forming lines to return to the ships that had brought them. "The passport regulations and the literacy tests have considerably increased the work of inspection at Ellis Island," the *New York Times* reported. "Nevertheless the number of inspectors remains the same as it was before the war, when the examinations of steerage passengers were much simpler. There is also congestion in the Courts of Special Inquiry and in the sleeping quarters at Ellis Island. Frederick A. Wallis, Immigration Commissioner, is trying to improve conditions."

But he couldn't. The Palmer-Hoover legislative mumbo-jumbo wouldn't allow him. The two men, exalted in position though they might have been, were themselves on the verge of becoming a perpetual joke. As for Palmer, he had by this time suffered the first in a series of heart attacks that would have kept him out of the White House even if his reputation had not. And in Hoover's case, although he might eventually turn into a perpetual joke, he would grow ever more mirthless and even vicious, as his power increased beyond the bounds of any elected official in the land.

EVENTUALLY, MOST OF THOSE IN the lines outside the Immigrant Inspection Station worked their way inside the building and, more important, into the country. For the most part, they stayed in the United States, despite the desire of Palmer and his legislative allies to exile them. In a very real sense, they would have had nowhere to go *had* they been exiled. Their own nations had been devastated by the Great War, turning those who clamored for entrance to America into the most lost of all generations.

The most reliable figures available tell us that Belgium lost between 1.34% and 1.95% of its total population; Italy as much as three and a half percent; France more than four percent; Romania about eight percent; Serbia somewhere between eleven and eighteen percent; and the nations of our foes, the Central Powers, consisting of Austria-Hungary, Germany, Bulgaria, and the Ottoman Empire, a combined percentage of between 4.89 and 5.82.

Most of the fighting on the Western Front occurred on French soil, where the landscape became unrecognizable in its ruin; homes and factories, shops and entire towns were leveled, becoming piles of rubble that would not stop smoking on the parched soil. Millions of acres of farmland were destroyed throughout Europe, with megatons of artillery shells having been dropped on them and measureless amounts of lethal gases having seeped into the soil. As a result, hunger and even starvation became as much a result of the fighting as death and injury. In Belgium, as well as northern France and various other nations, the terrain itself became victim to a kind of "friendly fire," as the soldiers defending the terrain dug into it themselves, creating hundreds of miles of unruly, unhealthful, and often useless troughs for the horrors of trench warfare.

The destruction of government buildings was the creation of chaos, at least in the short term. Without men to occupy those buildings, who was in charge? Who would sanction their leadership? What would be the basis of their rule? So many records were destroyed that boundaries of political units became a matter of guesswork, and titles to individual property simply no longer existed.

But the United States had suffered no such damage. There had been no fighting on U.S. soil. It had already been thought of as a land of plenty, rich where Europe was poor, new where Europe was old, bustling where Europe was stagnant, democratic where Europe was sometimes authoritarian. Now America became thought of even more favorably. The entranceways to Ellis Island became the mortal equivalent of the Pearly Gates.

In 1919, 141,132 citizens of other nations who passed through those gates achieved legal permanent-resident status. In 1920, the figure climbed to 430,001. In 1921, it almost doubled, reaching 805,228. Unfortunately for the Ku Klux Klan, between June 1920 and June 1921 more than half of the new Americans, about 520,000 of them, had previously been residents of southeastern Europe.

Many of the newcomers found employment in factories and as day laborers, adding even more brawn to the American workforce and the country's surging economy. But more often than not, the only jobs that welcomed them were so arduous that they seemed beyond the abilities of mere human beings, and left the men at the end of the day with aching muscles, bruised joints, and mouths so dry they could not produce saliva.

If only they could have stopped at a tavern after work for commiseration with their mates over a few cheap beers. But they couldn't. Alcoholic beverages were no longer legal behind the Pearly Gates.

PART TWO

CHAPTER THREE

The Long, Black Night of the Spirits

D OZENS OF FEDERAL EMPLOYEES BROKE the law because their boss, the attorney general, commanded them to do so in the name of national security. At the same time, millions of other Americans were breaking the law because they were thirsty. At midnight on January 16, 1920, a week after the Boston Red Sox sold the best player in baseball to the New York Yankees for $125,000, an event that was easily the worst investment any American would make until far later in the decade, and one that, known as the Curse of the Bambino, would have repercussions until early in the twenty-first century—at that appointed moment, eight months to the day before Wall Street exploded, the Eighteenth Amendment to the Constitution of the United States, having slipped through a back door of the state ratification process, took effect. The Volstead Act, named after a congressman from Minnesota, was the so-called enforcement arm, enumerating and occasionally even enforcing the penalties for breaking the law. America was now officially "dry." The sale, manufacture, and transportation, although, oddly enough, not the consumption, of alcoholic beverages, was henceforth forbidden.

The timing could not have been worse.

The groundwork for Prohibition had been laid forty years before the Great War, with the prim, pious, but ultimately untiring membership of the so-called Women's Crusade, whose tactic, ingenious in its way, was to pray saloons shut. A cleric from Boston who found himself in the small southeastern Ohio town of Hillsboro as the Crusade was getting started in late December 1873 could not believe what he saw.

> I came unexpectedly upon some fifty women kneeling on the pavement and stone steps before a [saloon]. . . . There were gathered here representatives from every household of the town. The day was . . . cold; a cutting north wind swept the streets, piercing us all to the bones. The plaintive, tender, earnest tones of that wife and mother who was pleading in prayer, arose on the blast, and were carried to every heart within reach. Passers-by uncovered their heads, for the place whereon they trod was "holy ground." The eyes of hardened men filled with tears, and many turned away, saying that they could not bear to look upon such a sight. Then the voice of prayer was hushed; the women began to sing, softly, a sweet hymn with some old familiar words and tunes, such as our mothers sang to us in childhood days. We thought, Can mortal man resist such efforts?

The answer, in the short term, was no. As men approached their favorite saloon and saw the women, among them their wives and daughters, kneeling not only on planked sidewalks but often in the dust that paved the streets, praying for abstinence, they were too embarrassed to enter the beverage emporium. They turned, feeling ashamed of themselves for what they had been about to do. They skulked away, hoping that loved ones had not seen them.

The result was the "Miracle of Hillsboro." In two weeks, all twenty-one saloons in town had been prayed out of business. For a while.

The Crusade spread: "east to Wheeling, West Virginia; northwest to Ripon, Wisconsin; southwest to Carthage, Missouri; and north to

Minnesota." The results, however, were not always similar to those in Hillsboro.

> Sometimes bartenders "baptized" the women with buckets of warm, sudsy beer, dumping the liquid over their heads so that they would return home from their labors smelling not of triumph but of conversion to the other side. On one occasion, and a bitterly cold one at that, a saloonkeeper turned a powerful spray of water on the crusaders, causing [historian Herbert] Asbury to remark that the "line of praying crusaders resembled a row of icicles." And in yet another town, a gang of thugs who had been deputized by the mayor to enforce a spur-of-the-moment decree against public praying threw a seventy-year-old woman down a flight of stairs and, after she landed, struck her on the arms a number of times with wooden clubs.

The problem with the Women's Crusade was that its effects could not last. There were almost always more saloons in a town than there were groups of women to pray before them. The Crusaders might close one establishment with their piety, but the next remained open. When the women moved on to the next, the imbibers simply sneaked out the back door of that joint and returned to the first. Their shame had been brief; their thirst endured. In the long term, especially when viewed from a distance, the Women's Crusade was little more than a game. Musical saloons. The habitués always won.

Nonetheless, a start toward a dry America, futile though it turned out to be, had been made.

IN 1873, THE WOMAN'S CHRISTIAN Temperance Union was created, and its strategy was not only different from that of the Crusaders, but much more effective. The group was largely responsible for the banning of demon rum and its kin in fourteen states. Most were Midwestern, surrounding Illinois; the WCTU headquarters was, and remains to this day, in the Chicago suburb of Evanston. But the membership has largely given up on a dry America and added to its roster crusades against tobacco and drugs, to which it devotes more time and money. Its guiding principle, then as now, was "organized mother love." In the wake of the failure of the Women's Crusade, it displayed that affection, free of charge, by providing educational materials to school systems whose budgets did not include enough money for needed books. Most American school systems were in that position and appreciated the WCTU's largess. But in return, the schools had to teach the lessons that the books, pamphlets, and posters taught. They were not the conventional three "r's."

"Tremble, King Alcohol, we shall grow up!" the youngest of students were instructed to say in unison—and an educator could certainly feel comfortable with a sentiment like that. The students *did* have to learn to read, after all, and to practice their elocution as they did. Then they were given pledges to sign, vowing not to imbibe when they had reached the legal age. Those who didn't want to sign were often chanted at in verse by their more compliant classmates.

> Young man, why will you not sign the pledge,
> And stand with the true and the brave?
> How dare you lean over the dangerous ledge
> Above the inebriate's grave?

IN ADDITION TO THE WCTU's fourteen states, a few more had outlawed booze during the Great War—temporarily, they thought at first—to provide U.S. troops with the grains they needed for their rations. But the real test for ridding the nation of alcohol would come after the war when, according to Congressional mandate, all states would vote on outlawing booze by means of a Constitutional amendment. To many, it seemed as if the government itself were conspiring against individual pleasure just when it was needed most, in the aftermath of warfare's horrors.

Support for the Amendment, which would be the Eighteenth, was gathering momentum, and the momentum was real; what it represented, however, was not. There was never a time when a majority of Americans supported Prohibition, never a time when they wanted, en masse, to deny themselves the satisfactions and consolations of beer, wine, and whiskey.

It was a tiny yet zealous group of non-drinkers that was responsible for Congress's decision to consider outlawing alcoholic beverages and the states' decisions to approve it—and that group would not be dissuaded by the thirsts of the multitude.

It was called the Anti-Saloon League, and the name was clever in its duplicity, as it implied that its only purpose was to rid communities of their most disreputable businesses. A saloon was not just a place that served alcohol but, by connotation, did so in unsavory surroundings. The talk was loud and obscene, the odor offensive, the décor un-decorous, the furniture scratched and stained, an uppercut to the chin the preferred means of settling disputes, and the behavior lewd—and even more lewd if purchased in an upstairs bedroom where both the sheets and the women were seldom changed.

And so the ASL won the support not only of non-drinkers, but of people who preferred to sip their beverages in more pleasant surroundings: well-tended taverns, restaurants, their own homes. The League seemed to support just that, only that. Yet its true purpose was not just to shut down saloons; it was to ban the products they dispensed. Such a sweeping vision would have come as a surprise to many of the League's less attentive members, those who might have skimmed the ASL's written material without paying attention to the fine print; but what they had signed on for was total abstinence, not a drop of the devil's beverages from sea to shining sea.

The League was headed by Wayne Wheeler, himself tiny yet zealous, a man whose wire-rimmed glasses rested upon a steely resolve: as a younger man he had been known to his college chums as a "locomotive in trousers," and he had never slowed down since in pursuit of his goals. It was because of Wheeler that the ASL turned into one of America's first all-powerful, government-bending, will-of-the-people-altering band of lobbyists—more powerful than the National Rifle Association, already in existence, would become midway through the twentieth century; more influential than the American Association of Retired Persons has been for several decades as this is written, early in the twenty-first century.

Wheeler was a remarkable fellow. He grew up lonely, with no nearby children of his approximate age as playmates, and few material possessions, on a small farm outside Brookfield, Ohio. In a book called *The Spirits of America: A Social History of Alcohol*, I wrote about Wheeler's early boyhood. It provided him, he claimed, with a life-changing experience:

> One day a laborer on the farm had a few belts of whiskey, then began feeding a bale of hay to some horses. Wheeler stood close to him, too close, and the man accidentally stabbed him in the leg with his pitchfork. Wheeler fell backward, crying out, then quickly clutched at the wound to stop the bleeding, which seems to have been profuse. Other farmhands rushed to help, carrying the boy into the house and getting the leg bandaged. If his later account of the mishap is accurate—and one cannot help but suspect a bit of tailoring for dramatic effect—what Wheeler said at the moment was, "I hope that some day there won't be any more liquor to make men drunk." He also claimed that, even after many years had passed, he could still remember the terrible alcoholic reek of the man with the pitchfork, and the shimmery flush of his skin.

Whether the account is true or dramatized, Wheeler had taken his first steps along the road that would lead him to the Anti-Saloon League, a well-financed group already in existence, founded by a minister named Howard Hyde Russell. In time, Russell would cede control of his mission to the young man who, upon his graduation from Oberlin College, Russell would come to consider his protégé. It was at that moment, when the baton was passed, that what had been just another collection of drys was transformed into a force that American lawmakers would find irresistible. Wheeler simply never tired, never ran out of ideas, never took no for an answer when he could respond with either reason or a threat.

For instance, at one point he communicated with A. Mitchell Palmer, not yet attorney general but rather the government's Custodian of Alien Property, a wartime office whose responsibility it was to seize and sometimes sell materials confiscated from the enemy in battle. Wheeler did not know Palmer but had made it a point to learn his sympathies, and played upon not only his latent xenophobia but, more specifically, his disdain for all things German that had resulted from the Great War. Wheeler sent a letter to Palmer, saying he had been "informed that there are a number of breweries in this country which are owned in part by alien enemies. It is reported to me that the Anheuser-Busch Company and some of the Milwaukee companies are largely controlled by alien Germans. . . . Have you made an investigation?"

It didn't matter to Wheeler whether an investigation had been made or not. *Of course* Germans owned breweries in the United States; the very name of their products made that clear, and the very nature of the German culture made it inevitable. Wheeler's intention was merely to call attention to the issue—to raise consciousness, as it would be said today—and, according to plan, he had done so with a man who was especially receptive to the dangers of outside influence in the United States.

Wheeler's first widespread effort to affect public opinion was as direct as could be. He instructed ASL members all over the country to stop their fellow citizens on the street and, once they did, writes historian Ethan Mordden, they "pleaded, they wheedled, they harangued, they threatened. And they appealed to voters' lambent Christian righteousness: 'Don't you want to end the distress of the wine widow and her starving children? Close the saloon and bring her husband home!'"

But the League was more effective operating behind the scenes than in being the scene themselves. To clergymen, for instance, Wheeler's minions privately suggested that a congregation whose members were not hung over from Saturday-night revels would be a more attentive congregation Sunday morning, more likely to take the sermon to heart, more likely to follow the paths of purity, more likely to drop coins into the collection basket. To the robber barons—Carnegie, Henry Frick, Henry Ford, Pierre du Pont, Gustavus Swift, John D. Rockefeller Sr. and Jr., and others—the ASL suggested that a sober workforce would be less likely to slow up production by getting body parts caught in machinery. Such an impression did this point make on the younger Rockefeller, it is said, that he "actually purchased, and then razed, several breweries and distilleries, the rubble a much-appreciated present for Wayne Wheeler."

And although Wheeler himself had never had any previous experience in government and never held any office, either elective or appointed, the

League under his tutelage was masterful at back-room political maneuvering. He proudly explained his method.

> I do it the way the [political] bosses do it, with minorities. There are some anti-saloon votes in every community. I and other speakers increase the number and passion of them. I list and bind them to vote as I bid. I say, "We'll all vote against the men in office who won't support our bills. We'll vote for candidates who will promise to. They'll break their promise. Sure. Next time we'll break them." And we can. We did. Our swinging, solid minorities, no matter how small, counted.

So effective did Wheeler turn out to be as a political manipulator that, according to biographer Justin Steuart, there was a point at which he

> controlled six Congresses, dictated to two Presidents of the United States, directed legislation for the most important elective state and federal offices, held the balance of power in both Republican and Democratic parties, distributed more patronage than any dozen other men, supervised a federal bureau from the outside without official authority, and was recognized by friend and foe alike as the most masterful and powerful single individual in the United States.

The hyperbole seems to leap off the page. But it is not as great as one might think; nor is it exaggeration to state, as Steuart does, that a number of political figures at the federal, state, and local levels "served under" Wheeler at various times. His power could be overstated, but it was real and it made a difference.

In fact, only once during the reign of the Anti-Saloon League did the trousered locomotive overreach himself. It happened when he approached the White House, only to have President Wilson refuse the ASL's plea "demanding," as I wrote in *Spirits*, "that a worldwide prohibition of alcoholic beverages be written into the Treaty of Versailles. Wilson did not agree. He did not even respond, nor discuss the matter with his advisers. He figured he had enough problems with the postwar world as it was.

Wayne Wheeler was not surprised. He had already suspected Wilson of cowardice.

THE ANTI-SALOON LEAGUE'S SUCCESS WAS, although unrecognized by most historians, one of the most significant and dismal episodes in all of American history. Political bosses had controlled their "swinging, solid minorities" long before Wheeler came along; and representatives of industries like steel and railroads had slipped wads of cash into the pockets of many a legislator. But these men were less an organized group than a series of powerful individuals paying for favors at different times for different reasons.

It was Wayne Wheeler whose efforts, it may be said, institutionalized the beginning of the end of the republic that the Founding Fathers had imagined. The point is arguable, but a strong case can be made for viewing the Anti-Saloon League as the death knell for majority rule in the United States, the end of the sovereignty of the people and the transfer of political power to passionately committed special-interest groups who began to sow both money and intimidation throughout the halls of government to achieve their ends. If this is so, then an equally strong case can be made for lobbying, in the modern sense, having been born in 1920, and having been brought into existence by a man who, unlike many of today's lobbyists, was not in it for the money, but for the cause. The tiny man with the iron-rimmed glasses was a true believer. They are, of course, the most dangerous kind.

In truth, Wheeler was a kind of robber baron himself. But he did not hoard money. What he hoarded was votes.

WITH PROHIBITION OFFICIALLY BEGINNING AT 12:01 A.M. on January 16, 1920, it is probably fair to say that attempts to avoid it began around 12:02. Since the ingredients to make ersatz kinds of beverage were still available on various black markets that had sprung up almost simultaneously with Prohibition's enactment, and available as well under drugstore counters manned by friendly pharmacists, many Americans had readied themselves in advance. They had purchased equipment as well as ingredients; they were able to start making their own alcoholic concoctions as soon as the need came upon them.

Most commonly, they brewed their own beer. It was far from being the real thing, but if a person had a good memory of the way beer tasted yesterday, he could get by with home brew today, could drink his way through the long, black night of the spirits now under way, recalling on his reminiscences as well as his taste buds. And if he had enough perseverance, enough zest for experimentation, he could keep making his product better, closer and closer to the beverage he had once known. For some who achieved proximity, brewing became a business, and they sold their surplus to friends, sometimes even to strangers who had not acquired the knack of manufacturing beer at home themselves. For others, beer production turned into a hobby, all-consuming and much more rewarding than collecting stamps or building those little ships inside tiny bottles. For most, though, home brew was just a means of slaking thirst, not quite satisfactory but better than the punchless alternatives.

So Americans had at it. They began malting, mashing, boiling, hopping, fermenting, siphoning, and settling. It was a complicated process, but few of the newly thirst-obsessed would be dissuaded. They took all the steps that a professional brewer would have taken, but did so amateurishly. A little less water, a little more malt. How to add the hops, what to do with the yeast? Or should it be *more* water and *less* malt? It was constant trial and error. Before long, some people noticed,

> [t]he air became thick with new kinds of industrial fumes; it was on some occasions possible for a person to walk an entire town or city block, if not more, without ever losing the scent of brew from the residences he passed. And after a man of unknown identity had paddled a canoe the entire length of the Mississippi River, he told the friends who greeted him in New Orleans that the telltale odors of home brew had been with him since Minnesota.

Actually, Prohibition would eventually be flouted to such an extent that a congressman from New York City named Fiorello La Guardia made a public exhibition of his disregard. One day he invited friends, fellow legislators, casual passersby, and reporters and newsreel cameramen into the lobby of that bastion of national lawmaking, the Office Building of the House of Representatives. He even invited the Capitol Hill constabulary, whose attendance was, to say the least, awkward. La Guardia wanted it to be. They stood in the back of the crowd, barely able to see. He asked them to step forward, wanted them to have a better view. They silently declined, fingering the handcuffs looped to their belts.

La Guardia went quickly to work, concocting his beverage by a simpler method than the one previously described, resulting in an inferior taste. But he wanted to keep the demonstration brief. "He blended two parts malt tonic, 'heretofore of interest only to anemics and easy to obtain at almost any drugstore,' to one part 'near beer [a brew with minimal alcoholic content, and legal under Prohibition].' He stirred the ingredients and allowed a few seconds to pass to heighten the suspense. Then he drank up and licked his lips. The cameras zoomed in. 'A brewmaster was standing by to sample the mixture,' historian Geoffrey Perrett records. 'He pronounced it delicious.'"

In all likelihood, he was exaggerating. But no matter—taste was not the point here: defiance was. The onlookers applauded lustily. All except the police, of course. La Guardia raised his glass in their direction, toasting their presence. Should they arrest him? they asked themselves. Each man looked to the next for guidance, but one blank face merely encountered another.

When no one formed his features into decisiveness, much less said anything, the cops concluded that taking a congressman into custody for violating an edict already held in such contempt by so many would not be wise, especially when he was surrounded by a mob of his supporters, a mob that might decide to show its support for La Guardia by menacing those in uniform.

After a few seconds, the cops dispersed, slowly walking away from the exhibition in the House lobby. The applause for the congressman still rippled as the gendarmes disappeared down the Capitol steps. As they did, the crowd closed in on La Guardia, hoping for a few pointers or, if they were lucky, a sip or two of his beverage.

It was perhaps the most outrageously contemptuous public display of lawbreaking ever committed by an American congressman. It didn't seem to affect his legacy. Two decades later, after five terms in the House of Representatives and notable service as the mayor of the country's largest city, the New York Municipal Airport was named LaGuardia Airport, and so it remains today.

Henry Louis Mencken, the most fascinatingly readable journalist ever to opine in the United States, was dismayed to report that he did not have as much luck as La Guardia. "Last Sunday," he related, "I manufactured five gallons of Methodistbrau, but I bottled it too soon, and the result has been a series of fearful explosions. Last night I had three quart bottles in my side yard, cooling in a bucket. Two went off at once, bringing my neighbor out of his house with yells. He thought the Soviets had seized the town."

By 1920, breaking the Prohibition law was such a common activity that entire families engaged in it, perhaps bringing themselves closer together as they might have done in an earlier generation by having Bible discussions, or perhaps playing a card game by candlelight after dinner. The historian John Kobler tells a commonly recited verse of the time:

> Mother's in the kitchen
> Washing out the jugs;
> Sister's in the pantry
> Bottling the suds;
> Father's in the cellar
> Mixing up the hops;
> Johnny's on the front porch
> Watching for the cops

IT WASN'T JUST BEER, THOUGH, that Americans turned into a do-it-yourself industry. The pastime also extended to liquor, and the most commonly reproduced variety was bathtub gin, so called because of the container in which it was sometimes stored, the quantities it could hold for mass consumption. The recipe was simpler than that for beer, although, depending on the amount a person wanted to produce, more time-consuming and physically demanding.

In a kettle, one heated corn sugar mash, a product used almost solely to make alcoholic beverages, yet, because of a loophole in the Volstead Act, still on the market. When the mash reached a temperature of 180 degrees Fahrenheit, the newly bred distiller slipped on a pair of gloves, trapped the steam with a cloth, and wrung the cloth into a bowl. He wrung as hard as he could, to get as much liquid as he could into the container. Then he kept trapping, kept wringing, trapping, wringing. The yield was pure alcohol, minuscule amounts of it with each wring, but too deadly to drink at that strength. It was, however, in sufficient quantity, an ideal base to create facsimiles of almost every kind of whiskey known to pre–Eighteenth Amendment man. For instance, something like gin could be concocted by adding the right amounts of water, glycerine, and juniper oil. The palate knew in an instant that it wasn't the real thing, of course, but these were extraordinary times, and one took what one could get. Bathtubs filled up and were just as quickly emptied. Glycerine and juniper oil could be purchased without difficulty or great expense.

Other liquors were created by adding different ingredients to the pure alcohol in the bathtub, ingredients as diverse as apples, oats, bananas, pumpkins, and parsnips. "In southern Florida," writes Perrett, "all that anyone had to do was take a coconut, bore a hole into it, leave the milk inside, add a tablespoon of brown sugar, and seal. Three weeks later they had a pungent, potent, treacly concoction called cocowhiskey."

As far as wine was concerned, it, too, had its substandard Prohibition versions, one of which went by the name of Bacchus Bricks, after their size and shape. First available to the public in 1920, they were usually sold in department stores and always by women of substantial physical gifts and smiles that reached back to their molars. Their sales pitches, coyly delivered, and almost always to a large crowd of shoppers, would go something like this:

"To get started, ladies and gentlemen, just dissolve one of our Bacchus Bricks into a bowl of water and *voila*, you have before you a sweet, tasty grape beverage.

"But," the woman would caution, holding up a large glass container, "after the brick is completely dissolved, you must be certain not to pour the beverage into this jug. And then you must be just as certain not to put the jug into a corner of the cupboard, away from the light, for twenty-one days. Because if you *do* store the beverage in a large glass jar for twenty-one days—*that's twenty-one days*—you won't have sweet-tasting, harmless grape juice anymore. What will happen is that the juice will ferment and turn into wine, into sherry or port or burgundy, depending on which of our Bacchus Bricks you buy—and then you would be breaking the law."

The Bacchus babe's listeners would elbow each other in the ribs and smile. A jolly old time, this Prohibition.

"And," the woman would continue, holding up a cork, "if you *do* slip up and put the grape juice into one of our containers for twenty-one days of darkness, be sure you don't stop up the jug with one of these corks, because if you do, you'll only be helping the juice to ferment. Have you folks got that?"

They had.

"Okay," the woman would conclude, "one more thing. The jugs and corks are for sale this week only when you buy three bricks for the price of two. Just don't use them for the wrong reason. May I take your orders?"

She was too busy filling out bills of sale and collecting money to indicate what the *right* reason might be.

OTHER PEOPLE, THOSE WHO COULD afford to pay more for their beverages than they ever had before and did not care to turn alcohol consumption into a do-it-yourself project, often drank in places called speakeasies, much more elegant establishments than saloons. They were like the velvet-roped, bouncer-guarded, trendy-for-a-week clubs of the present, entrance granted only to the special many, so that the tables were always filled, the bar always engulfed with patrons, and a number of people, unable to find seats, made up a throng around the more comfortable drinkers. But they were only people of the very best sort, which is to say that they could spend on liquor what others spent on rent.

The crème de la speakeasy customers sat in plush upholstered booths, on well-padded chairs, or on equally well-padded barstools. "Appointments varied, of course," I wrote in *The Spirits of America*, "but might include a solid oak bar with brass fittings, thick carpets, gilt-edged mirrors, and overhead, tinkling chandeliers with frescoed ceilings. Fine paintings or quality reproductions might hang on the walls, and small pieces of sculpture, perhaps busts of famous statesmen or warriors, men who would have had the fortitude to keep the Wayne Wheelers of the world from interfering with their pleasures, would be placed on marble pedestals in the corners, sometimes under specially installed spotlights that set them off dramatically."

Larger spotlights beamed down on the stage, in front of the elegantly set dinner tables, where the silverware was actually silver, the glassware crystal, and the fabric upon which they had been placed fine linen. At the speakeasies of top rank, entertainment would feature the most famous show-business names of the day: Josephine Baker, Rudy Vallee, Al Jolson, Ruth Etting, and Helen Morgan, the last of whom got her start in speakeasies and is thought by many to be the original torch singer.

And the staff at high-end speakeasies was always at one's service. "The headwaiters knew their customers' predilection for stone crabs or duck a l'orange," it has been reported, "and 'the doorman,' said *Fortune* [magazine], 'can always get you two or even four on the aisle if you feel like going to the theatre.'"

So much for the inside.

Since "speaks" had once been saloons, some carpentry was often required on the outside. "Door fitters were in especial demand," writes Henry Lee in a light-hearted volume on Prohibition, "for the high-minded new décor insisted on the elimination of the swinging doors that had graced the old, open saloons. In addition to decorum, the proprietors felt, thick oak defenses would slow down any raiders while the evidence was being poured down the drain. Too, when the Feds hit on the nasty device of actually padlocking raided premises, a need developed for several doors. No sooner was one locked with all the majesty of federal law than a second door was opened practically alongside, and the clientele suffered no inconvenience."

In addition to the extra doors, a speakeasy often donned a disguise, its owners hopeful that the cop on the beat would not recognize it for what it truly was. A sign might be placed in front that identified the establishment as a grocery, a tailor's shop, a barbershop, a bookstore, an art gallery, the International Hair Net Manufacturers' Association, or even a funeral parlor. The most memorable of the latter, a fake undertaking establishment in Detroit, "never saw corpses but used its hearses to bring in liquor for the ostensible mourners."

If a person was known at the speakeasy, he simply knocked at whichever door happened to be in service at the time and, after being sized up by an eye on the other side of the peephole just opened, was admitted. If he was a newcomer, though, he needed a password of sorts to prove he wasn't the law. "Joe sent me" is the stereotypical, cartoonish response for a prospective entrant; and if Joe was known to the former heavyweight boxer-cum-bouncer on the other side of the door, the man and his party were admitted. Otherwise, they were turned away, off to try Joe's name at some other establishment.

THE ORIGIN OF THE NAME "speakeasy" is not certain. It may be, as Mencken believed, that it derives from an old Irish word that means "speak softly shop." Speak softly, that is, so that if a few unbribed policemen happened to be passing by outside, they would not hear raucous patrons inside and be tempted to enter and make arrests. "Hush!" whispered the landlady at Rolliver's Inn in Thomas Hardy's *Tess of the d'Urbervilles*. "Don't 'ee sing so loud, my good man, in case any member of the Gover'ment should be passing and take away my licends."

It is said that in Manhattan, *The New Yorker* magazine's noted humorist "Robert Benchley once walked the north and south lengths of Fifty-Second Street between Fifth and Sixth Avenues counting speakeasies. He put the total at thirty-eight." In fact, "[f]ederal officials believed it to be the wettest block in America, populated by so many clandestine watering holes that a woman who lived in one of the block's few private residences had to put a sign on her door, pleading with people not to ring the bell."

Radio gossip and journalist Walter Winchell once appeared in a newsreel to claim that there were 1,600 speakeasies in a fourteen-block area of Manhattan, a figure impossible to believe, even delivered in Winchell's stentorian tones.

F. Scott Fitzgerald did not have so many choices. But he did not need them. He probably started his long, painful decline into alcoholism and eventual ruin in college, at Princeton, but was able to continue it in grand style in 1920, far from New York. Now selling his short stories to the *Saturday Evening Post* for $400 apiece, he could afford the best speakeasies that his hometown of St. Paul, Minnesota, had to offer. When he settled in the New York suburb of Westport, Connecticut later that year, and in Manhattan shortly afterward, his fee now up to $500 per tale and his first novel having been published, he could order whiskey delivered directly from the speak to his house or hotel suite.

It wasn't necessary to earn as much money as Fitzgerald to drink well during Prohibition, but it helped. "People made jokes about taking out a loan to take on a load," it was observed. "In some speaks, on some nights, a cocktail went for twice what it used to; on other occasions the mark-up could be a factor of ten—it depended on how much beverage was available at a given time and how difficult it was to procure." And how difficult it was to procure depended on the whims of law enforcement and the efficacy of criminal enterprise at any given time.

A speakeasy's profits, then, could be high. But so were its expenses. As has been calculated by the editors of *Time-Life* books, "it took money to make money—one New York proprietor put the cost at $1,370 a month. Of this, $400 was graft to federal Prohibition agents, the police department, and the district attorneys. The cop on the beat got another $40 to turn his back whenever beer was delivered." And if there was more than just one cop, and the police department often increased the number for no other reason than to spread the wealth among as many of their troops as possible, the speakeasy's costs went up even more. In fact, swears Sean Dennis Cashman, a historian of Prohibition, "New York speakeasy owners now paid more than $50 million every year from 1920 in graft to policemen and prohibition agents."

Most of the profits created by illegal alcohol went to organized crime, which filled the void previously occupied by legitimate businessmen, brewers, vintners, and distillers. And the federal government, which used to collect $500 million a year in taxes from alcoholic beverages, fully a tenth of the national revenue, suddenly found its various budgets harder to balance than they used to be.

But this is not to say that Prohibition created organized crime, as some people seem to believe. Stephen Fox corrects the misperception in *Blood and Power*, his history of illegal activity in America in the twentieth century.

> [O]rganized crime afflicted American life before the 1920s, but in small ways. Groups of crooks with entrepreneurial visions paid off the right cops and politicians, and in return controlled a neighborhood, or a section of a city, or at most an entire metropolis. But the enterprises under "protection"— mainly street crime, burglaries, prostitution, and gambling— were essentially restricted to certain places and people. Most good citizens could go their own way without being affected. A clear line divided the underworld from the upperworld. The gangs, confined by geography and relatively modest ambitions, did not operate on national or even regional scales. During occasional spasms of reform the cops and politicians, bribed or not, could still at their whim subdue the gangs for a while.

Once the Eighteenth Amendment took effect, however, everything changed. Prohibition turned organized crime into a growth industry; it was the greatest boon ever to the business of wrongdoing, the profits often utilized as seed capital, not only for other offenses of the time, but for future malfeasances, making certain that what had begun long ago, early in the nineteenth century, continued to prosper as a national franchise well into the future. Without the national ban on booze, organized crime would have remained organized, but would have been much less criminal, which is to say much less widespread, in its effects on society.

Historian Mike Dash provides a sweet summary of the effect of Prohibition on criminal enterprise. "Nothing like it had ever happened before," he writes. "An entire American industry—one of the most important in the country—had been gifted by the government to gangsters."

FOR PEOPLE WHO COULDN'T AFFORD high-class speaks, who could afford only the kinds of joints that reeked of saloons, the men and women of the lower classes, down on their luck, some of them so far down that they weren't even able to make their own hooch—for these men and women the Eighteenth Amendment would soon result in a far greater problem than price and availability. It would become, in effect, a means of legally sanctioned chemical warfare against the poor. Sometimes even the rich.

When a Cleveland, Ohio, businessman named Wilson B. Hickox was visiting New York and decided to have a nightcap before bedtime and his next day's sightseeing, he drank a beverage, source unknown, the volume of which had been increased by mixing it with strychnine. After less than a few minutes, Hickox began to feel "a tightening of the throat and chest, a kind of bitter pain spreading through his body. We may reasonably imagine the glass slipping from his hand and Hickox rising with difficulty and stumbling toward the door to summon help as his symptoms swiftly worsened. One by one his body systems were collapsing into paralysis as the toxic effects of strychnine swept through him. Mr. Hickox never made it to the door, but died slowly and wretchedly on the floor of his room, bewildered, frightened, and unable to move a muscle."

Before Prohibition ended, it would cost thousands of people their health and untold numbers their lives.

To Wayne Wheeler, however, the horrible turn that dry America was about to take was simply the will of God. He could see no reason to sympathize with those who defied it, regardless of their outcomes.

CHAPTER FOUR

Resolutions and Sentiments

A S THE EIGHTEENTH AMENDMENT WAS being defied, another addition to the Constitution was getting closer to passage, gaining support more rapidly than even its most optimistic advocates could have hoped. And in this case, unlike Prohibition, what the momentum represented *was* real.

Between January 6 and January 27, 1920, five states ratified the Nineteenth Amendment, bringing the number in favor to twenty-seven. Only nine more of America's states had to formalize their approval, and the three-quarter mark would be reached: American women would at long last be able to join men in the voting booth. In his healthier days, President Woodrow Wilson had made it known that he thought they belonged there, although he disappointed suffragists by not making his support more vocal.

Most members of Congress agreed with Wilson. A. Mitchell Palmer was another backer of the female cause, at least in part because he thought that women, by their very nature, would tend to vote more conservatively than men and help to safeguard the nation from anarchists and Bolsheviks and the continuing danger they posed. The Wall Street explosion was still a few months away, but Palmer and the BOI were as vigilant as they could be, still investigating previous acts of violence and taking into custody the occasional innocent with an Italian surname.

Palmer was especially encouraged by Carrie Chapman Catt, not only the sole woman in her graduating class at Iowa State University but the valedictorian. A member of the Woman's Christian Temperance Union, which seemed to Palmer further evidence of her conservative nature, she went on to succeed the better-known Susan B. Anthony as president of the National American Woman Suffrage Association. When that organization breathed its last in 1920, Catt founded the League of Women Voters to take its place, and that group has endured ever since, one of the most powerful nonpartisan political voices in the country for decades. A woman of many talents, Catt also edited the *National Suffrage Bulletin*, which later changed its name to *Progress*. Further, she managed two statewide campaigns in favor of the Nineteenth Amendment, winning them both. In Idaho, the vote was 122,126 in favor of suffrage, a mere 5,844 against.

But what particularly attracted Palmer to Catt was comments like this: "There is but one way to avert the danger," she declared, the danger being that more and more foreigners would take up residence in the United States, foreigners who might not have the best interests of the country at heart, and that is to "cut off the vote of the slums and give to woman . . . the power of protecting herself . . . the ballot."

A number of factors, both past and present, led to the Nineteenth Amendment's rapid approach. Even the Great War had a little to do with it. But very little. In his grand opus *The American Century*, the eminent historian Norman F. Cantor states that the Amendment was "a reward for what women had done during the war in ammunition factories and hospitals and on farms." It was true, but barely. A great deal of work had to be done before the fighting began to allow females into the polling place in 1920. But little known though it is, the majority of American women were already voting, at least part-time, before the Constitution was expanded for them.

The Nineteenth Amendment would make suffrage "universal," as both friends and foes alike agreed. But prior to the war it was already universal in almost every state west of the Mississippi River, Texas being the largest exception. Six other states, all in the vicinity of the Canadian border, allowed women to vote for president only. Even Texas allowed the female ballot in presidential primaries, but not in general elections. In fact, a mere nine states denied women the vote in all instances, and seven of those, to their inexplicable shame, were among the original thirteen colonies—which is to say, those soon-to-be states that were responsible for the Constitution and the Bill of Rights in the first place.

Bias against giving women an electoral voice, however, existed even before the nation's founding, long before. Miriam Gurko tells us that, as far back as 1638, Margaret Brent, "a large property owner and woman of many business affairs, demanded a vote in the [Virginia] House of Burgesses. It was denied, but not without a lively argument. This was probably the first demand for woman suffrage in America." Historian George Brown Tindall makes a further case for Brent, pointing out that even though she was so competent at her tasks that two of her brothers turned over the management of their acreages when they were away from home, no matter. "The governor, in response, acknowledged her gifts, but denied her request. When she became perhaps the first American suffragette, she had overstepped the bounds of acceptance."

In her study of the long, frustrating battle to grant women entrance to polling places, *The Ladies of Seneca Falls*, Gurko continues:

> In some colonies women did have the right to vote, since this was generally based not on sex but on ownership of property. Ironically, it was the arrival of independence and the spread of democracy that removed this right. As states adopted their constitutions or revised their laws under the new political conditions, voting qualifications were more clearly defined, usually spelling out the voter as a free, white, male citizen, in addition to whatever property or tax requirement there might be. Thus New York took the vote away from women in 1777,

Massachusetts in 1780, New Hampshire in 1784, and New Jersey, the last to do so, in 1807.

Gurko does not make clear the connection between independence for the country and the exclusion of women from voting booths; there seems no causal relationship. But she does point out that females, many times widows, continued to own property in what was now the United States, and that they were taxed on that property. Thus, after men had fought and won their battles against "taxation without representation," women were forced to fight their own battles—and against the very men who had been victorious against the British. They did so, however, with much less success.

The most significant step that women took toward suffrage occurred in 1848, exactly two centuries and a decade after Margaret Brent confronted sexism in Virginia. Women's-rights leaders summoned as many of their followers as they could to join them in the Finger Lakes region of New York for the Seneca Falls Convention, the first assembly of its kind in the United States and, to this day, still the most influential. Like the Founding Fathers, these Founding Mothers were determined to produce a document that would last the ages and inspire future generations. They did just that, even if less famously.

To make the point that the female was entitled to the same kinds of freedom as the male, they began their Declaration of Sentiments and Resolutions with familiar language: "When, in the course of human events. . . ." The second paragraph starts in similarly recognizable fashion: "We hold these truths to be self-evident: that all men *and women* [italics added] are created equal. . . ." The women of Seneca Falls were not copying the Declaration of Independence so much as trying to make the point that the document they were constructing was as basic to human rights as the one produced in Philadelphia by the Continental Congress. Further, they were slyly demonstrating that the Congress, in gainsaying female rights, was acting hypocritically, just as it was with Africans in American servitude.

That, at least, was the initial intent. But in continuing to make their arguments about treatment by males over the years, they resorted to language much less restrained, much less subtle, and even more incendiary than a previous generation of men had used against the British. I quote at some length from their Declaration:

> The history of mankind is a history of repeat injuries and usurpations on the part of man toward woman, having in direct object the establishment of an absolute tyranny over her. To prove this, let facts be submitted to a candid world.

> He has never permitted her to exercise her inalienable right to the elective franchise. . . .

> He has withheld from her rights which are given to the most ignorant and degraded men—both natives and foreigners. . . .

> He has made her, if married, in the eye of the law, civilly dead. . . .

> He has denied her facilities for obtaining a thorough education—all colleges being closed against her. . . .

> He allows her in church, as well as State, but in a subordinate position, claiming Apostolic authority for her exclusion from the ministry, and, with some exceptions, from any public participation in the affairs of the Church. . . .

> He has endeavored, in every way he could, to destroy her confidence in her own powers, to lessen her self-respect, and to make her willing to lead a dependent and abject life.

> Now, in view of this entire disenfranchisement of one-half the people of this country, their social and religious degradation,— in view of the unjust laws above mentioned, and because women do feel themselves aggrieved, oppressed, and fraudulently deprived of their most sacred rights, we insist they have

immediate admission to all the rights and privileges which belong to them as citizens of these United States.

The women at Seneca Falls unanimously approved the provisions of the Declaration—except, surprisingly, the article that seemed the least controversial, the request for the vote, which, as the above demonstrates, was not even phrased as a request but rather a plaint. The organizers of the convention were astonished by the opposition. "It was argued," writes Gurko, "that so excessive a demand would arouse such antagonism and derision that the movement would be killed before it even got under way."

The argument is perhaps correct. But it is strange that the Seneca Falls delegates felt voting might be perceived as "so excessive a demand"; there is much more in the Declaration of Resolutions and Sentiments that seems likely to arouse men to opposition and derision than its statement of implied support for suffrage.

There were four women in particular whose support for suffrage was not implied, but vocal and insistent. Their places in history would have been assured even if the ban against women in the voting booth had never been lifted.

ELIZABETH CADY'S FATHER WANTED A boy, and made no secret of his disappointment to either family or friends when his hard-laboring wife gave him the wrong choice. His daughter could have grown up feeling lonely and unwanted as a result; instead, she was motivated to succeed as a man might succeed, to satisfy both nature's product and her father's hopes. She might have been the first American female to insist that the word "obey" be omitted from her wedding vows. She did, however, take the name of her husband, the abolitionist Henry Brewster Stanton.

Like Thomas Jefferson, Stanton was the principal author of her convention's Declaration; but also like Jefferson, she generously accepted the contributions and criticisms of others. But it was Stanton who made suffrage the first of the Sentiments in the Declaration, writing it in such a way that it implied, rather than insisted, that the time had come for men to allow women to cast their ballots. It was, thus, also she who was the most mystified by her sisters' opposition to suffrage, and could not help but take it as a personal repudiation.

LUCRETIA MOTT, WHO WOULD EVENTUALLY become one of the founders of Swarthmore College, had no interest in women's rights until, as a teacher at the Nine Partners Quaker Boarding School in New York, from which she had graduated, she discovered that male teachers were being paid three times as much as she and the rest of the female staff. It did not seem possible to her; but no sooner did she confirm the information than she began to seethe, and her naturally dour expression made her dissatisfaction all the more obvious.

She spoke to school officials about the disparity in wages, but to no avail. She was not able to obtain from them either satisfactory answers or a raise in pay.

Her husband, an educator and abolitionist whom she met at Nine Partners, was on her side. So were the five of her six children who survived childhood, reformers all. Yet another fifteen years would pass before Mr. and Mrs. Mott formed the American Equal Rights Association, of which she became the first president. But the Association was dedicated to abolition no less than to suffrage, thus choosing to fight the two most strenuously uphill battles in all the nineteenth century. The former led to the Thirteenth Amendment to the Constitution, nominally ridding the nation of slavery, and Mott was delighted. That a full fifty-five years would pass before the Nineteenth Amendment, which guaranteed women the right to vote, gained the approval of the states would have been a particular heartache to her had she lived long enough to know.

Mott's grand oeuvre was the *Discourse on Woman*, still debated today among scholars, an integral part of the curriculum of various women's-rights programs in higher education. Mott began as follows:

There is nothing of greater importance to the well-being of society at large—of man as well as woman—as the true and proper position of women. Much has been said, from time to time, upon this subject. It has been a theme for ridicule, for satire and sarcasm. We might look for this from the ignorant and vulgar; but from the intelligent and refined we have a right to expect that such weapons shall not be resorted to,—that gross comparisons and vulgar epithets shall not be applied, so as to place woman, in a point of view, ridiculous to say the least.

Yet both before and after she wrote the *Discourse*, in fact all of her married life, Mott was a housewife and mother, and took great pleasure in both roles. She saw no conflict. She made her own choices.

IN 1847, LUCY STONE, THE daughter of a farm family with few educational interests running through its bloodstream, became the first woman from Massachusetts to earn a college degree. After teaching for a while, she achieved another first, becoming, it is said, the first American female to insist that she not change her last name after marrying. "The precedent was so unusual," writes Doris Weatherford in her history of the American suffragist, "that 'stoner' became a commonly used nineteenth-century noun to denote a woman who kept her maiden name." Poor Henry Browne Blackwell, in keeping rather than sharing his name with his wife, achieved what was for the time a most unfortunate distinction of his own.

Stone was tireless in her efforts to convince fellow academics that women deserved universal education no less than universal suffrage, but was not surprised to be met with indifference and opposition and ever more energetic rebuttal. In fact, according to at least one observer, she "protested her disenfranchisement in 1858 by allowing the seizure of her household goods at her Orange, New Jersey, home rather than pay taxes levied by a government in which she could not participate." The goods belonged to her husband, too. Mr. Blackwell made no complaint.

Prior to that, Stone was more seriously accused of slipping a knife to a former slave named Margaret Garner, who was on trial for murdering her child to prevent the little one from growing up into slavery. The knife, it was said, was for Garner to use on herself if she was sentenced to return to a life of being a white man's commodity. Given a chance to address the court in her own defense, Stone seemed rather to speak for the prosecution. "With my own teeth I would tear open my veins and let the earth drink my blood, rather than wear the chains of slavery. How then could I blame her for wishing her child to find freedom with God and the angels, where no chains are?"

Like Mott and so many other suffragettes, Stone was as well an abolitionist, believing that women deserved no more, no less, than Negroes of either gender. It was almost surely a joining of beliefs that worked against the woman's vote, but was also a connection that the more zealous of reformers simply could not sever. Stone died painfully, of stomach cancer, twenty-seven years before she would have known she was vindicated in her struggle for a woman's place in the institutions that governed society. "Ever the innovator," Weatherford tells us, "she was the first person in New England to leave orders that she be cremated."

SUSAN B. ANTHONY, THE FOURTH of the most powerful voices of Seneca Falls, was used to getting her way, even when her way was prohibited by law. She and her sisters Guelma, Hannah, Mary, and Eliza were among the few American women ever to have voted in a Congressional election before 1920, a feat that took remarkable cleverness and no less remarkable courage. It is one of the more fascinating little-known events in the history of the female march to equality.

In 1872, when the Anthony girls attempted to register at the polls in Rochester, New York, they were, as expected, told to go away. That was Susan's cue. She withdrew a copy of the Constitution from her purse, waving it as she spoke. "[T]all and slender, with a fine, erect carriage, and almost classically regular features framed by smooth, glossy brown hair," she captured the registration inspectors' attention from her first word. She claimed that the oft-ignored Fourteenth Amendment would not be ignored in her case, that its Due Process Clause gave her the "liberty" to vote as an American citizen, and that the same Amendment's Equal Protection Clause entitled her, as it entitled men, to participate in the process of electing public officials.

The voting inspectors did not know what to do, not at first. No one had ever made such an argument before, at least not in Rochester, New York. The officials talked among each other for a while; then, to Anthony's and her sisters' great surprise, their demand was approved. Two of the registration inspectors agreed "to take the responsibility" of allowing the Anthonys to vote, even though aware they might later be fined for their actions. By election day, realizing the fines could be as much as $500, the two registrars had changed their minds. But it was too late: the ladies' names, appearing as out of place as they could be, had already been printed on the roster of eligible voters. Taking the precaution of hiring a lawyer first, Susan led her sisters and the attorney to the polls on the appointed November day, and they "had the incredible experience of exercising the democratic right of all citizens to a voice in their government: they voted."

Two weeks later came a more expected experience. Susan, Guelma, Hannah, Mary, and Eliza Anthony were arrested. The trial, however, at which Susan, as the leader of her sisters' insurrection, was the only defendant, proved as much a burlesque as a legal proceeding could be. Susan was fined $100, but refused to pay and was not forced to do so. The registrars who had allowed her and the others to vote were fined, not $500 apiece, but a mere $25. When, as a matter of principle, they also refused to pay, they were sent to jail, where they enjoyed themselves immensely:

"The women who had voted," Gurko relates, "kept them fed with superb meals, and hundreds of Rochester residents came to visit them." After a week, President Ulysses S. Grant pardoned the two men, annoyed that he even had to deal with so trifling a matter.

According to social critic Gilbert Seldes, however, there was more to the leniency shown Susan B. Anthony than met the court record. "Knowing that she would be tried for this crime," he later wrote, "Miss Anthony took the precaution to vote the Republican ticket and so mollified the Republican prosecutor, judge, and jury." The Anthony sisters' counsel was himself a well-known Republican. These might have been the deciding factors in their favor.

In the late winter of 1906, approaching her eighty-sixth birthday, a year after having pleaded personally with President Theodore Roosevelt for an amendment allowing women to vote, Susan B. Anthony caught a cold from which she never recovered. She was "white and frail" as the end approached, and also greatly dispirited. "To think I have had more than sixty years of hard struggle for a little liberty," she said weakly, on her deathbed, "and then to die without it seems so cruel."

Had she been able to survive fourteen more years, to the nice, round, virtually impossible number of 100, she would not have felt her life's struggles so sharply.

BY THE WINTER OF 1920, American women had massed into an irresistible force and knew well their strength. It was just a matter of time, and not much more of it at that. Stanton, Mott, Stone, and Anthony would have been amazed that so equitable a request had taken so long to be recognized. A "founding document" of its own, it had proven much more controversial than the original of those papers.

Still, one of the problems faced by the early leaders of the movement, the indifference, or even opposition, of so many females toward voting, existed well into the twentieth century. As John Milton Cooper, Jr. writes in *Pivotal Decades: The United States, 1900–1920*, "Both the organized women's movement and the colleges drew from economically better-off, native-born whites, usually from the cities and larger towns of the Northeast and Midwest. Their concerns struck little response among poorer women, particularly blacks, newly arrived immigrants, and farm wives and daughters in the South and West."

For the accomplishments of their own lifetimes, Stanton, Mott, Stone, and Anthony must be credited, as much as any women alive in 1920, for bringing about the Nineteenth Amendment. Ironically, though, when it finally passed that summer after a brutally corrupt campaign in Tennessee, women would have no choice but to join their husbands and other male voters in dismissing from office the first—and up to the time of this writing, only—female to serve as "president" in the history of the United States.

CHAPTER FIVE

Civil Wrongs

A COLD FEBRUARY TURNED INTO A March that started out even worse. In the Northeast, snowfalls made highways and railroad lines impassable, and eighty-mile-an-hour winds knocked down trees and the poles that suspended electrical wires; as they fell, they blocked the frozen streets, stranding thousands at home in Maine and Massachusetts, Vermont and New Hampshire. Pedestrians in New York were blown off balance as they walked, even though the canyon walls of skyscrapers should have protected them. As far south as Washington, D.C., temperatures sank to levels that most people had never felt before.

But springtime finally made its appearance in 1920, earlier in New Orleans than in New England, of course, and that was when the crowds started getting bigger again at the clubs where Louis Armstrong led his band by playing a beat-up old five-dollar cornet he had bought in a pawn-shop. He did not make much money yet. He did not live on the right side of town yet. He did not even live in the right town. But he was closing in on all of those goals.

"We were *all* poor," he later wrote of those days. "The privies [the toilets] were out in a big yard, one side for the men and one side for the women." His neighbors were "churchpeople, thieves, prostitutes, and lots of children. There were bars, honky-tonks, and saloons." And there was one night in particular, young Louis recalled, when "a woman hollered out into the yard to her daughter. She said (real loud), 'You, Marandy, you'd better come into this house, you laying out there with nothing on top of you but that thin nigger.' Marandy said, 'Yassum.'"

The blues *had* to be born in a place like New Orleans. "Chastized as the devil's music" by the pure of heart but weak of knowledge, it was, in fact, just the opposite. "Does Jazz Put the Sin in Syncopation" asked an article in the *Ladies' Home Journal,* then proceeded to answer in the righteous, but erroneous, affirmative.

In his definitive *The History of Jazz,* Ted Gioia relates that jazz did not begin in New Orleans's red-light district, the infamous Storyville, but in the city's Baptist churches. Says banjoist Johnny St. Cyr, "Those Baptist rhythms were similar to the jazz rhythms, and the singing was very much on the blues side." And trombonist Kid Ory, who would later figure importantly in Armstrong's life, believes that "[Buddy] Bolden [believed by some to have been America's first real jazz instrumentalist], got most of his tunes from the Holy Roller Church, the Baptist church on Jackson and Franklin. I know that he used to go to that church, but not for religion, he went there to get ideas on music."

But like children leaving home to see the wider world, in the early twentieth century jazz became a passenger riding the rails, the music too undertaking a journey, finding its way to bigger cities where African-Americans were living the lowdown life, and to the occasional small town where poverty was so plentiful, it might as well have been a crop. For instance, cotton, the picking of which was sufficiently onerous that only blacks would do it, and for pennies a day and still end up owing the boss for food and other supplies; the picking of which would soon find itself with not nearly enough hands.

As for Louis, he had his eyes on Chicago, where the real tunes were being played these days. The best musicians were heading there, including many from New Orleans. In baseball terms, the Crescent City was the minor leagues—Triple-A ball, the top of the rung, but still the minors.

Chicago was the majors. It was bigger, more diverse, a more expansive environment for the new music than its birthplace, in large part because blacks were freer in the North than in the South and their music could not help but reflect the lack of restrictions. Jazzmen were pouring in not only from New Orleans, but from the Mississippi Delta, the cotton fields of Alabama—from points all over the South. Anyone could sit in with anyone else at any club at any time—the more the merrier, yes; but of greater importance, the more who played the music, the better for both its evolution and its spread. As Southern musicians settled near Lake Michigan and joined in the party, jazz started to become a new kind of music, separating from its roots in the blues with something distinct and previously unknown resulting from the process, something purely American but a product created purely by American outsiders, by Americans whose dreams hadn't come true and never would, not unless they told the tale of their sorrows and joys with just the right notes, just the right beat, just the right feeling. And even then there were no guarantees.

Louis Armstrong, though, had some magic in him. He was only eighteen at the time in 1920 but was the year's boy wonder, already becoming a jazz master, even without musicians of Chicago caliber sitting in to influence him, urge him on. Always a prodigy, Armstrong was remodeling jazz into something that he could play like no one else. The influences on him could not have been more varied than just a neighborhood Baptist church. As Lucy Moore points out, they included the rhythms and melodies that were in the very air of New Orleans: "the mournful energy of the freed slaves' blues; the calypso rhythms of the West Indies; the syncopated beat of plantation banjo music, known as ragtime; the mysticism of Negro spirituals, the lyricism and sophistication of the Creole tradition; and the local love of marching brass bands—fused on the streets into an entirely new type of music."

But Armstrong's was the newest of all. Biographer Laurence Bergreen writes that his subject was his own inspiration, his own source of encouragement. "Satchmo," short for "Satchel Mouth," a tribute to the size of his opening,

"entered just a fraction behind the melody," as he told [his second wife] Lil, and then caught up to the other musicians and finally got out in front of them. . . . Sure, it was "wrong" by the standards of classical music, but in jazz, with its relaxed tempos and polyphony, the technique added tension to the music, as the ear waited for the soloist to enter. In Louis's hands, this was more than just a gimmick; he used it to imply notes that carried as much musical meaning as the actual notes. His horn engaged the ear and the mind, making the listener hear things that were only suggested, never stated. Eventually, he learned to alternate between the melody and his variations on it, until the melody gradually disappeared behind the notes suggesting it, and the ear supplied what his horn left out. His method was rebellious, yet it conformed to a ruthless inner logic. He embroidered and invented tunes within the tune, rhythms within the rhythm.

The result was that he "transformed whatever piece he happened to be playing into an extension of his psyche," and, as it turned out, his psyche would soon become the national rage.

But when?

Patience, he told himself; patience. He might have been but a teenager in the spring of 1920, but already the cats knew about him in Chicago; some had heard him in his hometown, and their amazement quickly turned to the more solid foundation of respect. They not only spread the word about him up North, but belted out their own versions of Louis's licks.

It would just be a matter of time until he got the right offer and joined them. He knew it. What he did not know was that two more years of waiting were ahead, although he would later say he had not minded. He already *was* New Orleans, in most of the ways that mattered, was already leading the way in Chicago—and that wasn't bad for someone his age.

When Kid Ory headed North from the bayou in 1920, his departure opened up the Southern throne for Louis. But before the Kid left, in a rite of passage, he gave his successor some advice. The Kid told Satchmo to "'put a new piece together. Words and music. Even put in a little dance.' The song," Bergreen continues, "was an unashamedly filthy thing called, variously, 'Keep Off Katie's Head' or 'Take Your Finger Outta Katie's Ass.'

When Louis sang this to a packed house at Pete Lala's one night, 'Man it was like a sporting event. All the guys crowded around and they like to carry me up on their shoulders.'"

The cornetist Joe Oliver was nicknamed "King," and that was precisely his rank in the Chicago blues scene. It was he who had summoned Ory to join him, and in 1922 he would call for Louis, waiting those extra two years, perhaps, because he wanted more time at the top. Once Louis came to Chicago, the city would eventually be his every bit as much as New Orleans was now, and the King knew it. It would be a momentous event, a transfer of power. The King was in no hurry.

But like Ory, Oliver would be gracious. It was the music that mattered, after all, the music more than the man, and both Oliver and Ory could see that the music was about to belong almost solely to Satchmo. An entire generation and more would grow up trying to copy his sound. To a man, they would fail. No one can copy a legend. From Terry Teachout, another Armstrong biographer:

He really did perform with everyone from Leonard Bernstein to Johnny Cash. He really did end his shows (some of them, anyway) by playing 250 or more high Cs capped with a high F. He wrote the finest of all jazz autobiographies—without a collaborator. The ranks of his admirers included Kingsley Amis, Tallulah Bankhead, Jackson Pollock, Jean Renoir, and Le Corbusier ("He is mathematics, equilibrium on a tight-rope. He is Shakespearean!"). Virgil Thomson called him "a master of musical art." Stuart Davis, whose abstract paintings were full of jazz-inspired images, cited him as a "model of greatness." Is it any wonder, then, that so many musicians longed to play the way he played and sing the way he sang? It was no accident that they usually referred to Armstrong not as "Satchmo," his own favorite nickname, but as "Pops." He was the father figure of jazz, and what his children wanted was to *be* him, or at least come as close as they possibly could.

But Armstrong was not merely different, an exception among exceptions. Most other men and women of his race lived a different life, a life that

ERIC BURNS

remained the same from cradle to grave—and such a short, hard period of time it seemed. It was the blues that they lived, never able to play it. It was the blues that they lived; they would never make it to jazz. For Armstrong and a fortunate few others, it was the music to which they would devote their lives in willing servitude—not the white massah, no more of the white massah standing in cotton fields with a whip in one hand and a cooling drink in the other. But he was about to become a rarity, just like old-fashioned church music once the jazzmen got hold of it.

ACCORDING TO GOVERNMENT FIGURES, 111,888 men and women of African descent in the United States made their way northward in 1920. But they were just the latest in a much larger number of internal immigrants. As James R. Green tells us, "The black population in Northern cities grew by 35 percent between 1910 and 1920 and topped 100,000 in New York, Philadelphia and Chicago. In other industrial cities, this population multiplied dramatically, by over 600 percent in Detroit and over 300 percent in Cleveland. The number of blacks working in manufacturing increased by 40 percent in the same decade, while black employment in agriculture dropped by 25 percent."

African-Americans were escaping from conditions they found intolerable, assuming that their lives could only be better at the top of the country than they had been at the bottom. In the South, everything from public toilets to hospitals, from parks to schools, was segregated, and those who dared step across the lines of racial separation faced reprisals from the law and, worse, from the Ku Klux Klan, which was in places a law unto itself. It has been claimed that the Klan gained more than a million members during the twenties, a number that is probably much too high. Nonetheless, it *is* true that as African-Americans departed from the legally sanctioned racism of the South for hopes of welcome in the North, the Klan was close behind, making a migration of its own, determined not to let the black man escape its own particular brand of justice.

BLACKS WERE ALMOST TEN PERCENT of the population at the time, yet less than five percent of the military. And of the military men, only one in five saw action in the Great War, clearly the result of prejudice, a prejudice that U.S. officials not only encouraged, but taught. "The French allied forces, for example," writes James Oliver Horton, "were instructed to see that the French civilian population respected American racial etiquette. To treat black soldiers as equals or to show them respect would, they were told, offend white American soldiers. This was especially true when French women socialized with black men."

Many more African-Americans were waiting their turns in uniform as the war ended. If they had been called upon earlier, perhaps the fighting would have ended before it did. The little-known, but nonetheless legendary, "Battle of Henry Johnson" suggests the possibility.

Johnson and Needham Roberts were on sentry duty in Germany on the night of May 15, 1918, when a noise caught their attention.

About 2 A.M. [Johnson] heard the Germans cutting the wire that protected his post, so he sent Roberts, in an adjoining sentry post, to alert their troops. Johnson lobbed a grenade and the "surprised Dutchmen" began firing, so he recalled Roberts. Roberts was soon incapacitated by a German grenade. Two Germans tried to take Roberts prisoner but Johnson beat them off. Roberts could not stand but he sat upright and passed grenades to Johnson.

With grenades exhausted, Johnson grabbed his rifle. He inserted an American clip in his French rifle but it jammed. At that point, a German platoon rushed him and the fighting became hand-to-hand. He then "banged them on the dome and the side and everywhere I could land until the butt of my rifle busted." Next he resorted to his bolo knife. "[I] slashed in a million directions," he said. "Each slash meant something, believe me." He admitted that the Germans "knocked me around considerable and whanged me on the head, but I always managed to get back on my feet." One German was "bothering" him more than the others, so he eventually threw him over his head and stabbed him in his ribs. "I stuck one guy in the stomach," Johnson continued, "and then he yelled in good New York talk: 'That black _____ got me.'" Johnson was still "banging them" when his friends arrived and repulsed the Germans. Johnson then fainted. The fight had lasted about an hour.

Johnson and Roberts were taken to a French hospital. Johnson had a total of 21 wounds to his left arm, back, feet, and face, most of them from knives and bayonets.

The Battle of Henry Johnson, as far as I know the Great War's only eponymous struggle, resulted in all manner of accolades for its African-American hero. At the one extreme was the awarding to Johnson of the highest of all French military honors, the Croix de Guerre with a gold palm. Roberts received a Croix de Guerre sans gold palm. They were the first two American soldiers, out of tens of thousands who fought in France, to have been so recognized.

There were no honors awaiting either of them in the United States.

At the other extreme was the story called "Young Black Joe," written by Irvin S. Cobb, one of the most famous journalists of the time, and published in the *Saturday Evening Post* on August 24, 1918. Cobb presented his encomium to Johnson awkwardly, both in phrasing and feeling: "I am of the opinion personally, and I make the assertion with all the better grace, I think, seeing that I am a Southerner with all the Southerner's inherited and acquired prejudices touching on the race question—that as a result of what our black soldiers are going to do in this war, a word that has been uttered billions of times in our country, sometimes in derision, sometimes in hate, sometimes in all kindliness—but which I am sure never fell on black ears but it left behind a sting for the heart—is going to have a new meaning for all of us, South and North too, and that hereafter n-i-g-g-e-r will merely be another way of spelling the word American."

More than anyone else, Cobb, in his own distinctive manner, had created a hero. As much as anyone else, Henry Johnson deserved to be one.

AND SO WHEN JOHNSON AND other African-Americans returned to the United States, many of them joining their families who were now living in the North, they expected hearty shows of gratitude at the most, a "welcome back" or a slap on the shoulder at the least. They expected freedom from segregation, or at least a lessening of its impact. They expected better career opportunities than had existed upon their departure, if nothing so grand as a position in the executive offices. They did not believe in the sudden appearance of gold streets in the ghetto, nor even streets in which the ruts had been filled, maybe even paved over—not in the black neighborhoods. They were, however, counting on paper, green paper, more of it than they had been able to earn in their old lives. Simple, dignified, fairly compensated employment. Nineteen twenty, they hoped, as most soldiers had finally been mustered out of service by then, would be the start of new lives for them.

It did not happen, almost none of it. For the most part, African-Americans were faced with the same demeaning jobs and insulting wages they had left behind to take up arms against the Hun. In the South, they had earned their daily crumbs by cleaning toilets in public buildings or sweeping the streets in front of them, streets which, because of horse droppings, often smelled more like the toilets than the great outdoors. They tended horses, shined shoes, toiled at the most repetitious and mindless jobs in factories, and carried bags through hotel lobbies or along train platforms to seats in the "Whites Only" cars. They kowtowed to the white man and woman in both their language and their demeanor.

But for the returning black serviceman, as for the black families who had departed from their tenant farms, things were no better in the North; there was no dignity to be found in the Chicago area workplace either. The jobs they secured were horrifyingly similar, and sometimes even identical, to those they had left behind. And, on occasion, no employment awaited them at all. As Meyer Weinberg reported,

> In Chicago, "International Harvester, the packinghouses, and steel mills all carefully monitored quotas on the number of blacks that could be hired." With respect to anti-black prejudices of European immigrants, "employers . . . took pleasure in fueling the flames of this discord, doing whatever they could to incite the prejudices and fears of native workers."
>
> Beginning in 1924, the management of U.S. Steel established quotas for black employees. The new policy was part

of a broad racial program for the Gary [Indiana] community: "In the 1920s . . . Gary saw the growth of 'jim crow' housing, public accommodations, recreation, and education [begun] by United States Steel corporation executives running both City Hall and the decisive community organizations to an extent unknown prior to . . . [World War I]."

Nor did there seem to be any likelihood of change—not yet, at least. There was no nationwide campaign to improve living conditions for blacks; no such phrase, or even notion, as "civil rights." The country's best-known black leader, despite being a man of unusual accomplishment, inspired derision at least as much as he raised alarms. His is an extraordinary story for its time. If only it could have ended differently.

MARCUS MOSIAH GARVEY WAS ONE of the rare blacks who had made a wide-ranging success of himself in 1920, perhaps the widest: entrepreneur, journalist, poet, publisher, and lecturer. Born in Saint Anne's Bay, a small town on the north coast of British Jamaica, Garvey had been a playful, sometimes rambunctious boy—once jailed for being part of a gang that threw stones at the windows of a local church, breaking every one. He was, afterward, ashamed of himself; he vowed it would be his last act of vandalism, and it was.

Always intelligent, always curious, Garvey took elocution lessons and entered public-speaking competitions at a young age. He read constantly in his father's library, where, according to historian Jules Archer, he "learned about the colonization and partition of Africa by European powers. He became aware of a worldwide pattern of oppression of those with black skin by those with white skin."

Moving with his family to the United States, to Harlem, New York's largest black neighborhood, which was actually a series of neighborhoods shoved up against each other, and a part of town that would, in 1920, change the very meaning of American culture, Garvey began to dream. "But," as biographer Colin Grant tells us, "when Marcus Garvey closed his eyes in the middle of the year [1919], he did not imagine the saccharine luxury of a Sugar Hill [Harlem's priciest neighborhood] penthouse with a chauffeured Cadillac parked outside and a Scandinavian maid to open the front door. No, what he saw were ships, not one or two but a whole line of Negro-owned steamships sailing across the Atlantic. It was an impossible idea. There had been no hint of anything like it in recent history."

By 1920, Garvey had founded a group for the advancement of African-Americans in the United States; and when he lectured, he spoke frequently about both the group and the exalted position he had given himself as its head. "I am President-General of the Universal Negro Improvement Association," he would say at the beginning of his presentations, by way of justifying the fees he collected from those whom he addressed. "There is always a charge for admission, in that I feel that if the public is thoughtful it will be benefited by the things I say. I do not speak carelessly or recklessly but with a definite object of helping the people, especially those of my race, to know, to understand, to realise themselves."

In addition to collecting money for the UNIA, Garvey also edited a weekly newspaper called *Negro World*, one of the rare journals of the time that advocated women's rights as well as those of African-Americans. Every issue, which cost a nickel, included a full page titled "Our Women and What They Think." Also included were poetry by Garvey, and reviews of theatre, music, and literature. The paper would play a major role in the Harlem Renaissance, that dramatic change in American culture that is the subject of a later chapter.

It was during the Renaissance, as another Garvey biographer relates, that the paper "eventually claimed a circulation of one hundred thousand, making it the most widely read black weekly of that day. Following Marcus's policy of glorifying blackness, it refused ads for hair straighteners, skin bleaches, or any product that promised to make the user look whiter. It was the only black publication to reject such ads."

Black is beautiful, Garvey believed, well ahead of his time. Further, he insisted that his people could most improve themselves by departing from the hostility and indignities that beset them in the United States and establishing a nation of their own in Liberia, a nation in West Africa and one of only two countries on the continent that had no history of European colonization. Liberians, as it happened, were not in favor of Garvey's idea; he would clean up details like that later.

The first step was to bring into being the Black Star Steamship Line, the fleet he saw when he closed his eyes. So determined was Garvey to make the dream come true that he sought money from those Americans who, in his opinion, would be most likely to support the venture. Not all of them were black. And not all of them were friendly.

One day in 1920, Marcus Garvey, without any advance notice, "did what no black person in America had ever contemplated." So we learn from biographer Grant. Garvey had made an appointment with someone who was stunned to hear from him but, once learning the reason, was willing to meet. After their time together, Garvey explained what he had done and why he had done it. Opinion was divided. A number of UNIA members and other African-Americans came to regard him as a death-defying genius, while others now thought of him as a fool, perhaps even a traitor to the causes of black America, striking secret bargains of some sort with the devil.

> Have this day interviewed Edward Young Clarke, acting Imperial Wizard Knight of the Ku Klux Klan. In conference of two hours he outlined the aims and objects of the Klan. He denied any hostility towards the Negro Improvement Association. He believes America to be a white man's country and also states that the Negro should have a country of his own in Africa. He denied that his organization, since its reorganization, ever officially attacked the Negro. He has been invited to speak at forthcoming convention to further assure the race of the stand of the Klan.

And that was it. Garvey said no more, having answered some of the questions raised by his visit to the Klan, but having ignored others and raised a few more. He did, however, allow a spokeswoman to tell reporters that "Garvey intends to reorganise the Black Star Line shortly, and it is possible [Imperial Wizard] Clarke may buy stock in the new company."

Possible, yes—but not certain. And to this day no one seems to know for certain whether or not the Ku Klux Klan became a stockholder of the Black Star Steamship Line. It remains, though, intriguing to contemplate;

the possibility of Klan money helping to ship Africans back to their home-land is as stunning as it is . . . well, sensible.

GARVEY'S ATTIRE WHEN HE VISITED the Klan made him look pompous, even laughable. It was, in fact, the same outfit he wore at all the formal occasions he attended, all the speeches he gave, and it could not have been more different from Mrs. Martin's bedsheets and pillowcases. If the Klansmen looked like a child's notion of a ghost, Garvey looked like a small nation's potentate or a large parade's grand marshal.

His silliest adornment was his hat, a Napoleonic bicorn with fluttering plumage; beneath it he wore white gloves and a dark blue uniform with gold epaulets and tassels and brass buttons bright enough to make a passerby blink. A belt crossed his chest at a forty-five-degree angle. A sword hung in a sheath from his waist, a sword he had never used, in part because he had no idea how to wield it. It slapped against his leg as he walked.

But just as the Ku Klux Klan was to be taken seriously for its violence, Garvey and the UNIA were to be taken seriously for both their persistence and their ability to raise money. Whether the Klan contributed or not, Garvey gave speech after speech in support of the Black Star Line, collecting thousands of dollars from African-American families who could barely afford contributions of any denomination but were determined to show their support. And, if possible, to sail back to Africa, their native land, once the steamship line became a reality.

Garvey also sought money for his Negro Factories Corporation, "to encourage black economic independence."

Slowly but surely his ideas began to catch on. The end of segregation, the beginning of self-rule—it sounded better and better to African-Americans weary of their mistreatment. Self-reliance was, in fact, the theme of one of Garvey's best-known poems, "Have Faith in Self."

> Today I made myself in life anew,
> By going to the royal fount of truth,
> And searching for the secret of the few
> Whose goal in life and aim is joy forsooth.
> I found at last the friend and counselor

That taught me all that in life I should know;
It is the soul, the sovereign chancellor,
The guide and keeper of the good you sow.
I am advised—"Go ye, have faith in self,
And seek once more the guide that lives in you. . . ."

IN NEW YORK, A UNIA rally attracted 25,000 men and women eager to learn of Garvey's plans to weigh anchor. It was a large turnout, larger than expected, and J. Edgar Hoover didn't like it. Already behaving as if he were the head of the BOI, which he would be before long, he had several times in the past sent agents to listen to Garvey and observe those in attendance. Although he could not publicly admit it, Hoover, along with the Klan, favored the whitest America possible, and he probably would have invested in the Black Star Line himself if he could. He was certainly in favor of the idea behind it.

Still, he was troubled by Garvey, saw him as a rabble-rouser, and feared him for his ability to attract large crowds of black people. J. Edgar Hoover did not like large crowds of people with dark skin, especially when they were listening to a lecturer who whipped up their passions and raised the energy level as they slapped hands with one another in brotherhood and shouted out "Amens!" They might be peaceful now, and they were just that on their night in New York—but who knew what would happen in the future, what those crowds might do if they were all worked up, agitated and inflamed, for some other reason? As Hoover was well aware, they had reasons aplenty for dissatisfaction.

"Garvey is a West Indian Negro," he jotted down in a memo,

who [has] been particularly active among the radical elements in New York City agitating the Negro movement. Unfortunately, however, he has not as yet violated any federal law whereby he could be proceeded against on the grounds of being an undesirable alien, from the view of deportation. It occurs to me, however . . . that there might be some proceeding against him for fraud in connection with his Black Star Line propaganda.

As it turned out, there was. Or so ruled the judge and jury that heard the case Hoover brought against Garvey. The defendant was indicted on charges of mail fraud for selling stock in the Black Star Line after it had gone bankrupt. It might have been true; then again, the conviction might have been the result of Hoover's bigotry as much as Garvey's illegal behavior. Historians debate the charge even to the present.

Nonetheless, Garvey was sentenced to five years in prison, and he did not take the verdict with equanimity.

> "Mr. Garvey immediately burst into a storm of rage," reported the *Kansas City Call.* "An undignified tirade of foul abuse and low language followed," according to [socialist] Hubert Harrison, in which "both judge and district attorney [were described] as 'damned dirty Jews.'" And the *Call* painted a final pitiful picture of the convicted UNIA leader "escorted to the elevator . . . by eighteen marshals through a crowd of sobbing sympathizers."

Eventually it was decided that Garvey's sentence would be reduced to three years, but only if he could provide $15,000 for bail. It was money he did not have, had never had—but Amy Jacques would not be dissuaded. Perhaps the most supportive of Garvey's supporters, she hectored some of her friends and associates, pleaded with others, threatened still more, and within a few weeks had raised the entire amount in either cash or promissory notes.

The money was handed over to authorities and Garvey was free. But not happy. He began a speaking tour of the country on which he spoke more venomously than ever about the treatment of blacks in the United States. Among those who cheered him on were men and women whom he had rescued from poverty by providing them jobs with the UNIA. Among those who didn't were the tyrannical Hoover and members of the almost comically corrupt Harding administration. For them, it was all too much. Garvey had to be silenced.

In fact, he was deported. Speaking out as angrily as he had when first sentenced, Garvey continued to insist on his innocence, to fume at such treatment for a President-General. But his words would soon be heard no more.

Garvey's voyage back to his homeland of Jamaica, according to biographer Grant, was a sad occasion for more than just the deportee. Its implications were much greater.

> Garvey's and the Black Star Line's failure was every aspiring black American's failure. Months, sometimes years later, it produced a dull referred pain, whose source was not always immediately obvious, but was reminiscent of so many aches that had gone before. James Saunders Redding recalled how the collapse of the Brown and Stevens Bank—"the richest and safest Negro bank in the world"—in which the Black Star Line had some deposits brought his father to the verge of tears "not because he lost money in that disastrous collapse—he didn't— but because that failure cast dark shadows over the prospects of a self-sustaining Negro culture."

Garvey stayed in Jamaica for a few years, then took up residence in London, where he died in 1940. He suffered two strokes, at least one of which came, supposedly, after reading an obituary of himself that was, in addition to being slightly premature, full of mistakes and highly critical of his life's work. His body was taken back to Jamaica for burial and enshrinement.

In the United States, it was not an especially sad occasion for the "black intelligentsia," which, according to historian Page Smith, had always been embarrassed by Garvey's "spectacular antics—words big with bombast, colorful robes, Anglo-Saxon titles of nobility to his staff (Sir William Ferris, K.C.O.N., for instance, was his editor, and Lady Henrietta Vinton Davis, his international organizer); his steam-roller-like mass meetings and parades and lamentable business ventures."

His work, however, would be more appreciated, and his excesses overlooked, as time went on. Schools in a number of countries, including the United States, have been named after him, as have numerous streets and public parks. In 1965, Dr. and Mrs. Martin Luther King, Jr. visited his shrine in Jamaica, with Dr. King, who would be compared to Garvey as an orator, later receiving the first Marcus Garvey Prize for Human Rights.

In 2011, the Obama administration was petitioned to pardon Garvey for his mail-fraud conviction. The decision was announced at a press conference. The administration had refused, on the grounds that, as a matter of policy, it did not offer pardons posthumously. Obama was not asked for an opinion of Garvey's life and times, nor did he volunteer one. The next reporter to ask a question changed the subject.

DESPITE THEIR BEING CLOSE FRIENDS, Carter G. Woodson was as different from Marcus Garvey as it was possible for one person to be from another. He did not hatch unrealistically appealing plans like the Black Star Line. He did not dress outrageously or speak with overly practiced elocution; in fact, on those rare occasions when he addressed public forums, his voice was so soft that it was hard to hear at times. Despite his color, and the influence that would eventually be his among learned African-Americans, he never seemed a danger to the white establishment, was never the subject of a memo by J. Edgar Hoover; Woodson was too earnest and scholarly to attract large groups of followers. But his imprint, if not his name, has long outlived him, and after all these years his legacy remains a surprisingly important part of the black experience in the United States today. If only anyone knew.

Woodson, born in Virginia in 1875, is the first American of slave parentage to have earned a Ph.D. in the United States. He may, in fact, be the only one. Neither of his parents could read or write, but they managed to influence their boy's academic yearnings nonetheless—all the more, probably, for they could not bear the thought of their son suffering through their own deficiencies and being fated to similar employment. His father, Woodson would one day relate, insisted that "learning to accept insult, to compromise on principle, to mislead your fellow man, or to betray your people, is to lose your soul."

Woodson studied at the Sorbonne in Paris, and afterward received his M.A. from the University of Chicago and his Ph.D. from Harvard. By that time, he was well on his way to a conclusion that would influence his entire career: that history "was not the mere gathering of facts. The object of historical study is to arrive at a reasonable interpretation of the facts. History is more than political and military records of peoples and nations. It must include some description of the social conditions of the period being studied."

The social conditions of 1920 were difficult, painful, even de-humanizing for African-Americans. Yet Woodson, with his training in the great sweep of history, its emphasis on the dispassionate overview rather than the heat of the moment, was able to look at those conditions with an almost detached equanimity. It was not, in many cases, what his fellow blacks were hoping for from him. As far as they were concerned, Woodson contemplated the period with a certain passivity, and much too forgivingly. Even as a young man, he had concluded that racial prejudice "is merely the logical result of tradition, the inevitable outcome of thorough instruction to the effect that the Negro has never contributed anything to the progress of mankind." It was hardly the talk of a firebrand.

But if Woodson had truly been a passive man, he would not have been able to change that perception. Change it, though, he did—not entirely, but more, it seemed, than any one man possibly could.

Finished with his formal schooling, Woodson began his life's work by forming the Association for the Study of Negro Life and History (although the organization still exists, the "Negro" has since been changed to "African American," without a hyphen). After a few years, the Association started to publish an immediately influential magazine called *The Journal of Negro History*, which concentrated not on polemics but profiles, bringing to life notable black figures of the past and calling attention to their contributions to men and women of both races. In addition, Woodson founded the Associated Publishers, the first African-American publishing company in the United States. Headquartered in a row house in Washington, D.C., the first two stories served as office space and printing facilities. The third floor was where Woodson lived. It was all he could afford at the time, but he did not mind. His life and work were one; there was no reason for them not to share the same abode.

In addition to publishing the magazine, he was able to continue working "on two scholarly projects he had begun the year before: the research on free blacks in the antebellum period and a study of blacks during Reconstruction." It is no wonder that despite his relative youth, Woodson was by 1920, at the age of forty-five, known as "the Father of Black History." By those who know his work, he continues to be so regarded today.

It sounds like achievement enough for one man. But there was more. Woodson was also an author, and black self-esteem was a principal theme of his two texts, *The History of the Negro Church* and *The Mis-Education of the Negro*, books that continue to be widely read in academic circles. The latter, in fact, is a particular favorite of Garvey's UNIA, which still exists, and to this day urges African-Americans to study the Woodson volume, finding it "a key to our freedom as a people." Another of his books, *The Negro in Our History*, had sold 90,000 copies by 1966, by which time it had been published in eleven editions.

Woodson worked closely with schools—those schools that would have him, at least—in emphasizing the historical importance of the black man and woman to our nation's founding and growth. He felt certain that, if he could only carve out a place for the achievements of African-Americans in the curricula of a few institutions, more would surely follow. He could not have imagined the extent of that following. Today, Black Studies, or African-American Studies, is a recognized major in almost every college and university in the United States. No man is more responsible than Carter G. Woodson.

Further, and perhaps of equal importance, Woodson was also the guiding force behind "Negro History Week," the second week in February, which he chose because within those seven days both Abraham Lincoln and Frederick Douglass had been born. According to a brief publication of the NAACP, of which he was a member, "Dr. Woodson often said that he hoped the time would come when Negro History Week would be unnecessary; when all Americans would willingly recognize the contributions of Black Americans as a legitimate and integral part of the history of this country."

That time has not yet come. But one cannot help concluding that Woodson would have taken some degree of pleasure in knowing that, beginning in 1976, America's bicentennial year, all of February became Black History *Month*—and not only in the United States, but in the United Kingdom and Canada as well.

Nineteen twenty was Dr. Carter G. Woodson's year, the peak of his influence, but he would remain there for the rest of his life. The enduring strength of his achievements and the anonymity of the achiever would have been exactly what he desired.

CHAPTER ʃIX

The Robber Barons and Their Serfs

W OMEN, IT SEEMED CERTAIN, WOULD soon have the right to vote; as spring began to turn up the temperature into summer, it was just a matter of days, and enthusiasm, already in the air, continued to build. But many of their men, husbands and sons and brothers who toiled day after day both above and below the ground to earn the most meager of wages, would not be able to get away from work long enough to cast their ballots. For them, the right to be counted at the polling place was as hollow as the mineshaft responsible in May, 1920, for the Matewan Massacre, one of the most ferocious labor–management conflicts in American history.

Disputes of one sort or another had been simmering for a long time, going back to the previous century, when strikes were few but the animosities that would eventually make them commonplace were becoming more and more virulent. The working man versus his employer: it was a drastic change in the American workplace—the robber barons no longer so intimidating to the people they had hired, those who labored so arduously finally rebelling against those who paid them paltry wages and demanded so much of their lives in return. The rebellion was, many believed, too long in coming.

For the most part, the strikers were first- and second-generation Americans, men who had been falsely encouraged in their vision of the United States, not only by their own yearnings and the rare success story of a countryman, but, all the more, by the propaganda of the steamship companies who desperately needed passengers, not just cargo, to make their transatlantic routes profitable.

So they promised El Dorado. People eager for New World fantasies listened with more longing than reason. Pamphlets published by the shipping lines showed princely homes, velvet lawns, and spectacular views of other such manses from afar; the implication was that such living conditions could be had by all. Other pamphlets hinted at dignified and highly remunerative employment, also available for all. Still others mentioned the educational opportunities that awaited the children of immigrants, who would then grow up and be able to find positions of wealth and power for themselves, perhaps even international renown.

How many people truly believed the ballyhoo is impossible to say, but more often than not the ships that crossed the Atlantic were packed with dreamers fore to aft, the prices reasonable because amenities, even necessities like toilets, were nonexistent. For the passengers, the moment they were herded onto ships and assigned their own almost immovably tight spaces, it was the beginning of doubts that the dream would come true.

The role of steamship companies in breaking the hearts of Europeans bound for America is little acknowledged in volumes of history, as is the fact that many of those Europeans, having arrived in the United States and found themselves treated as menial labor at best, now began to look longingly toward the Russian Revolution as well as to listen attentively to the preaching of anarchists, many of whom were their own countrymen.

Hopes were also being shattered for native-born Americans, among whom internal immigration was increasing dramatically, and not just because of African-Americans who found the South so unwelcoming. Young white farm boys with similar dissatisfactions were also deserting their homes and heading north. The result of all this, the so-called Great Migration, was a stirring of the melting pot such as there had never been before. The United States was changing in population, in demographic makeup, and in values and means of cultural expression.

And in even more ways: 1920 was the first census year in which the country's urban population surpassed the rural. It was a landmark in U.S. history, a sign that the only way of life generations of earlier immigrants had ever known was slipping away and would eventually be gone forever. It was as well an omen: there would be changes ahead of such magnitude that few people could even imagine them now.

Farms were no less important to America's economy and dinner tables than they had been before; but even in agriculture's lush years, the barrenness of life surrounding the fields—the tedium of the plains and endlessness of the skies—was becoming harder and harder for young people to endure. They had been fleeing, leaving their homes behind them, little by little since before the Civil War. By 1920, the pace had picked up exponentially, and the Midwest, outside of the cities, was beginning to crumble. Populations shrank in some villages as if they had been ravaged by the plague. Once-prosperous stores shut down for good, while others, already long closed, had begun to cave in on themselves, with their timbered roofs sinking and the planks that made up the outer walls collapsing; the result was that many once-bustling communities looked as flimsy as if they were fronts for movie sets that had been left behind after shooting. As the deterioration continued, a few towns became so small, so inconsequential, that they were condemned to the ultimate indignity: officially removed from the map by Rand McNally. Much of the cotton went unpicked, the wheat unharvested.

The young men and women who turned their backs on agriculture headed to places like New York, Chicago, Boston, Philadelphia, and even out west to the newly exciting movie capital, Los Angeles. Some did so with their minds full of the kinds of visions written down by F. Scott Fitzgerald: tales of reckless love and even more reckless deeds; of parties at which almost fatal amounts of alcohol drowned inhibitions; of sophisticated women in daring attire and sophisticated men whose apparel was just as daring in its own way and, like that of the women, brightly bejeweled where appropriate.

Further, there were tales of nightclubs and speakeasies and midnight rides to Harlem, the white kids gathering up their gumption as they eased their way cautiously into after-hours black enclaves, perfumed and smoky dives where, after a few minutes, the dark-skinned people stopped staring at them and made room for them and their money at the bar. Soon, all eyes went to the stage. And all ears listened as men both black and white, smooth and wrinkled, played their jazz, played *with* their jazz, the notes running all over the joint, as if deciding for themselves where they would land—yet still, miraculously, under the musician's control. Did any of the white boys want some weed? There was always a seller, the air thick with his product, the dives not smoky just because of tobacco.

And the young adults from farm country had seen Fitzgeraldian visions not just in his books but in his ever more popular short stories in the *Saturday Evening Post*; they had read of wealthy couples strolling through the eternal shadows of skyscrapers to assignations on Park Avenue or the Upper East Side, afternoon sex on silk sheets covering king-size beds in penthouse apartments. Then home to their spouses. And they had read about mansions in the Hamptons, to which one drove in touring cars with their running boards and rumble seats and the tops down, vehicles that cost more than a lifetime's yield on the back forty. How ya gonna keep 'em down on the farm after they've read "Bernice Bobs Her Hair" and "The Rich Boy"?

FOR THE MOST PART, JOBS were available for whites in the North, certainly more than for blacks; employment opportunities might have spiked during the war, but they remained high afterward, as factories that had previously converted to war materiel converted back to the consumer goods that were necessary for an eventually booming postwar economy. But, like the young African-American men from the South, the whites were crushed to realize that they had traded the variety of demanding tasks on the farm for the sameness of tasks in industry. They worked on the railroad, and toiled "with the regularity of machinery, dropping each rail in its place, spiking it down, and then seizing another." Or they signed on for backbreaking assignments in steel mills; mind-numbing duties on automotive assembly lines, which required them to perform the same simple task all day; stomach-churning chores in meat-packing houses, or days spent in the perpetual night of coal mines, swinging picks into solid walls of rock, hefting loaded shovels into overflowing trams. Men worked six days a week, maybe six and a half; they spent twelve hours a day on the job, maybe longer; they made less money in a month than their bosses spent for lunch on some days.

The Northern cities of 1920 were the great low-levelers of American life. In 1920, historian David Kyvig had learned, "Between a third and two-fifths of the American population could be classified as poor even by the modest standards of the time." These people did not need Bolsheviks to tell them that their working conditions would lead to early graves. They did not need anarchists to tell them that the buildings in which they worked were unsafe, poorly ventilated, and lacking proper escape routes in case of emergency.

This last flaw proved especially tragic in the Triangle Shirtwaist Factory fire of 1911. One hundred forty-six employees were killed, most of them women, recent immigrants, Jews and Italians, virtually none of whom had ever seen a factory in the farmland and villages of the old country. One of the youngest of the casualties, an especially hard-working, empty-eyed little girl, her name and land of origin unknown, was eleven years old. Yet one more voice in a cacophonous chorus of screams as the fire grew like mushroom clouds would grow later in the century. Not until 9/11 in the first year of the following century would New York suffer a disaster to surpass the blaze at Triangle.

It was the owners of the company, ever trying to save money so they could make more of it, who were responsible for the disaster. They had locked doors which, if unlocked, would have allowed most of the women to escape the rampaging flames. But the owners had secured them precisely for that reason, to prevent escape by women who wanted to sneak away from their tasks for a few minutes to smoke, sneak in a snack, or maybe just take a few breaths of cleaner air, which they would suck in like handfuls of water on a fast-drying oasis.

And with this we arrive yet again in this volume at the great paradox upon which the United States was built: So many of the men who made the country into the world's greatest power—from those who paid for the railroads to be built to those whose steel mills provided the necessary metal; from those who provided the munitions for the Spanish-American War to those who financed the Panama Canal and other major construction projects, such as bridges and dams, mills and ever-taller office buildings; from those who owned the coal mines and oil wells, the appliance factories and the newly automated clothing plants—it was on too many occasions the men in such positions, the very men creating the wealth of the nation, who were destroying the lives of their workforce in the process. The dark side of Andrew Carnegie and his ilk was their willingness to inflict a perpetual midnight on the lives of their workers, the brawn that made America's place in the sun possible. It was not radicals from abroad who most seriously threatened the United States in 1920, not the Bolshies, not anarchists: it was the capitalists at home. And their behavior was not only ignored by legislative bodies and police officials; it was often *supported.*

It was further supported, much later, by a British historian whose body of work is voluminous, eminent, and enduring. Yet somehow, his view of American labor in the early twentieth century ran off the rails of logic. I include it here, in paraphrased version, almost as comic relief. The italics are mine; the punch line, so distant from the truth, demands emphasis.

> As the historian Paul Johnson reminds us . . . so-called robber barons such as the Vanderbilts, ruthless though they undoubtedly were, not only left magnificent monuments in their wake but also created the vast national enterprises into which the teeming multitudes of immigrants were absorbed *and uplifted by the engine of prosperity.*

The engine did not uplift most immigrants: it ran over them.

Far closer to the truth is William James, the most prominent American philosopher of the twenties, perhaps of any time. A scholar who often wrote obtusely and virtually never with vulgarity, James excoriated the robber barons in an uncharacteristically succinct phrase for their willingness to kneel before "the bitch-goddess **SUCCESS.**"

Or, as the prominent socialist economist Henry George put it—briefly, but at the end of a long treatise, the "association of poverty with progress is the great enigma of our times."

IN 1920, THERE WAS THE almost inconceivable total of more than 3,600 strikes in the United States. Less than a century earlier, there would not have been any of them; now there were ten *every day!* They had become staples of employee–employer relations, but for the former were more of a series of small wars that seldom achieved the goals of the strikers' war. They gave the men a chance to state their grievances publicly, and to adversely affect their companies' profits for a time, but the strikes simultaneously cost the workers badly needed income and sometimes even their jobs, as, when the battles ended, new workers might be hired to take the place of those who had previously turned their backs on the factories. The power of capital did not yield to the power of the man with the sweating brow.

In fact, the strikes almost always ended up solidifying the power of the company while at the same time weakening the power of the union, if there even was one and if it had ever had any power to begin with. The strike might have been a weapon for the employee, as people still liked to think, but its edge was dull, and most employers were too strong to be permanently affected by its thrusts.

Nonetheless, the anti-management, anti-establishment momentum had long been building among America's working men, and after the Great War it would reach a peak that it would not attain again for several decades.

THERE ARE FEW JOBS AS demoralizing as coal-mining, and so it is no surprise that it was probably the most strike-riddled of occupations. In 1902, the industry made headlines and struck fear into the marrow of Americans, when more than 140,000 miners in Pennsylvania laid down their picks and shovels. They did so just as an abnormally cold winter was about to begin, "to protest low wages, harsh working conditions and long hours." It took the possibly unconstitutional mediation of President Theodore Roosevelt to settle the walkout on the verge of a great national freeze-out.

In 1920, although in better weather, coal miners in West Virginia decided they had had enough. It was the year after the much-publicized Boston Police Strike, in which many of that city's law enforcers watched for two or three nights, without so much as flinching, as store windows were smashed, the stores' contents looted, and violence awaited anyone who tried to make the case for order. And so it was the year in which Massachusetts governor Calvin Coolidge, best known for seldom opening his mouth, opened it long enough to denounce the police with the famous words "There is no right to strike against the public safety by anybody, anywhere, anytime." The phrase caught on, and as a result so did the previously—and continuously—nondescript Coolidge; in 1920, he was selected by the Republicans to be their vice-presidential nominee.

The year after the police strike, with Americans on edge, wondering which laboring men would strike next, disrupting capitalism, and perhaps even threatening civil war, it turned out to be West Virginia coal miners. They made their case against the owners eloquently. But the very nature of their duties made justice almost impossible for them. How do you fairly compensate a man who spends his entire day underground, descending before dawn, climbing out after dusk, never seeing so much as a ray of sunshine? How do you compensate him for breathing air that is thick with pollutants and chemical fumes, rather than crisp with the breezes of spring or autumn? How do you compensate him for feeling his health and strength slip away week by week, month by month, actually feeling himself get older more quickly than the calendar seems to permit? He will die young. He knows he will die young. Almost all miners do. Pick a miner at random, and the odds are that he has replaced his father, who went to his grave early. His son or sons will replace him when *his* grave is dug, and their lives too will end prematurely. It is the way of things in coal country, and in 1920 West Virginia was its heart.

But coal was one of the key ingredients in the American recipe of success, growth, and domination. And so it would remain for many years to come. Nothing, then, could be allowed to interfere with removing it from the ground, and there was as yet no other way to do it than to send men down into the earth to get it.

Back in 1920, when the West Virginia miners struck, Attorney General Palmer, who sensed the influence of radicals underground as well as atop, was among the most concerned. It was the last gasp for the anti-American forces, he seemed to think. It was also his own last gasp as a presidential candidate, what with other politicians having surpassed him in the public consciousness and his health having noticeably begun to ebb. So great was the matter, Palmer believed, that he insisted on talking personally with President Wilson. Mrs. Wilson agreed to give him a few minutes with her husband, but she was not happy about it. He, on the other hand, was not happy about so short a period with the chief executive. Biographer Robert K. Murray speculates on their conversation:

> What actually was said at this meeting is not known. However, we can guess what happened. Palmer impressed upon the president the seriousness of the impending strike, pointing out its unquestionable effect on the nation's economy and its radical overtones. He then urged the president to take a strong stand and suggest that the government enjoin the miners from striking. Whether President Wilson accepted this latter proposal willingly or reluctantly is a matter for conjecture. Josephus Daniels, secretary of the navy, later maintained that had Wilson been a well man he most certainly would never have consented to Palmer's suggestions.

It hardly mattered to West Virginia miners that the government was going to enjoin them from striking. It was just talk. *No one* was going to enjoin them from striking, and when the specter of the Bolshies inevitably entered the discussion, it is likely that most of the miners rolled their eyes in confusion. Some had never heard of Bolsheviks. Some had never heard of Russia's 1917 uprising. A few had probably never even heard of Russia. There were no newspapers in the underground world, and few miners had the energy to read them at home, if there *was* one at home, when they were lifted out of the mine after dark. They might have known even less about anarchy and those who advocated it.

They were, nonetheless, smart enough to know who their antagonists really were: it was those who employed them and cared not a whit for their hardships—who, in fact, deliberately caused many of them. They referred to their employers, sometimes, in the disdainful singular. The people who ran the mines were "the man." Said one West Virginia miner, summing up his reasons for striking, "We work in *his* mine. We live in *his* house. Our children go to *his* school. On Sunday we're preached at by *his* preacher. When we die, we're buried in *his* cemetery."

As the miners became ever more dissatisfied with their lives under the earth, the man, early in 1920, had become ever more penurious, trying to break the United Mine Workers, the union that the coal men had recently joined, by cutting the salaries of all who belonged to it, promising to restore the money if the miners severed their ties with the UMW. They would also have to sever ties with the American Federation of Labor, or AFL, with which the UMW had recently aligned itself.

It was a tempting offer. But it was the man's offer; it could not be accepted, not even considered rationally. The miners would stick together in their refusal. They were fighting for something larger than a mere pay raise; it was dignity they wanted as well, dignity and respect and a voice in all decisions related to their precarious employment. The man, after all, had no idea what it was like deep in the shaft, walking around in what could so easily turn into a flaming, toxic tomb, his cries echoing to no purpose. The man probably grew timid when he walked down the stairs to the basement of his home.

On May 19, 1920, several members of the Baldwin-Felts Detective Agency, the latter of whom were two brothers, arrived in the town of Matewan, in Mingo County, West Virginia. Miners there were striking. Management had ordered violence in response. The Baldwin-Felts goons stepped off the train and went straight to work, no instructions necessary. They evicted families from company-owned housing. They had been doing this kind of thing for years, and it came to them as naturally as going to church on Sunday. In a number of West Virginia coal towns, they had "forced striking miners from their homes, dumped their meager belongings along the railroad, and [driven] the families at gunpoint from the hollows."

To Baldwin-Felts detectives, the sudden homelessness of a mining family was another successful day for themselves.

They were successful in Matewan. Most of the miners' shacks had been emptied of possessions and those possessions scattered not atop the railroad tracks this time but along the town's unpaved main street. Finishing their tasks, the Baldwin-Felts men collected their money at the mine's headquarters, then stopped in the town's lone restaurant for a self-congratulatory dinner. They were awaiting the last train of the day back to civilization. They would never be on it.

Sid Hatfield, sheriff of Matewan and one of the legendary Hatfield-McCoy feuders, had been born just a few years after "the Hatfields had tied three McCoys to a pawpaw bush and shot them dead, and he grew up with that meanness in him." But his meanness was on the side of the miners. Sid— everybody called him by his first name—was one of the people, and the people, *his* people, were coal miners. As historian Lon Savage writes, Sid

> had been only a boy during the Spanish-American War, when the nation lost some three hundred men in battle, but he became aware in the ensuing years that West Virginia had lost more men than that in a single year of coal mining accidents. After one of his family's friends was crushed to death, the widow and children were evicted without compensation from their company home to make room for a replacement miner. . . . [Sid] watched all this happen and was as much a part of it as the river and the coal.

He grew up to be a "rather handsome young man, slender, no more than 150 pounds in weight and five feet six in height." But Sid was tougher than he looked. He had to be. The same was true of C. C. Testerman, the equally slight mayor of Matewan and another friend of the miners. Both were wiry, not much body weight but all of it muscle, able to take on opponents of far greater dimensions. Especially when Sid and C.C. held guns in their hands. Tonight, both did.

Accompanied by a small posse, they stood in the shadows of twilight outside the restaurant as the Baldwin-Felts men ate their evening meal that day in Matewan. Stood resolutely. Inside, the detectives finished eating, paid their bill, and started walking toward the front door. The chugging of the last train of the day became faintly audible in the distance.

By then, Sid and C.C. had seen and heard even more than they had expected about the activities of the past few hours. "The report circulated," according to Savage, "that a family with several children had been forced at gunpoint from their home, their furniture set out in the rain, the children left to stand in the drizzle. The stories grew worse: the detectives had thrown out a pregnant woman, a sick child, a tiny baby in its crib, all with nowhere to go. The miners' fury rose."

It didn't matter to Sid and C.C. whether these particular stories were true or not. If they weren't true today, they would be true tomorrow or the day after, as they had been true yesterday—either in Matewan or a community nearby; the Baldwin-Felts methods were well known, oft-repeated. Someone had to take a stand against them, and who better than a Hatfield? When better than now? C.C. agreed and, like Sid, was ready to put his life on the line for the cause.

The train was visible in the distance, its whistle breaking the prickly silence. The detectives, obviously content with their supper, departed from the restaurant and turned down the street toward the depot. Had the miners not been on strike, they would still have been working, would not have seen what Sid was about to do on their behalf. He called out a warning to the Baldwin-Felts boys, waited for a response. The detectives stopped, but none of them said anything. Sid shifted his position slightly for a clear shot and drew his gun. The detectives drew their guns too, but the sheriff had the split-second advantage. He pulled his trigger twice, at two specific targets. His aim was unerring. The two targets, both named Felts, vanished in that instant from the world of the living; Baldwin-Felts was suddenly Baldwin and a bunch of other guys whose names nobody knew.

The gunfire was returned, and the sound of bullets being exchanged caused more people to head for the action, most of them miners who had nothing else to do with their time and had been standing around the fringes of the action as Sid and his men gathered outside the eatery. By the time the shooting ended that night, seven detectives were dead and another had been wounded and taken to a nearby hospital at less than breakneck speed. Two miners were killed, and Mayor Testerman, who had also caught a bullet, maybe more than one, lay in the main street, rolling back and forth in the dirt, clutching at life with all his energy. It was not enough. He became the third casualty from Matewan. Four other residents of the town, men who happened to be in the wrong place at the wrong time, were injured by stray shots.

But there was more to come. The Matewan Massacre is not as famous as many other labor–management clashes, but it was longer, deadlier, and in many ways more dispiriting.

Some days later, relates Geoffrey Perrett, in *America in the Twenties*, the coal diggers would march south from Matewan, "cutting telephone and telegraph wires as they went. The governor mobilized the state police to stop them. The coal operators joined in by organizing a four-airplane air force that bombed and strafed" the miners, killing untold numbers. It was the first strike in American history fought, at least in part, from above.

The miners were horrified by the planes. They believed their own country had gone to war against them. Which, in a sense, it had. The miners sought and found refuge, but hiding was not what they really wanted. They were not that kind of men. It was retribution they sought, and with the help of friends and neighbors the miners were able to arm themselves with all manner of weapons, including submachine guns and homemade grenades. They fired at the planes, heaved the grenades into mobs of state police pursuing them on the ground. It took the lawmen, virtually West Virginia's entire force, to restore order and persuade some of the miners to return to work the next day.

But only for a time. Although the first shots had been fired in May, Matewan was still a battlefield in July, when the miners struck again. This time, though, they went after the owners in a different way. Although a number of the original strikers had returned to the caverns of their employment, resigned to a continuation of the worst, those who had not returned had found a new vocation. Working in the secrecy of their cellars, they put together crude but effective bombs and, in the middle of the night, hurled them into the railroad cars that waited for shipments of coal—which was once again coming out of the ground; but now, with so many of the cars having been blown to pieces, it had nowhere to go.

In retaliation, the company fought back like a cell of terrorists. Unable to find the miners who had actually made the bombs, the man took his revenge on the miners who were now toiling for him again, who had had nothing to do with the destruction of the cars, who had in fact been intending to fill the cars for transport. The man's goons beat his employees into dizziness, unconsciousness, and in a few cases to death. Meanwhile, the families of all miners were imprisoned in tent cities at the foothills of nearby mountains, with armed guards making sure they did not leave. They begged for permission to depart briefly, to find out about loved ones who had gone to war against the man. They were told to stay where they were.

It was not until the first breaths of autumn that the strike finally ended, and for reasons that, at least in part, had nothing to do with labor–management relations. As Savage relates,

> The demand for coal was falling dramatically. Non-union fields undercut those that were unionized. Wage cuts and unemployment eroded the miners' determination. [A.F.L. head John L.] Lewis stopped the organizing drive before it failed.
>
> The coal operators now delivered the coup de grace: an injunction. It bore the names of 316 complainants, nearly every non-union coal company in West Virginia. The injunction restrained the miners in every conceivable way. They were even barred "from further maintaining the tent colonies of Mingo county or in the vicinity of the mines of the plaintiffs."

The next year, 1921, most of the violence moved to coal mines in "Egypt," the nickname for the stretch of land where southern Illinois meets Missouri and Kentucky. In Matewan, most of the miners were on the job again, although at a slightly lower wage than they had been making before the strike. It was all too typical.

What was different about Matewan, although it did the miners no good in the long run, was that the local government sided with labor. In virtually all other cases, government and management were virtually a team, with the former sometimes providing weapons and manpower to the latter so they could defeat the miners. When defeat inevitably came for them, they were left to wonder how they would survive, much less prosper, against the wealthy establishments that both hired and vilified them.

To former president Roosevelt, who had died the previous year and who had been as perceptive a historian as he was a chief executive, it all would have seemed preordained. In one of his many books, he had stated his position with a heartlessly succinct eloquence. History, he wrote, is an ongoing struggle "between the men who possess more than they have earned and the men who have earned more than they possess." He left no doubt about the victor's identity.

IN 1921, ONLY ONE INCIDENT of strike-related violence was reported near Matewan, but, inevitable though it probably was, it hit the town hard. While walking up the steps of the town hall in nearby Welch, West Virginia, where he was to stand trial on trumped-up conspiracy charges related to another strike, Sid Hatfield was accompanied by a second defendant and their wives. Suddenly gunshots shattered the early-morning quiet. One of them hit Sid in the arm and another three or four in the chest. He was dead before he hit the ground. Mrs. Hatfield almost fainted, then began crying, wailing her husband's name over and over, eventually lunging forward and hugging him one final time, kneeling on the steps beside him and holding him tightly, as if to squeeze life back into him. Those who sought to carry the body away had to fight off Sid's sudden widow, as gently as they could.

No one ever caught the killer or killers. It was not surprising, but what *was* surprising was that there were no attempts to avenge Sid's death. Someone knew who had pulled the trigger; someone knew who had ordered the hit. But Sid was dead; nothing would change that, and efforts to get even would only lead to further efforts to get even, and at some point it all had to end; life had to go on in the southwest corner of West Virginia without the innocent living in constant and pointless fear.

Besides, by this time Matewan was spent, emptied of the energy that revenge demanded. The town had gone back to work, and the old, familiar grimness through which they lived had long since draped itself over the people who lived on the land above the mines.

DRIVING INTO MATEWAN TODAY ON State Route 49, one does not see a sign that says "Welcome" or boasts a slogan like "Home of the 1972 West Virginia Class AA Wrestling Champions." Instead, one sees a historical marker with the words "Matewan Massacre" serving as the headline:

> In 1920 area miners went on strike to gain recognition of UMWA. On May 19 of the same year, twelve Baldwin-Felts Agency guards came from Bluefield to evict the miners from company houses. As guards left town, they argued with town police chief Sid Hatfield and Mayor Testerman. Shooting of undetermined origins resulted in the deaths of two coal miners, seven agents, and the mayor. None of the 19 men indicted were convicted.

It takes almost as long to read the marker as it does to drive through the town. The population is less than five hundred today, and to many of them coal-mining doesn't seem so bad when there's nothing else to do. New equipment has made the job less physically demanding than it used to be: much of the heavy-duty digging is done by machines, and fleets of powerful fans keep the air circulating below the ground, reducing toxins and stagnation. Still, it is coal-mining, and coal does not grow on trees, ripe and easy for the picking. Those who dig for it remain men who have but a nodding acquaintance with sunshine.

CHAPTER SEVEN

The Beginning of Ponzi's Dream

THERE WERE, HOWEVER, MORE HUMANE ways to mistreat the American working man than to damage his body and perhaps terminate his existence. There were ways to steal from him without affecting his employment at all, especially the man who had a good enough job to have put some money away for his family and the future he was hoping to provide them. An Italian named Carlo Pietro Giovanni Gugliemo Tebaldo Ponzi, sometimes known by the aliases Charles P. Bianchi and Charles Ponei, discovered one of those ways.

Ponzi, who became better known by the Americanized version of his first name, Charles, was born in 1882 in the northern Italian province of Ravenna, the small town of Lugo, in "a decidedly working-class neighborhood; down the street was the ghetto where Lugo's large Jewish population had been required to live since the 1700s. At the other end of the street was the Church of Pio Suffragio, a gloomy sanctuary filled with baroque stuccos of cherubs and frescoes depicting the deaths of saints."

No wonder he wanted to get out. Nor is it any wonder that others wanted to get rid of him. As a boy, virtually his sole interest was discovering how much trouble he could cause in the neighborhood, how many little crimes he could commit without getting caught, how many saints he could appall even though they had passed from the realm of the living. Biographer Donald H. Dunn tells us "that relatives weary of paying his fines for gambling, petty theft, and forgery, had put up the money to get the young man out of the country." It was the United States to which they exiled him, not in hopes of his finding golden streets, but in hopes that American law-enforcement officials would keep him either in line or in prison.

Ponzi felt no guilt about his relatives' chipping in to get rid of him. In fact, he could not have been happier. Not so his mother. When Carlo was but a child, Mrs. Ponzi "dreamed aloud about the illustrious future she wanted for him, building what he called 'castles in the air' in her stories of the glory she hoped he would achieve. A favorite notion was that her smart, pampered boy would follow the example of one of her grandfathers and become a lawyer and perhaps even a judge." Instead, poor Mrs. Ponzi found her son *in need* of lawyers and *facing* judges. As for the "castles in the air" that floated through Ponzi's dreams, he would build them, all right, but then he tried to sell them—and that was when his problems began. Many years, however, awaited that sorry occasion—and its sorrier results.

In the meantime, Mrs. Ponzi was disconsolate. She had always hoped her son would succeed in Italy. She wanted the family to see him triumphant, to enjoy the neighbors' envy of her; she wanted to be a witness to his life, not someone who learned about it long-distance in letters. When he was shipped across the ocean, she chose to believe that *he* was the one who had decided on the voyage, not virtually the entire *villaggio* of Ravenna. Yes, that was it; he had simply made up his mind to achieve his success on a grander stage than Ravenna. His vision was ambitious; so, too, must be his *teatro*.

Mrs. Ponzi might have admired her son's ambition, but no sooner did his boat pull away from the dock than more tears began to flow down her cheeks than her flowered handkerchief could absorb. As for Ponzi, he too felt the immediate sting of absence. Later in life, he would conclude that leaving his mother was the most sorrowful event of his younger days, and in some ways one from which he never fully recovered. Other than that, though, he was pleased with his expulsion—this despite the fact that he passed through Ellis Island in 1903 with but a few dollars, a few shirts and pairs of pants, and a train ticket from New York to Pittsburgh.

But even then, Ponzi's belief in his ability to fleece his fellow man never wavered. His ambitions far outran his years, and he could realize those ambitions only with the big score, the ultimate scam. In the meantime, like anyone else on the make in the land of liberty, he would work his way up the ladder, mastering a variety of small deceits. Pittsburgh would be his starting point. He had been told that a distant cousin awaited him there, a man who would be able to provide employment, something to get himself started.

But Pittsburgh was not the place for him, and his dissatisfaction was evident after a matter of days. He and his relative did not get along with each other—and, to make things worse, the relative did not, as advertised, have a job for Ponzi. He did not even have any suggestions, other than the steel mills, and these Ponzi would not even consider. Further, the cousin did not have a spare room for him; he told Charles he would have to find somewhere else to stay.

After a few weeks of searching for employment and being forced to live in a shabby Italian rooming house, he gave up on Pittsburgh and went back to New York, where he took any work he could find: as a grocery clerk, a road drummer, a factory hand, a dishwasher.

A bright young man, and a quick learner when he applied himself, Ponzi learned to read and write his new language, albeit with the occasional glitch, within a year. It was at about that time that he got a job with another distant relative, this one in Boston. The man, Joe DiCarlo, was cordial, welcoming, and absent an honest bone in his entire body. Now *this* was a man to whom Charles could look up. "I ship stuff on the railroad for the food companies," he told the young man, a second cousin of a third cousin, "takin' it off at this end and splittin' it up among the stores or movin' it on east. It's paperwork mostly. 'Cept now and then I do a little sellin' of my own." He winked, then went on to explain that "a crate o' tomatoes here, a barrel o' flour there"—would sometimes get lost in transit. "There are ways to cover it up," DiCarlo told his apprentice, "if you got the right papers. The letter I got says you had enough schoolin' to be good with numbers. You'll be helpin' me."

Ponzi smiled. He liked the idea of cheating, just on general principles. And he seemed to have a natural gift. He got better and better at it as he improved his command of English, but he also grew more and more disenchanted, for "with his growing skills came growing profits—profits that seemed only to vanish in his employer's pockets. When he announced in late fall that he was leaving for New York [DiCarlo] nodded understanding." And likely chuckled. Charles had started out his career as an American con man by being conned himself.

For the next sixteen years, Mrs. Ponzi's beloved only child grew to manhood, struggling at one small-time con after another. He once stole 5,387 pounds of cheese that he intended to chop into small pieces and sell for 45 cents a pound. But he was quickly arrested, and then just as quickly released when the clerk who had written out his warrant misspelled his last name, making him, according to the letter of the law, a different person from the one who had been charged. The prosecutor was enraged. Ponzi took it as a sign, skipping out of the courtroom.

On another occasion, Ponzi offered to save a failing bank by promising the president money that he did not have and could not possibly obtain. His hope was that he and his partner, through various machinations, could gain control of the bank, operate it for a few months, and then empty it of its contents. Ponzi was undeterred by the fact that he knew no more about how to run a financial institution than he did how to turn a double-play on a baseball field. But he would learn as he went along; his confidence, he was certain, would carry him to skill, and the eventual result of the skill would be a financial windfall.

It did not work out that way. The bank president saw through Ponzi's ignorance and refused to hire him. Further, certain that the young man's intentions had been dishonest all along, he called the police. Ponzi barely escaped prison again. He was developing a skill in outrunning the law; so far, he had shown no indications of any others.

In New Orleans, he teamed up with a minister of dubious repute, and the two of them claimed they would rid the city of criminals who were harassing the local businessmen; the city council had only to pay Ponzi's "secret society" a fee of $10,000. It was a lot of money, but city officials seemed almost ready to hand it over. At the last minute, though, they changed their minds when they discovered that the secret of the secret society was the total of its membership: two—Ponzi and the parson, and neither of them had ever confronted an organized-crime ring before, nor did either possess the know-how or courage to do so. As was the case with the bank, Ponzi had anticipated more on-the-job training, but members of the city council decided not to give the dubious pair of crime-fighters a chance. The two crooks were told that neither their services nor their presence were wanted any longer in New Orleans, and off went the Italian again, separating from his partner at the city limits.

Working his way through the South, Ponzi ended up in Brocton, Alabama, where he once again refused to be discouraged by his ignorance. He came up with a plan to provide the town, small but growing, with electric light and running water. "I have no figures to submit at this time as to the cost of the plan," he admitted before a meeting of the town council. "I have no money to pay for any of it. What I propose to do is form a corporation and ask each member of this fine community to subscribe to one or more shares of its preferred stock—enough to pay for the cost." And on he went, doing more to talk himself out of employment in Brocton with every sentence he uttered. The council, most of its members yawning, said it would discuss Ponzi's offer, but he knew better. Rather than wait for its decision, he thought the wiser course was to hit the road again.

This time, though, it proved to be not so wise after all. Heading north, so far north that he was no longer in the country, he was arrested for forging checks in Montreal. Shortly after regaining his freedom, he found himself in jail down south again in Atlanta, charged with smuggling Italians into the United States illegally. He denied the charge, but the five men who were now residents of America because of Ponzi all testified against him, and to that there was no defense. Writes biographer Mitchell Zuckoff,

> Ponzi was given a job in the prison laundry, but his linguistic skills soon won him a transfer to the mail clerk's office. He impressed his boss, prison record keeper A. C. Aderhold, as

smooth, smart, and congenial, a clever young man with a gift for figures who kept error-free books without complaint. The only peculiarity Aderhold noticed was what he called Ponzi's "obsession for planning financial coups." Aderhold thought his assistant took so much pleasure from plotting elaborate moneymaking schemes that he might someday put one into play simply to see if it would work.

After four years in the Atlanta Penitentiary, Ponzi was back in the Northeast, and perhaps more upset than he had been at any other time since arriving in the United States. It was not that he had set such corrupt goals for himself and still not achieved any of them; what troubled him was that he still had nothing about which to brag to his mother. He was, at least in one sense, a good Italian boy; he loved his mama, "thin, graying, tiny, but oh, so beautiful still, back in Italy. Someday, someday he would send for her, mail her a prepaid ticket for the finest stateroom on a transatlantic steamer, along with a thousand dollars cash for a new wardrobe and incidental expenses. Charles Ponzi's mother would come to America like a queen."

But when?

Seventeen years had now passed since he had last seen her, seventeen years since Ellis Island, and Charles Ponzi, so sure of his prospects when he had come ashore, had yet to make good—or, in his case, to make bad profitably. There had been times when he felt so depressed and desperate that he forced himself into legitimate employment again. "He sold groceries and insurance," we are told by Donald H. Dunn. "He worked in a factory. He repaired sewing machines. He pressed suits in a tailor shop. He waited on tables in cafes and hotels. His vocabulary grew, but his bankroll did not."

Especially at his next job, in 1912, working part-time at an Appalachian mining company as a nurse, another position for which he had no qualifications. But although his bankroll remained stagnant, his humanity, barely revealed at all in the past, displayed itself in a manner so courageous and startling as to suggest an incident from a totally different man's biography. In a life remarkable for a variety of reasons, this was to be the most atypical, and heroic, occurrence of all—excessive in its kindness, almost unendurable in its pain. And impossible to figure out.

A woman named Pearl Gossett, a full-time nurse for the miners, was cooking dinner one night in 1912 when the gas stove on which she was working unexpectedly blew up, leaving her with serious burns on the left side of her torso: arm, shoulder, and breast. A few days later, Ponzi heard about the mishap and asked a Dr. Thomas, who was treating Gossett, about her condition. Thomas told him she was near death; traces of gangrene had begun to appear on the burns, and these would almost certainly prove fatal. Ponzi asked whether anything could be done. The only possibility, Thomas said, was a skin graft, but Thomas had asked almost everyone who worked in both the hospital and the mining company to donate skin, and no one was willing. The doctor was saddened, even angry. If only everyone to whom he had spoken would have parted with one inch, just one tiny square inch of epidermis, Pearl Gossett would survive.

Ponzi wanted to know how much skin she needed altogether.

Forty or fifty inches, Thomas said, a substantial amount which would require numerous donors.

Except in this case. Ponzi told Thomas that he would provide all the required skin himself. Thomas was stunned. Is she a friend of yours? he asked after a few seconds to regain his composure.

Ponzi said he didn't know her, had never met her. She wasn't even a *paisan*. But that wasn't the issue. How quickly, he wanted to know, did she need the skin?

The doctor tried to talk Ponzi out of a procedure that would be so painful to him, but could not. Ponzi demanded an answer to his question. She needs the skin as soon as possible, Dr. Thomas finally conceded.

The donor said he was ready.

One more time: Didn't he want to think about it some more? the doctor asked. It was such a drastic measure for one man to provide so much skin.

No.

Was there anyone he wanted to notify, any next of kin, close friend?

No one who could possibly come to his side, he said, thinking of his mother. The doctor nodded, then began striding toward the operating room, telling Ponzi to follow him. Both men cleaned up, prepared for the ordeal ahead of them, and, as soon as he gave one final go-ahead, Ponzi was anesthetized. From Dunn again:

> That night, doctors removed seventy-two square inches of skin from his thighs. Ponzi spent the next few weeks in the hospital, bandaged from hip to knee. When he had nearly recuperated, Ponzi got another visit from Dr. Thomas. The nurse needed more skin.
>
> "Go as far as you like," Ponzi answered.
>
> On November 5, another fifty square inches were taken from his back. He spent most of the next three months in the hospital, battling pain and pleurisy. The donations would leave him with broad white patches of scar tissue on his back and legs. Gossett remained scarred as well, but she recovered.

At the hospital, Ponzi was a savior. Several people there brought him to the attention of various award committees, including the Carnegie Hero Fund, which had been established eight years earlier to honor precisely the kind of civilian valor that Ponzi had just performed. But the fund did not even reply. Neither did other organizations with medals or plaques to present in cases like this. With the exception of a single newspaper article, Ponzi's remarkable display of selflessness went unacknowledged. It is not known whether Charles sent the article back to Italy.

Others at the hospital were happy to care for Ponzi as he slowly recovered, both at the institution and in their homes, and he was grateful for their kindness. They brought him food, flowers, tiny gifts of all sorts. But kindness is not riches. When he finally healed, at least enough to be on his feet and on the go again, he was back to his old priorities. Perhaps he thought that, after what he had gone through in almost complete anonymity, society finally owed him something, and Ponzi was determined to collect. Regardless, the heroic phase of his life, as brief and inexplicable as it had been, was over.

AN INVESTMENT BANKER NAMED CHARLES W. MORSE had been serving a fifteen-year term in the Atlanta Penitentiary for misappropriation of funds at the time that Ponzi was also incarcerated there. The two of them became friends and often played chess together, with Morse constantly giving Ponzi advice about matters other than the game. "Always have a goal, Charlie, my boy," was how Morse began the counsel Ponzi found most memorable. "A goal that keeps getting bigger. If you think that a thousand dollars is enough the first time around, an hour later you'll realize that you might as well go for ten thousand. In another hour, you'll see that you might as well go for ten million. The risk is the same, isn't it? If you have the nerve to go for the first bundle, you have the nerve to go all the way."

Ponzi nodded, thinking it over.

And then, late in 1919, the moment seemed to come.

IT WAS A COMPLICATED IDEA, and it speaks well of Ponzi's intelligence that he could have figured it out. He would not have been able to do so, however, had it not been for something that had happened almost fourteen years earlier. "In April 1906," biographer Zuckoff explains succinctly, "representatives of the United States and sixty-two other countries gathered in Rome with the goal of making it easier to send mail across national borders. . . . A key item on the Rome agenda was to create a way for a person in one country to essentially send a stamped, self-addressed envelope to someone in another."

The problem, of course, is that stamps cost different amounts of money in different countries, and one nation cannot be expected to accept the postage of another's at face value, any more than it can be expected to accept another's currency at face value. But after working through a number of obscure and complex details, and spending numerous hours at the negotiating table, officials in Rome were able to overcome their problems, and the Universal Postal Union was created. All member nations would accept something called the International Reply Coupon of any other member nation. The coupon, as *Business Week* put it, "could be purchased in one country and redeemed for postage stamps" in another. It might have been, as Zuckoff believes, that a "more mundane and obscure financial instrument [than the International Reply Coupon] is hard to imagine," but Ponzi could see the possibilities.

Especially in the wake of an event that was totally unforeseen when the Universal Postal Union was created. One of the results of the Great War was that the economies of most European nations had taken a pounding, and as a result were left with money worth considerably less than it had been before the fighting broke out. One day, Ponzi was reading an article about different currency values in the paper; at the same time, there lay on his desk a coupon from Spain which he planned to use to send a publication called *Trader's Guide* for a businessman in Barcelona. He was just about to go to the post office when it occurred to him that, because of the war, the Spanish International Reply Coupon was no longer worth what it had been earlier. So instead of mailing the *Trader's Guide*, Ponzi decided to do some math. It wasn't easy.

Zuckoff again:

> The coupon had cost the Spaniard thirty centavos, or roughly six cents. After a penny processing fee, it could be exchanged in the United States for a stamp worth five cents. Ponzi knew that the Spanish monetary unit, the peseta, had been devalued after the war, so he began figuring how many pesetas he could buy for a dollar. Using exchange rates published in Boston newspapers, Ponzi concluded that a dollar was worth six and two-thirds pesetas. Because there were one hundred centavos to a peseta, Ponzi calculated that a dollar was worth 666 centavos. If each International Reply Coupon cost thirty centavos, a dollar could buy twenty-two of the coupons in Spain. If Ponzi brought them to the United States, those twenty-two coupons would be worth five cents each, or a total of a dollar and ten cents. By redeeming them in Boston rather than Barcelona, Ponzi would earn a profit before expenses of ten cents, on each dollar's worth of coupons he bought in Spain and redeemed in the United States.

Through a friend in Italy, Ponzi knew that the lira, his homeland's basic monetary unit, had been even more thoroughly devastated than the centavo, and his manipulations could earn three times as much money as would be provided by wheeling and dealing in Spain. "Sixty-six coupons purchased in Rome for a dollar," writes Donald H. Dunn, "would be worth $3.30 in Boston. Ponzi's mind reeled at the thought—he was looking at profits of $2.30 on every dollar spent, or 230 percent, before expenses. Other countries might have even more devalued currencies, and the profits would be even more astronomical. One example was Austria. . . . If redeemed in the United States, Ponzi's initial thousand-dollar investment [in Austria] would yield stamps worth more than twenty-five thousand dollars."

There were complications to work out, of course, even more mind-bending than those that had already presented themselves; but after a few days Ponzi believed he had unbent them sufficiently and was left with nothing more than one final complication: how to get enough money to buy the coupons in bulk—and therefore make profits in bulk. It did not bother him that, so far, what he was proposing to do was legal.

He started a firm called the Securities Exchange Company, which had just the right sound to him. Respectable, trustworthy, and accurate; the company was, after all, exchanging securities. He rented a suite at a prestigious location, the Niles Office Building in downtown Boston, and set up shop. He was unable to afford either the office or the furniture; he had to borrow the money for both. But thanks to a loan from a friend, the office was ready for business in a few days, and its occupant, as he had always been at the start of one of his ventures, was once again optimistic. This time there was reason.

A mere five feet, four inches tall, the little man never lost the bravado of one much larger. Dunn compiled a list of what he believed to be Ponzi's principal attributes: "A confident tone of voice, for example; a tone that indicated its owner knew precisely what he was doing at all times. A dapper appearance, too; an appearance that said—from the well-shined shoes, the pristine celluloid collar above the tightly knotted tie with its small diamond stickpin perfectly centered, the casual breast-pocket hand-kerchief, and the rakish straw hat—that here is a man who, if he is not already successful, will latch on to success at any moment."

And he had better latch on to some quickly. Ponzi's first bill for the office and furniture rental would be due in less than a month, and right now he could not even make a down payment on either. He needed a client, and he needed him fast.

Enter Ettore Giberti, a grocer from the Boston suburb of Revere at whose store Charles and his wife and mother-substitute Rose, née Gnecco, bought their food. Giberti had heard Ponzi brag about the investment opportunities of International Reply Coupons until the subject rang in his ears. Sometimes, he had to admit, he wished Mrs. Ponzi did more of the shopping, but perhaps it was his good fortune that Charles was the customer after all. Giberti, who had a wife, a son, and a net worth of $1,200, was worried about the future. He wanted his boy to go to college, and, God willing, there would be other sons, and perhaps even a daughter or two. Such a joy they would be—but such an expense. And then there was his wife, whom he wanted to see wearing nothing but the finest clothes. As for himself, he wanted to retire before he was an old man, to enjoy life before infirmity caught up with him. Twelve hundred dollars would simply not do, and Giberti could not see a way to make a significant improvement in his financial standing without playing the stock market, which to him was the same thing as gambling. He could not afford to "play" with money that had such important tasks ahead of it.

Finally, he decided to go to the Niles Building and let Ponzi make his pitch with proper documentation in suitable surroundings. Giberti's knock on the door was to Ponzi more than just the sound of opportunity: it was the sound of a fortune about to begin building. With a thumping heart, Ponzi admitted his first customer.

At first, the conversation did not go well. Despite the glib banter he had previously displayed in Giberti's grocery, the dialogue now was different: the grocer was no longer just a food vendor but a potential client, and Ponzi had not yet had any practice in polishing his spiel to the point of making a sale. He feared he was being much too complicated in his explanation of International Reply Coupons, that he was losing Giberti, who had in fact begun squirming in his chair, giving the appearance of a man who would much rather be slicing a rib roast.

So, in a burst of enthusiasm—and irrationality—Ponzi offered Giberti a fifty-percent return on his investment. Just blurted it out. Giberti was astonished. So was Ponzi. Had he *really* promised fifty percent?! Was he *crazy?* Fifty percent was, of course, a possibility, given the vagaries of different countries' exchange rates, but to promise it was quite another matter. As for Giberti, he might have been just a grocer but, like Ponzi, he followed the investment news in the papers and was aware that a fifty-percent profit on an investment was not only out of the ordinary but, as far as he knew, outside the realm of possibility.

Yet Ponzi was his customer, his friend, neighbor; the grocer trusted him. He sat in his chair for what seemed to Ponzi the rest of the afternoon—thinking, calculating, squirming even more than before. Then, despite how fantastic the coupons sounded, or more likely *because* of that, Giberti, a cautious man with his money, decided to hold on to it; he would not make the investment. He thanked his countryman for his time, then prepared to leave.

Ponzi panicked. His first sale, and he was about to lose it. But he was nothing if not a quick thinker. He rose from his desk and, before Giberti could depart, he not only assured him of a fifty-percent return on his money, he offered him employment as the first sales agent for the Securities Exchange Company. Giberti was dumbfounded. What did he know about selling International Reply Coupons?

Charles Ponzi, huckster by trade and instinct, pooh-poohed him. *He* knew what it meant to be a sales agent; he had spent much of his life selling, often the "castles in the air" about which his mother had fantasized—but selling nonetheless. He would teach Giberti what to do, and, before Giberti could decline, Ponzi started in on him, spending the next hour or so instructing his first employee in the intricacies of the scam that had not yet become a scam, giving him information about the product and advice about persuading others to buy: "salesmanship and psychology," he kept repeating; those were the key words, "salesmanship and psychology."

Giberti began warming to the offer. Yes, he wanted the best for his children, but he wanted the best for himself too; and salesman sounded a lot better than butcher.

Ponzi then assured him that he was in the perfect position to sell the coupons. Dozens of people came into his shop every day; if they trusted his judgment on what cut of meat to buy, why wouldn't they also believe him when he suggested an investment? All right, so it was a bit of a reach, but for his trouble, Ponzi said, Giberti would receive a commission of ten percent on each sale. How could he possibly lose? Even if the International Reply Coupons turned out to be a bust—and Ponzi assured him there was no chance of that—he now had a second job that required almost nothing in the way of additional time and effort.

When Giberti finally left Ponzi's office, careful not to have made a firm commitment, he was nonetheless smiling. Two weeks later, in January 1920, he returned positively exuberant. So far, in addition to the money Giberti himself had invested, he had talked eighteen of his customers into handing over at least a portion of their savings to the Securities Exchange Company—and he was just getting the hang of it! The result was that, in addition to his own profits, Giberti was able to present $1,770 to Ponzi.

SEC was officially in business. More than that, it was about to become the thriving enterprise of which Ponzi and the two women who depended on him, his wife and mother, always knew he was capable.

Or was it?

MUCH TO HIS SURPRISE, PONZI suddenly had competition. The Old Colony Foreign Exchange Company had not only joined SEC in figuring out how to make money on International Reply Coupons, but had taken a suite of offices in the Niles Building—and in what Ponzi thought was an inexcusable display of effrontery, had done so on the same floor as his own firm. So appalled was Ponzi that he went to see a fellow Italian on the police force, expressing his fear that people would think these Old Colony impostors, whoever they happened to be, were somehow associated with him, and that such an association could only damage SEC's reputation.

As a favor to his countryman, the cop looked cursorily into Old Colony's methods and the dividends it paid to its investors and determined that its practices, at least so far as he could tell, were perfectly legitimate: Old Colony, providing exactly the same opportunity that the Securities Exchange Company was providing, had done nothing to break the law. And that is the important point to realize at this stage in the development of the Ponzi scheme, a point that too many historians ignore. Such investments as were being accepted in International Reply Coupons were not against the law. It was beginning to look as if, with ultimate irony, Ponzi would be able to line at least his own street with gold and not break the law. Who would have guessed!

He was still worried, though, about the competition from Old Colony. He assured his friend on the force that the company would eventually turn crooked, and pleaded with him to keep an eye on them. The cop said he would. What he did not say was that he would also keep an eye on Ponzi. There was something about the business of both firms that did not smell right to him, nor to other authorities who were starting to become suspicious by the returns the companies offered and, in fact, had in a few cases already paid. They started to gather information, ask questions of clients.

No sooner had Ponzi begun to fret about Old Colony than all eyes in the Boston financial community suddenly turned toward the newer firm. It had taken out an ad in Boston newspapers, summarized as follows by historian Michael E. Parrish:

> For every $10 invested with the firm for ninety days, it promised $15 back. . . . Potential customers were told that Old Colony intended to buy International Postal Union money orders in some foreign currencies and later redeem them in others, reaping profits from the daily and often substantial fluctuations in exchange rates from country to country. Old Colony assured the curious that its activities were perfectly legal and that all who entrusted their funds to the firm would become very rich, very soon.

A ten-dollar investment would bring fifteen dollars in return? Old Colony was promising fifty percent! Ponzi had, of course, made precisely the same guarantee, but he had done so in private, in a face-to-face conversation; he could easily talk the neighborhood butcher into waiting another week or two for his dividends if need be, offering arcane but impressive-sounding explanations for the delay. Then he could pay him back out of future investments—which was, of course, precisely the course of action that would lead Ponzi down the road to thiefdom.

But it was something else altogether to make a public vow of such riches. It was, among other things, too much pressure to place on SEC, which would now have to match Old Colony's figure in just as public a manner, or tumble to the status of also-ran. Ponzi was livid. Had these Old Colony swindlers done their homework? Rates of exchange on foreign currency were constantly varying, and although they were just as constantly favoring Americans, and would continue to favor them for years to come, the percentages were sure to fluctuate. A fifty-percent return simply could not be guaranteed on a regular basis.

Nonetheless, Ponzi authorized his newest salesman, Charles Ritucci, who worked out of the newly opened Plymouth, Massachusetts, office, to print flyers in English, Italian, and Portuguese and paste them onto store windows all over town:

> **Securities Exchange Company, No. 27,**
> **School Street, Boston, Mass.**
> **NOTICE**
> **Do you want to get rich quick? See our agent, Charles Ritucci, 301½ Court Street, Upstairs in Plymouth Theatre Building, who will explain how you can get fifty percent profit on your investment, payable forty-five days from date of investment. Our bank office in Plymouth opens every night from 6 to 8. Yours truly, Securities Exchange Company.**

SEC and Old Colony, the two little firms on the same floor of a Boston office building, were paying the highest dividends of any companies in the country, more than United States Steel, more than Ford Motor, more than J. P. Morgan. Even in capitalism's homeland and primary feeding ground, it didn't seem to be the kind of thing that could last.

It might have been Old Colony that took out the first ads, but it was Charles Ponzi and the Securities Exchange Company that seemed most to benefit from them, perhaps because Ponzi had started making money for his clients before Old Colony, and just as likely because he was such a charmer that neither prospective clients nor hard-bitten newspapermen could resist him. Journalists, in particular, found themselves captivated by the dashing little fellow, and Ponzi delighted in the power he so deftly wielded over them.

That power was never more clearly demonstrated than on a day in the early summer of 1920. A reporter for the *Boston Post* made an appointment with Ponzi to talk about a lawsuit filed by Joseph Daniels, a furniture dealer and once a friend of Ponzi, who had loaned him the money to make the initial payments on his office and furniture. Ponzi had repaid him in full, but now that the Securities Exchange Company had become such a success, he was suing for more. It was a fool's mission; Daniels had absolutely no case against Ponzi and would have been advised so by every lawyer he had consulted, if he had bothered to seek counsel in the first place. The most for which Daniels could hope was publicity as an annoyance.

Nonetheless, Ponzi was happy to talk about the matter, was happy to talk about anything with the press, and invited the *Post* reporter to his home. By the time the interview was over, the reporter had fallen completely under Ponzi's spell, the result of which was that he ended up writing a story that resembled a press release more than an exposé.

DOUBLES THE MONEY WITHIN THREE MONTHS
50 Per Cent Interest Paid in 45 Days by Ponzi—
Has Thousands of Investors
Deals in International Coupons Taking Advantage
of Low Rates of Exchange

A proposition fathered by Charles Ponzi, as head of the Securities Exchange Company at 27 School Street, where one may get 50 percent in 90 days, on any amount invested, is causing interest throughout Boston.

Yesterday his offices were crowded with people trying to loan him money on his personal note.

The proposition has been in operation for nine or ten months, rolling up much money for the man behind it and rolling up much money for the thousands of men and women who are tumbling over themselves to entrust him with their money on no other security than his personal note, and the authorities have not been able to discover a single illegal thing about it.

Ponzi, starting last October or November with hardly a "shoe-string," to so speak, is today rated as worth

$8,500,000—purchaser of business blocks, trust companies, estates, and motor cars. His investors—and they run the gamut of society, rich men and women, poor men and women, unknown and prominent—have seen their money doubled, trebled, quadrupled.

"The story went on merrily from there," writes Mitchell Zuckoff, "liberally and generously recounting the Horatio Alger version of [Ponzi's] life." As for poor Joseph Daniels, even though the story was supposed to be about him and the victimization he claimed to have suffered, he was not even mentioned in the article, his name appearing not so much as a single time—making him feel even more victimized than before. The reporter had, according to his lights, stumbled across a much better story than a small-stakes lawsuit from an undoubtedly jealous plaintiff. He had, rather, found an immigrant who had in turn found the American dream, a poor boy from Italy who had scrambled through almost two decades of insulting employment now amassing a fortune for both himself and those who had believed in him.

Profits were tumbling over profits. There was no apparent end in sight. According to one account, people begged him to take their money, inundated him with it; "Ponzi literally couldn't bank it fast enough. It was packed into shoe boxes and stuffed in desk drawers. In April he took in $120,000 . . . and in July over $6 million." Most of the money was legitimately, if precariously, invested. The remainder, save for $100,000, was spent on a rich man's necessities: house and furnishings, car and clothes. The $100,000 was a gift to an orphanage.

As of June 1920, Charles Ponzi was America's financial wizard nonpareil. But the year had more than six months to go; and, as Ponzi had already discovered, a lot of money can change hands in a short period of time.

PART THREE

CHAPTER EIGHT

The Ignoble Experiment

SSUES OF LEGITIMACY AND ETHICS aside, there seemed no end of ways to make money in the United States in 1920. And by the time the Securities Exchange Company had reached its apogee of profit-making, bootleggers (a term that had originated in the colonial era when it referred to a man's hiding a flask in the long leather sides of his footwear) had figured out how to soar to an apogee of their own. They, however, would remain at their peak much longer than Ponzi, and the damage they inflicted would affect far more people.

What they did, simply put, was to increase their customer base. Prohibition was the greatest seller's market in American history, and the purveyors of illegal alcohol not only began to reach a class of drinker they had never reached before; they provided him with a kind of product he had never consumed before, one with a much better profit yield than the top-shelf liquor that went to top-shelf customers for top-shelf prices.

Eventually, this kind of alcohol and the increased revenue it brought would lead to violence. In 1920, though, the wide-scale killing associated with such mobsters as Al Capone, Dutch Schultz, Bugs Moran, and others was still a year or two away. It would not start in earnest until organized crime had had more time to organize its bootlegging activities; for fiefdoms to be established, which sometimes required importing hired guns from other cities to enforce boundaries; and for even greater greed to inspire the merger of fiefdoms under the control of a Capone, a Schultz, a Moran, all of whom spent much time in the twenties in murderous competition with one another.

A different kind of violence, though, one that did not involve revolvers, machine guns, and speeding getaway cars, had begun to occur in earnest in 1920, and for a while relatively few people knew about it: the victims, in this case, were not newsworthy and they did not die in spectacular fashion. Rather, these were men and women who drank the toxically doctored alcohol that now seemed to control the market, and far more of these lost souls would die during the reign of the Eighteenth Amendment than the crooks who were later portrayed in movies and TV shows. It was the ultimate tragedy of the ultimate in legalized folly.

PROPORTIONATELY, THERE WERE NOT THAT many high-class speakeasies. There were not that many individuals with enough money to patronize them, or to buy the same quality liquor for private use. Nor were there that many individuals with the time, money, and energy to brew or distill their own alcoholic beverages. But there were countless millions of others during Prohibition who were just as desperate, if not more so, to satisfy their thirsts: alcoholics, or close to it; penniless, or close to it. These were the people who patronized the kind of speaks that Wayne Wheeler tried to evoke by calling his group the Anti-Saloon League, speaks that have been described as having "a Hogarthian degradation" to them.

Then there were the people who bought their liquor by the bottle, or even the glass, from equally ragged men who prowled the sidewalks after dark. These were the people who begged for change on street corners during the day, and then, when darkness came, sought out their suppliers, their "pushers," and turned over their earnings for as much booze as they could stomach. They were putting their health and even their lives at stake. They did not always know it. As statistics show, they did not always care.

The number of arrests for drunkenness and disorderly conduct in the United States during Prohibition increased 41 percent compared to figures before January 16, 1920.

The number of arrests for drunken driving went up 81 percent.

Homicides, assaults, and batteries climbed 13 percent.

The population of federal prisons was up an unprecedented 366 percent and included, among others, both customers and vendors of alcoholic beverages.

And federal expenditures on penal institutions of all sorts soared a thousand percent!

What it all meant was that the downtrodden had quickly become much more valued customers to organized crime than the elite. Unlike the latter, the downtrodden were everywhere, quantity over quality; and because what we would today call the "street person" often had sorrows of one sort or another to drown because he was unemployed or poorly employed or luckless in love or even mentally ill, he was often thirstier than the man of means and the woman at his side. The bootleggers who made the kind of liquor sold to these people knew that their beverage did not have to meet the same kind of standards required by the sophisticated tippler. Some of them jokingly referred to the booze they manufactured for the low-end market as "rotgut." But it was not a joke: it was an accurate description of the effect of the bottle's contents.

A RULE OF THUMB FOR the unscrupulous bootlegger was that one bottle of good whiskey could be "cut" into five bottles of rotgut.

> Most often, the cutting was done in the middle of the night, in plants that were set up in warehouses or storage facilities that looked deserted, and therefore not suspicious. The tools of the cutter's trade were water, flavorings, and alcohol. The water increased the quantities of beverage; the flavorings restored the diluted mixture to something approximating its original taste; and the alcohol replaced the lost pizzazz. . . .

[S]cotch, for example, after being watered, might be restored with caramel, prune juice, or creosote, and then spiked back up again with industrial alcohol.

There are few ingredients more dangerous to the workings of a person's internal organs than industrial alcohol. That it had to be manufactured, though, was never disputed, even by Wayne Wheeler, as it was a necessary ingredient in products that were themselves necessary, like cleaning agents, insecticides, and explosives for military use in battle and civilian use in construction. For this reason, an exemption was granted to those firms that manufactured industrial alcohol; they could continue to do so despite the Eighteenth Amendment.

But the Anti-Saloon League, which monitored even the smallest details of Prohibition, was especially wary in this case. "It did not quarrel with the exemption," I wrote in *The Spirits of America*, "but fearful of its misuse, insisted that industrial alcohol be made into an even more deadly compound by requiring that manufacturers add methanol, or wood alcohol, to it. This, reasoned the league in public statements, would ensure that no one, no matter how crazed, would use the product as a beverage base."

That the people who drank industrial alcohol, unaware they were doing so, would also be unaware of the addition of methanol seems not to have occurred to Wheeler and his fellow moralists. With a mantle of rectitude draped over his conscience and worn as proudly as a minister's raiments, Wheeler was as indifferent to the life or death of his fellow man as were the crooks who catered to their thirsts. "The person who drinks this industrial alcohol is a deliberate suicide," Wheeler declared, and to one who might have pointed out that a person didn't *know* he was drinking industrial alcohol, Wheeler would have been unmoved. A person might not have known what specific poison he was ingesting, but he knew he was drinking alcohol of some sort, and that was against the law. It was justification enough for the suffering or death of the customer. According to author Stewart H. Holbrook, Wheeler's attitude "seemed a notice that the [Woman's] Christian Temperance [Union] of Miss Frances Willard had lost out and that an Old Testament God of savage determination had taken over the business in characteristic style."

Even more extreme, and viciously inhumane, than Wheeler, was the comment of one John Roach Straton. Told that a doctor in Indiana had ordered small doses of whiskey to be given to close relatives of the state's governor and attorney general, whose deaths were imminent, he replied, "They should have permitted the member of their family to die, and have died themselves, rather than violate their oaths of office." By profession, John Roach Straton was a minister.

The variety of lethal or near-lethal ingredients that found their way into beverages during Prohibition was a tribute to the perverse creativity of perverse human beings, criminals who made certain that none of the people who bought from them knew precisely what it was they were drinking, or what form of interior demolition it would leave behind. It might not be industrial alcohol that they used as a base, for its legitimate uses sometimes depleted supplies for the nefarious ends of gangsters. In that case, they might have to resort to rubbing alcohol, engine fuels, brake fluids, kerosene, nicotine, shellac, sulfuric acid, formaldehyde, camphor, chloral hydrate, benzol, ether, and even perfume and hair tonic as bases— it made no difference. All were gut-rotters to one extent or another.

They might even add antifreeze to their product. "Bootleggers claimed it was a flavorful additive," I discovered, "especially when it had been newly drained from an automobile radiator, because the pieces of rust in it gave the solution a rich, full body."

And, of course, the same pieces of rust would provide the recommended daily amount of iron.

In the shabby Hell's Kitchen neighborhood of New York were establishments that sold a beverage called smoke, "a no-frills mixture of raw alcohol and water. . . . At ten cents a slug, most folks could obliterate themselves and still get change for a quarter. Other New Yorkers bought jellied cooking alcohol and squeezed it through a rag to produce a liquid that they either guzzled down themselves or sold to the unsuspecting. Perhaps this is what gave Russian soldiers the idea, many years later, to satisfy their own satanic urges by draining brake fluid from their tanks, filtering it through some kind of fabric, and chugging down the remainder straight."

In Philadelphia, a favorite thirst-quencher was Soda Pop Moon, sold in innocent-looking soft drink bottles and comprised mainly of rubbing alcohol. A Chicago favorite was Yack Yack Bourbon, which contained virtually no bourbon at all—but rather large portions of iodine. The undiscerning in Kansas City, Missouri, ingested Sweet Whiskey, a wholesome name but "a distillation of alcohol combined with nitric and sulfuric acids that soon destroyed the kidneys." And an Atlanta woman, arrested for public drunkenness, had been brought to her sorry state by the almost inconceivable combination of mothballs and gasoline. "She just liked to drink, she explained, liked to get a different take on reality, and this was the best she could do during Prohibition. Was it her fault that safer beverages were so much harder to find these days, and so much more expensive?"

In various other parts of the South, "people wet their whistles and scorched their esophageal linings with White Mule, a form of clear moonshine so named because it could do as much damage to the unsuspecting as a flying pair of the creature's back legs." There was a ritual attached to the consumption of White Mule, which began with storing the liquid in a fruit jar.

> The experienced drinker kept the fruit jar tightly closed until he was ready to drink. Then he held his breath while he unscrewed the lid and quickly lifted the jar to his lips, gulped the clear liquid, replaced the lid and screwed it tightly into place again. Only then did he attempt to breathe. Frequently this was difficult. For a few moments he coughed and shuddered violently. Slowly, his breathing began again, his eyes opened, and the strained, anxious expression on his face was replaced by an equally strained and anxious smile. He wiped the fusel oil from his lips and, if it was then possible for him to speak, said: "Boy, that's got a kick—and how!"

"Farm hands in the Midwest," writes the estimable historian Herbert Asbury, "drank a fluid drawn from the bottom of a silo, where silage had rotted and fermented for perhaps several years. No viler beverage can be imagined." Unless it is Old Crow whiskey, which had been legally bottled and sold under that name for many years. But then, after the Eighteenth

Amendment was passed and bootleggers got their hands on the stuff and cut it with their various industrial decoctions, it was suddenly known as Old Corrosive. Ingredients not known, name sufficient.

"I call it legalized murder and the Government is an accessory to the crime," thundered Edward I. Edwards, a United States senator from New Jersey. His was a lonely voice, and often ridiculed—but as early as 1920, when Prohibition was as new as the latest pay cut from Andrew Carnegie for the men who worked the infernos called blast furnaces, it spoke the truth.

AND THEN THERE WAS JAMAICA gin, or, simply, Jake: 180 proof, which is to say ninety percent alcohol. In some states, Jake could be obtained with a prescription because, in minute doses, it could relieve an upset stomach. Bootleggers, of course, managed to pilfer more than minute doses, and in such cases Jake concentrated its wrath on the extremities of the victim's body, leaving the stomach as upset as it had been before.

In the July 26, 1930 issue of *Collier's Weekly*, journalist William G. Shepard described the effect of Jake on the tippler.

> The victim of "jake paralysis" practically loses control of his fingers. . . . The feet of the paralyzed one drop forward from the ankle so that the toes point downward. The victim has no control over the muscles that normally point the toes upward. When he tries to walk his dangling feet touch the pavement first at the toes, then his heels settle down jarringly. Toe first, heel next. That's how he moves. "Tap-click, tap-click, tap-click, tap-click," is how his footsteps sound.
>
> The calves of his legs, after two or three weeks, begin to soften and hang down, the muscles between the thumbs and index fingers shrivel away.

Jake-steppers, they were called, or Jake-trotters. At one time there were said to be 800 cases in southern Tennessee, a thousand in Louisiana, and, according to national estimates, between 15,000 and 20,000. No one ever died from Jamaica gin, but no one ever recovered, either. "In fact," I learned in working on *Spirits*, "so vicious a poison was it that, in researching its origins, government scientists learned some of the principles that would lead their German counterparts to develop nerve gases in World War II. It is an appalling thing to say about a substance that human beings willingly, and so frequently, put into their bodies a couple of decades earlier."

Sometimes Jamaica gin and other forms of lethal liquid found their way into the most elegant speakeasies, as well as into the finest stemware at the most soigné of private parties. Anyone, at any time, could be fooled by a venal bootlegger. Thus even the more cautious of high-end drinkers, not always trusting their sources, would on occasion add safe ingredients to their alcohol, just in case. The result was the blending of newly conceived mixtures, some of them ad-libbed as the host for the evening's revels went along, depending on what was in his refrigerator or cupboard.

In his study of the upper crust at the time, Stephen Birmingham, who made a career of writing about different elements of different upper crusts at different periods, wrote as follows about 1920 and the years immediately following: "Recipes were invented, sampled, and quickly passed around. Into the shakes went whites of eggs, yolks of eggs, milk, honey, Worcestershire sauce, orange-flower, wines, herbs, spices, and mixes of every and the most incomparable variety. Weirder grew the drinks, scarcer got the real stuff, and higher went its price. Still people cried, 'Come for cocktails.'"

Some who have written on the twenties have concluded that thus was the cocktail born. Not so. A few cocktails, most made with rum, existed as early as colonial times: the Rattle-Skull, the Bombo, the Mimbo, the Sillabub, and the Whistlebelly. They were never, however, very popular, sometimes a last resort when one did not have enough liquor to fill his glass. It was during Prohibition that the cocktail first became the rage— not because some Americans found them tasty so much as because they were survivable. For the former reason, of course, people have been drinking them in enormous amounts ever since. In other words, what started out in life as a precaution has since become a staple for those who prefer alcohol rather than other forms of liquid refreshment.

IN THE OCCASIONAL DRUG STORE, wood-alcohol milkshakes were whipped up behind the counter, a bizarre mixture of innocent sweets and poisonous libation. Straight wood alcohol was also sold, without the presence of a mixer, and referred to in Connecticut and parts of New York as a Coroner's Cocktail. It is inconceivable to think of someone seating himself on a barstool and asking for a drink with such a buyer-beware name, yet during a single four-day period in 1928, thirty-four people died in New York City from placing orders for Coroner's Cocktails. Just four days. Just Manhattan. Just wood alcohol. "In 1925, a reported 687 New Yorkers went to their eternal rewards long before they had intended because of venomous beverages; a year later, the total climbed to 750. It seems fair to assume that comparable percentages of the population became fatalities in other cities."

In his history of the twenties, *That Jazz*, Ethan Mordden says, "In 1927, the death toll from the imbibing of 'liquor' containing poisoned alcohol stood at 11,700."

It seems the final judgment on Prohibition's first seven years. Further, it appears to point to the enormity of Prohibition's eventual tally, and the proportions of plague that it almost achieved. Both statements are false.

To begin with, common sense alone tells us that both popular perceptions and a number of historians are erroneous; there *had* to be less drinking during Prohibition than before. Consider: For some people, after January 1920, alcohol was simply too expensive. For others, it was too hard to get. For yet others, those who made their own booze at home, it was too much work for too inferior a product. For others still, it was too lethal. And finally, there were those afraid of the penalties that the law brought with it or the respect that they still maintained for the principle of law—even, somehow, this one. (See the figures provided by law enforcement agencies and cited at the beginning of this chapter.)

Thus, hundreds of thousands of people who could take booze or leave it, to whom we today refer as "social drinkers," would simply have given up the stuff, drinking not at all or, more likely, on far fewer occasions than they used to. It would not have been worth the money, the trouble, or the gastric peril.

More specifically, with regard to Mordden's figure of 11,700 deaths in seven years, although it may well be true, it does not take into account the mistake that so many students of the twenties have made, which is to consider the lives that Prohibition saved. Yes, the law was impossible to enforce. Yes, it was contrary to human nature. But also yes, it had a salutary effect on many Americans. The number of people who were spared illness or death surely does not compare to the number of victims, but all stories have two sides, and, as is usually the case, the second one casts a different light on the first.

For some reason, it was not until a half century had passed that the truth of Prohibition was finally established, and one of those responsible was the historian David Kyvig. In his book *Repealing National Prohibition*, published in 1979, he provides the following figures. As you read them, you must keep in mind that no numbers are available for the years during which the Eighteenth Amendment was in effect; since alcoholic beverages were illegal then, the government was not able to keep figures for purposes of taxation and measurement of economic patterns.

> During the period 1911 through 1915 . . . the per capita consumption by Americans of drinking age (15 years and older) amounted to 2.56 gallons of absolute alcohol. . . . In 1934, the year immediately following the repeal of Prohibition, the per capita consumption measured 0.97 gallons of absolute alcohol distributed as 0.64 gallons of spirits, 0.35 gallons of wine, and 13.58 gallons of beer (4.5 percent alcohol after repeal). Total alcohol consumption, by this measure, fell by more than 60 percent because of national Prohibition. Granting a generous margin of error, it seems certain that the flow of liquor in the United States was at least cut in half.

Prior to that, in 1976, another historian, Norman Clark, "reviewed the literature and concluded that estimates that placed the annual absolute alcohol consumption rates at between 50 and 33 percent less than those of the preprohibition years were essentially correct."

Economist Jules Abels used a different method to arrive at the same conclusion. From the Census Bureau, he obtained figures on gallons per capita consumption before and after Prohibition—compressing his findings into the following table.

YEAR	SPIRITS DISTILLED	LIQUORS MALT	WINE
1914	1.44	20.69	.53
1918	.85	14.87	.48
1935	.70	10.45	.30
1940	1.02	12.58	.66

"Obviously," Abels sums up, "drinking declined during Prohibition, since in 1935, the year after repeal [Abels is in error here; 1934 was the year after repeal], per capita drinking was far below that of 1914, and even though it picked up five years afterward, except for wine it was still below the 1914 level."

Yet another means of gauging the efficacy of Prohibition is by an examination of the nation's health records.

In 1943, Forrest Linder and Robert Grove compiled mortality figures for the Census Bureau in *Vital Statistics Rates in the United States.* They found that from a high of 7.3 deaths from chronic or acute alcoholism per 100,000 population in 1907, the rate fell gradually (possibly as a result of prohibitory laws and war prohibition) to 1.6 per 100,000 in 1919 and then to 1.0 in 1920, the first year of National Prohibition. The rates then climbed slowly again, probably reflecting the gradual increase in illegal (and often poisonous) liquor supplies . . . peaking at 4.0 per 100,000 in 1927—although in 1932, the last full year of Prohibition, the figure was down once again to 2.5.

Anecdotal evidence also supports the case for the Eighteenth Amendment's being beneficial to the health of a significant number of Americans. Hospitals reported fewer cases of cirrhosis of the liver and fewer admissions as a result of alcohol-related violence. College administrators found their students to be more sober, more often, than they used to be, and business executives reported to those conducting surveys that their employees "seemed more clear-headed and quick-witted after lunch than had previously been the case."

In addition, sales of Coca-Cola and Canada Dry ginger ale soared during Prohibition, as did sales of grapefruit and orange juice. "The Welch Grape Juice Company," historians Mark Edward Lender and James Kirby Martin tell us, "sold a million more gallons of juice annually during the 1920s than it had in 1914." Almost totally, these increases can be attributed to the rising popularity of cocktails, which means that alcoholic beverages were watered down to an extent never known before. Far fewer people drank their whiskey straight; it was simply too perilous. Their glasses might have been filled to the top, but a lot of that liquid was fizzy and bubbly and, save for the vast amounts of sugar it contained, absolutely harmless.

The Anti-Saloon League, although not aware of this information at the time, began to make outrageous claims on behalf of the Eighteenth Amendment. It boasted that few Americans were drinking any longer and, because of the great national abstinence, they were saving more money than they ever had before, while spending a higher percentage of disposable income on necessities—food, shelter, and clothing, rather than beer, wine, and whiskey. It further stated that bootleggers were going out of business at a prodigious rate, that they were finding it almost impossible to obtain either good liquor or poisonous forms of alcohol for use as bases. Yet when asked to provide either numbers or sources for this information, the League could do neither.

Actually, in some cases its claims were true but factors other than Prohibition were responsible. In 1920, for instance, the United States was more prosperous than ever before, which allowed for different patterns of both spending and saving than had existed prior to the Eighteenth Amendment, which was completely irrelevant to the change in behavior. And as the twenties ended, spending on necessities and saving as much as possible was mandatory because the Great Depression was beginning.

In summary, though, there were positive aspects to Prohibition that are too often ignored by those who write about the twenties. Although it did not prohibit, Prohibition *did* reduce. Was it, then, as the Anti-Saloon League and others insisted, a law that deserved more respect than it received? This is a risible claim. No law that results in more deaths than occurred before the legislation was passed deserves any respect at all from the populace. Perhaps the best summary of the era, certainly one of the briefest, was offered by an unnamed friend of Winston Churchill. The man had visited the United States during its dry years, and observed carefully before reporting back to England. "There is less drinking," Churchill quoted his friend as saying, "but there is worse drinking."

THE TWENTY-FIRST AMENDMENT TO THE Constitution of the United States was ratified on December 5, 1933. It repealed the Eighteenth, thereby making the latter the only Constitutional Amendment ever acknowledged to be an error and tossed into a Capitol Hill wastebasket.

Yet for all the arguments pro and con that had been offered during the thirteen years, eleven months, and eleven days of the "Noble Experiment," its demise was assured by a factor that had been little discussed for the majority of that time: money. The Eighteenth Amendment simply cost too much. According to the Association Against the Prohibition Amendment and the Women's Organization for National Prohibition Reform, admittedly biased groups, the United States treasury lost an estimated $861 million in tax revenue from alcohol during the period when it had been illegal. The groups also claim that another $40 million a year was tossed to the winds in Prohibition enforcement, which was lax at best, dishonest at worst. Whatever the figures, by December 5, 1933, America was deep in the throes of the worst economic crisis in its history. It was finally time to make the booze safe to drink again—and, no less important to the nation's future, it was time to get tax dollars, tens of millions of tax dollars annually, back into the Treasury.

Wayne Wheeler had no comment.

CHAPTER NINE

Planning Parenthood

T WAS MID-AUGUST, WITH HEAT waves swooping over the country, almost as if undulating, and the Nineteenth Amendment still had one more state to go.

Carrie Chapman Catt arrived without fanfare in Nashville, as Tennessee would be the next to decide on the Amendment and the final vote needed for ratification. Catt, however, was not there to take a starring role in the campaign, as might be expected of someone so eminent in the suffrage movement; rather, she would work behind the scenes where, in this case, she believed she could act more effectively. For the most part, she would send telegrams to prominent politicians of both parties, pleading with them to make public announcements of their support for woman suffrage. She was a hard woman to say no to.

Warren G. Harding, one of the Republican prospects going into the convention, replied promptly to Catt's request, writing that "if any of the Republican members should ask my opinion as to their course I would cordially recommend immediate favorable action." Harding's fellow Ohioan, James M. Cox, who would end up being his opponent in November, expressed "confidence that the Legislature will act favorably, which will greatly please the national Democratic Party."

With support like this, and even more from politicians almost as influential as the presidential candidates, it appeared almost impossible that women would continue to be barred from America's polling places. But anti-suffragist forces were not yet willing to concede. In early August, they too gathered in Nashville for one last stand. Most of them were men, as might be expected, but not all. "Many women also went to Nashville to oppose their own enfranchisement," writes feminist historian Doris Weatherford, "among them officers of the Southern Women's Rejection League, and of antisuffrage associations from Delaware, Maine, Maryland, Massachusetts, and Ohio." In the case of these ladies, their "devotion to states' rights proved greater than their commitment to women's rights"; that, at least, was the company line, briefly recited to all reporters who wondered about their negative position.

Whether or not it was true, the anti-suffrage forces were so upset about what had happened around the country earlier in the year, when by January 27 the universal vote for women was but nine states short of passage, "that they filed suits in a number of states against the legislatures' ratification. Inventing points of law that had never been considered in the cases of the first eighteen amendments to the Constitution, they went to court."

The cases made no sense. The legislative actions in the states named in the suits had been conducted in strict accordance with procedures for altering the nation's founding document. Yet, somehow, one of the suits managed to sneak itself all the way up to the docket of the United States Supreme Court. It did not stay there long. The court ruled dismissively, several of the justices joining millions of other Americans in wondering why they were wasting their time on a matter whose guidelines had been so rigorously enforced and whose outcome was so patently obvious. At that point, supporters seemed to believe, the battle had been won; they could relax.

They were wrong. More struggles remained, none so great as the one in the Tennessee Legislature in mid-August 1920. Although initially seen as a state solidly behind the women's cause, when the votes were counted, to the shock of all except lobbyists who had exchanged untold amounts of cash for support, the total was forty-eight in favor of the Nineteenth Amendment, forty-eight against.

The state house exploded in anger, the tumult stilled only after the Speaker of the House pounded the gavel so many times, the head might well have flown off. A few minutes later, with the house still noisier than usual, the call was sounded for a second vote. In the gallery—standing room only, mostly women, mostly desirous of the vote—people let out long, audible sighs; those who had seats took them again after having sprung to their feet but were fearful of an even worse outcome. Would an aye, just a single aye decide to change his vote to a nay? How could a cause that made so much sense, that threatened no one, that would alter the functioning of the Constitution not a whit, possibly have become so controversial?

The legislators below the women in the gallery visibly tensed.

One did so more than anyone else. According to Doris Weatherford, it was at this point that "conscience struck 24-year-old Harry Burn," who had been elected to the state legislature at the age of 22. He had promised his political bosses, who were against ratification, that he would support their position only if his vote were needed to deny the amendment the first time the roll was called. Afterward, he would follow the counsel of his mother, who wrote him a letter, urging him to

> Vote for suffrage and don't keep them in doubt. I notice some of the speeches against. They were very bitter. I have been watching to see how you stood, but have noticed nothing yet. Don't forget to be a good boy and help Mrs. Catt put "Rat" in Ratification.

It was, of course, those who opposed ratification who were the rats, in Mrs. Burn's view, but never mind her slogan; her intent could not have been more clear.

As the second vote began, Burn decided to be a good boy. He would change his mind. He would help Mrs. Catt. The result was even more uproar in the House, but this time it signaled happiness more than confusion. "After Burn switched his vote to the affirmative, antisuffragists charged that he had been bribed," but so much blacker was the pot than the kettle that the statement played as a punch line more than an accusation. Perhaps Burn *had* been bribed, but if so it was by sentiment, not dollars. The *New York Times* reported on the jubilation when the official vote was announced: forty-nine in favor of the amendment, forty-seven opposed.

> Women screamed frantically. Scores threw their arms around the necks of those nearest them and danced, so far as it was possible to do so, in the mass of humanity. Hundreds of suffrage banners were waved wildly, and many removed the yellow flowers they had been wearing and threw them upward to meet a similar shower from the galleries.
>
> There were few tears of joy shed by the suffragists. Some wiped their eyes, but on the whole, they considered it no time for weeping. Their happiness was far beyond that stage.

This time the Speaker of the House did not even attempt to wield his gavel. It might not have been heard anyhow.

Burn waited patiently until the large hall was at least relatively still again, then told the Speaker he would like to make a statement for the official journal of the hearing. It was "a point of personal privilege," he explained, and he had the right to express just such a sentiment. The House became even quieter. The war was over, but the final strategic thrust was about to be revealed. Burn coughed, cleared his throat, took his time. "I changed my vote in favor of ratification because I believe in full suffrage as a right; I believe we had a moral and legal right to ratify; I know that a mother's advice is always safest for her boy to follow and my mother wanted me to vote for ratification."

From the gallery came an eruption every bit as loud and tearful—if differently motivated—as the first one.

From those aghast at the notion of woman's suffrage, one of the leaders of whom was a fellow named Seth Walker, came what movement historian Eleanor Flexner has called a display of *opéra bouffe*.

> Unable, despite threats and bribery, to bring the bill up for reconsideration, thirty-eight members of the losing minority

crossed the state line into Alabama to try and prevent a quorum until the majority had somehow been undermined. Their hosts in Decatur [Alabama] had even wired those planning the move: "Send them on. We will be proud to entertain Seth Walker and his opponents of suffrage as long as they wish to remain and it will not cost them a penny."

The action was promptly ruled illegal.

STRANGELY, THERE WERE NO MASS celebrations by newly enfranchised women, no demonstrations from coast to coast. To Alice Paul, a leading strategist of the Nineteenth Amendment, went the honor of sewing the thirty-sixth and final star on the National Woman's Party suffrage banner, as half a dozen of her supporters looked on, but that appears to have been the extent of triumphant display. There was certainly nothing like the gathering of eight thousand women who marched through Washington on the day before President Wilson's inauguration in 1913. Some of the protesters carried placards, others shouted out slogans; all seemed exuberant and determined. And they were in the streets, of all places, not in the kitchens! The policemen assigned to duty along the route simply could not condone what they saw. Because they "had no experience with such unladylike behavior," we are told, "they failed to protect the women from assault. A portion of the parade route turned into a mob scene so serious that it ultimately cost the police chief his job. Public sympathy swelled for women who were willing to take such risks for rights."

But history does not record anything on a grand scale (assuming eight thousand women can be considered a grand scale) after the Tennessee decision. A small parade here, some small parties there and there, a few speeches at various civic occasions—but there seems to have been nothing more exuberant. Perhaps women, and the men who supported them, were fearful that their foes would turn to the Supreme Court in an attempt to overturn the Nineteenth Amendment. And, in fact, they did; the Amendment was not finally institutionalized until 1922, when the Court made a final ruling in its favor. Perhaps, believing that women had been entitled to the vote since Margaret Brent insisted on it in 1638, they believed congratulatory displays were gratuitous. Or perhaps they were simply weary from an incomprehensibly long ordeal.

Carrie Chapman Catt summed it up. Since the 1848 Seneca Falls call for the vote, she counted: 480 campaigns in state legislature; 56 statewide referenda to male voters; 47 attempts to add suffrage planks during revisions of state constitutions; 277 campaigns at state party conventions and 30 at national conventions; and 19 biannual campaigns in 19 different Congresses. Literally thousands of times, men cast their votes on whether or not women should vote. Literally millions of women and men gave their entire lives to the cause and went to their graves with freedom unwon. No peaceful political change ever has required so much from so many for so long. None but a mighty army could have won.

But even a mighty army, by 1920, would have been exhausted, satisfied more than celebratory.

Another reason that at least some supporters of suffrage did not feel like marching through the streets victoriously was that they were still enraged at the tactics of their opponents, who had done everything they could to undermine the woman's vote by undermining both law and justice.

Catt was among those who could not rid herself of fury. In Tennessee, she had watched in something close to horror as the Speaker of the House called for an adjournment at the precise moment when the woman's vote seemed a certainty. The reason was obvious. The anti-suffragists needed time to collect the money for even more bribes than they had already paid out, and Catt could not help but watch these frantic, last-minute transactions as they were conducted in the open, legislative business as usual.

She was watching, thought Catt, money being put to its worst possible use, the purchase and alteration of a man's integrity. She had never seen anything like it before. A couple of days after ratification, unable to remain silent any longer, and irate at others who had also seen the the corruption without speaking out against it, she took to a podium in Nashville and kept it until she had made headlines:

Never in the history of politics has there been such a nefarious lobby as labored to block the ratification in Nashville. . . .

Strange men and groups of men sprang up, men we had never met before in the battle. Who were they? We were told, this is the railroad lobby, these are the manufacturers' lobbyists, this is the remnant of the old whiskey ring. Even tricksters from the U.S. Revenue Service were there operating against us, until the President of the United States called them off. . . . They appropriated our telegrams, tapped our telephones, listened outside our windows and transoms. They attacked our private and public lives.

Still, even if everything Catt had stated was true—and there was no reason to doubt her—the opposition had failed. The Nineteenth Amendment, by the narrowest of margins, had been accepted on August 18, 1920, and in a few months women were finally going to enter the voting booth. With Prohibition having become law in January, 1920 is the only year in American history in which two amendments were added to the United States Constitution.

AT LAST, FEMALES HAD SOME control over the lawmakers who would represent them. Now it was up to 41-year-old Margaret Sanger, she believed, to take the next steps in a campaign long since begun, to give women control over their own bodies. It would be a shorter struggle, but even more vituperative.

A nurse by training, Sanger coined, or at least was the first person to make common usage of, the term "birth control"; she was the nation's first prominent advocate for it; she opened the first birth-control clinic in the United States; and she would go on to found Planned Parenthood. Few movements are the labor of a single person; but, to an uncommon degree, the freedom that women have today in the procreative process is due to Sanger's perseverance a century ago.

Born in 1879, Sanger was the daughter of Michael Hennessey Higgins, a stonecutter who specialized in angels and saints for tombstones. It was precise and tiring work; but unfortunately for Mrs. Higgins, her husband still had a great deal of virility left at the end of the day, enough to impregnate her the astonishing total of eighteen times in twenty-two years.

Eleven of the children grew to adulthood. Their mother, however, died at fifty, exhausted from having created so much life, and was presumably laid to rest under an example of her husband's handiwork.

Little Margaret had paid careful attention to her mother's unceasing labors, a life that had alternated between pain and enervation, and although she never spoke or wrote publicly about the subject, it is hard to believe that the mother's suffering was not the spark of the daughter's vocation.

Described as "fine, clean and honest" when she was a young tomboy, Sanger appears in her later photos to be rather a prim lady, even timid. She was anything but. Her courage, thought to be an inheritance from her father, was evident from childhood, when, having decided she was plagued by too many fears, she set out to conquer them.

The cause of one fear was darkness, and she met it by forcing herself to go to sleep without a candle. At first she stayed awake most of the night, on the alert for menacing creatures who themselves feared the day. But weeks passed, and outside of some unidentified noises from outside and the random sounds of her house settling, she heard nothing to alarm her. She saw nothing to alarm her. In time, she dozed peacefully.

She was also afraid of heights, which her brothers delighted in pointing out. After enduring all the taunting she could, she joined her siblings in jumping from the barn rafters to the hayloft below, a distance of thirty feet. She shook so much she could hardly breathe before her first few attempts; but soon the leap became, as was the candle-less bedroom, more of a habit than it was a test of courage.

"Then," according to biographer Emily Taft Douglas, "she faced her worst test, an ordeal that [Sanger] thought important enough to repeat at some length in her two autobiographical accounts."

Douglas continues:

> In Corning, [New York], the Erie Railroad crossed the Chemung River on a narrow iron span which men used as a short cut. Margaret's father had once helped her across by lifting her over the wide gaps, but the experience had terrified her. For that very reason, and in spite of the fact that it was forbidden, she decided that she must cross the bridge alone.

Halfway over she heard the dreaded hum of an oncoming train, and she stumbled. Perhaps that saved her life. She fell between the iron ties, over which she instinctively curled her arms. Unable to pull herself up again, she dangled there over the deep, rapid river. In a moment, the cars rushed down upon her and the wheels crashed over her head. Numbed and helpless, she hung there as the train thundered across the bridge. Providentially, a fisherman below saw the child and rescued her. He gave her two smacks on the rear, faced her toward home and went back down to his line.

Her fears now under control, she was prepared for any threats and opposition she would face as an adult. As it turned out, she would probably face more than any other woman of her time.

WHEN SANGER WAS IN HER early thirties, the standard line about birth control in the ghetto of Manhattan's Lower East Side was: "Have Jake sleep on the roof tonight." It was a joke that always brought a smile, or at least a nod of agreement from the women fanning themselves at their apartment windows or on the fire escapes. Sanger didn't think it was funny. She began to address the public on a woman's right to manage her natural "resources," and so fervent was she that she offered herself as a speaker to any women's group that would have her, asking for no compensation. Few accepted, afraid of repercussions from the law. Sanger was reduced to begging for forums and, little by little, found them. They were seldom large, never attracted the press; but she was beginning to spread the word.

"Her standard lecture in these days," writes biographer Ellen Chesler, "embraced a panoply of arguments for birth control—from the health, welfare, and personal rights of women and children, to the eugenic inheritance of the society, to global peace and prosperity."

Sanger also began writing a series of articles on birth control for the socialist publication *New York Call.* "What Every Girl Should Know" was the name of her column, and there were readers who did not want their girls to know any of it. But only one of those readers canceled her subscription. Others, however, were pleased by Sanger's remarkably direct language on so important and forbidden a subject, finding her work "indicative of a higher, purer morality than whole libraries full of hypocritical cant about modesty."

Eventually, though, sentiment against Sanger began to build, finally reaching the point at which the *Call* had to act. Sanger's column was simply too controversial, even for a socialist paper, a paper opposed to virtually everything for which the government and conventional society stood. In what turned out to be her final piece, she "insisted that existing economic and social arrangements fundamentally compromised and degraded women by forcing them to rely on men for support. She set forth a rudimentary but nonetheless radical argument demanding economic and social freedom for women so as to permit greater autonomy in choosing a mate and bearing children."

Postal authorities disputed the argument, or at least Sanger's right to make it through the United States mail. As Nathan Miller informs us about the publication's last issue, "The editors printed the column's head, 'What Every Girl Should Know,' and under it, 'NOTHING! By Order of the Post Office Department.'"

Sanger was upset at first, but soon saw her termination by the *Call* as an opportunity. She had had too many disputes with her editors about content and language, and was tired of reining herself in, which to her was a breach of trust with her readers. She wanted even more direct expression, an even higher, purer morality. In 1914, she began to publish an eight-page monthly newsletter entirely on her own called *The Woman Rebel*. It contained such passages as the following: "The marriage bed is the most degenerating influence of the social order, as to life in all of its forms—biological, psychological, sociological—for man, woman and child. . . . Let this institution, then, be anathema to all thinking minds."

In another article, even more provocative, she attacked the views of the Roman Catholic Church, something simply not done in those days, regardless of one's faith.

> *The Western Watchman* (Catholic) says, according to *The Menace*: "We say, a young girl's business is to get a husband. Having got a husband, it is her business to beget children.

Under ordinary conditions of health a young wife ought to have a child in her arms or on her bosom all the time. When she is not nursing a child she should be carrying one. This will give her plenty to do, and she will have no time for political meetings or movements."

How do the women like that program for a life vocation? According to this authority a woman is to look upon herself merely as a vehicle for the breeding of children. . . . This editor would not even give her the protection that is bestowed upon cattle (when he says) "when she is not nursing a child she should be carrying one." The home of such a couple, instead of being a place of comfort and refinement with food for mind and the amenities of social life, is to be a rabbit warren, a sty filled with anemic, underdeveloped children, . . . and so continue until she drops into the grave the victim of man's distorted and perverted sense of duty. Out upon such a theory! For the protection of the female sex, let her be taught how to defend herself against such teachings as these.

It is obvious that Sanger is recalling, and denouncing, her father's heedless lust for her mother.

Friends of Sanger warned her that various legal authorities were watching *The Woman Rebel*, and may have been preparing to pounce. At which point this most notable of woman rebels, long used to the fearlessness she had developed in childhood, forced the law to take action. She wrote two front-page editorials for the *Rebel*, one of them under the pseudonym Herbert A. Thorpe. The column expressed its support, posthumously, for three anarchists who, experimenting with bombs in the basement of a Manhattan home, ended up destroying both the home and themselves in the process.

The second editorial was called "In Defense of Assassination," a position she took in general terms only, eschewing any references to specific incidents or victims. The piece was, in part, an open letter to Anthony Comstock, a United States postal inspector and, as the head of the New York Society for the Suppression of Vice, a surprisingly powerful figure in the struggle against public sexuality. We do not know Sanger's true feelings about the killing of prominent persons; she had published the article specifically to provoke, to make Comstock and the postmaster general try to suppress *The Woman Rebel*. And if what she had published so far did not spur either of the two men to act, she had decided, she would write an article in support of arson!

She did not have to go that far. Action was finally taken. Late in August 1914, she was presented with three subpoenas, two for publishing sexually explicit material and the third for advocating assassination, charging that it was incitement to murder and riot.

As should be clear, Sanger was a hellion as both a writer and a speaker. She wanted people to pay attention to what she had to say and, in her methods to do so, was uncompromising and incendiary.

"In court, however," as biographer Madeline Gray states, "Margaret was so charming and demure that when she asked for a postponement in order to prepare her defense, the judge readily consented. The case was held over until the fall term, giving her six weeks of grace."

She was also granted bail a few more times, these postponements of shorter duration, and she used the time not so much to prepare her defense as to stay on the offense. She began a new publication called *Family Limitation*, as bland a title as she could devise for opinions that continued, as far as her opponents were concerned, to be almost as controversial as arson advocacy. And more physiologically explicit than anything she had written in her previous pamphlets. "Don't wait to see if you do not menstruate (monthly sickness) but make it your duty to see that you do," advises *Family Limitation*.

It also urges a woman to start taking a laxative several days before she expects her period. "If there is the slightest possibility that the male fluid has entered the vagina," drink hot water with quinine in addition to the laxative. "By taking the above precautions, you will prevent the ovum from making its nest in the lining of the womb." Following, in the pamphlet, are sections on douches, condoms, and vaginal suppositories. Subjects like this had never appeared in print before, at least not where members of the general public could obtain them. In all likelihood, they were seldom even whispered between husband and wife.

And once she had gotten *Family Limitation* up and running, and was convinced it had said all it needed to say for the time being, she did something even more shocking, and shockingly unethical. To the dismay of all who believed in her and were grateful for her defiance of authority, and to the special dismay of those who had put up the money for her temporary freedom, she decided to jump bail. It was totally out of character for Sanger, a woman who had always behaved with the utmost responsibility toward friends and supporters.

She later explained, however, that she had seen no choice. She believed, mistakenly, that she faced a maximum of forty-five years in jail if she was found guilty on all the counts against her, and so decided that the better course was to pack her bags and take a train to Canada. She intended to pay back the money she owed over time, she said, but the promise was never put to the test.

As a final gesture of defiance to the man who had been assigned to serve as the judge of her case, as well as to the prosecuting attorney, she wrote to these two officers of the court and told them she was skipping the country under an assumed name so they would never be able to stop her, and, in the hope of raising their blood pressure even higher, enclosed with her letters the most recent issues of *Family Limitation*.

Sanger's husband played a minor role in all of this, and in fact played a minor role in her entire life until, a few years thence, she divorced him, relegating him to the most minor role of all. Before departing for England, though, she yielded to his pleas to see her for a final good-bye. At that same time, she deposited her three children with him, showing no signs that she would miss them, and then sailed from Canada to Liverpool on November 3, 1914. From Liverpool she journeyed to London. She expected to be gone a few months. It turned out to be a year, one of the most instructive of her life.

BY THAT TIME, THE GREAT War had broken out; but Sanger, refusing to be intimidated by the violence around her, made a trip from London to the Netherlands, "where," according to historian J. C. Furnas, "a new system of birth control clinics meant the world's lowest death rates for mothers and town-born babies. There she met and brought home the

Dutch secret weapon—the Mensinga pessary, still a good nonbiochemical contraceptive to protect against regardless husbands." Another attraction of the Netherlands to Sanger was the work of birth-control pioneer Dr. Johannes Rutgers. She was able to arrange a meeting with him, and both pronounced themselves impressed with the other, with Rutgers calling *Family Limitation* "a brilliant pamphlet."

He explained to Sanger that, even with the war raging nearby, the Dutch had been able to enlist the services of forty-eight nurses who fit more than 1,700 women with diaphragms. "However small this operation," biographer Chesler recounts, "it constituted a substantial health presence in the gynecological and obstetrical fields and was widely credited for the country's superior maternal and infant mortality statistics."

The size of the Netherlands' operation didn't matter to Sanger; it was the effort expended on the behalf of women's freedom that impressed her, as well as the encouraging results. But Rutgers insisted to Sanger that the results were encouraging only because those who administered and monitored the birth-control program had had extensive medical training. Sanger took notes. "No other class of men or women," she wrote, "are so AWARE of the NEED of this knowledge among working people as they."

Returning to the United States, where criminal charges against her for *The Woman Rebel* had earlier been dropped, she soon found herself in trouble with the law again. On October 16, 1916, Sanger opened the first birth-control clinic in the country, in the Brownsville section of Brooklyn. On its ninth day of operation, the clinic received a visit from a female police officer. On the tenth day, the woman returned with some male members of the city's vice squad. They arrested Sanger and Fania Mindell, one of the clinic's volunteers, and then began disassembling the operation, impounding furnishings, supplies, copies of *Family Limitation* and other publications, and case histories of the clients who had previously visited the clinic, even though Sanger screamed at the invaders that they were private, that the police had no right to such information without approval.

As she watched the pillaging of her life's work, she lost her temper in a manner that she had never done before in front of others. It was Mrs. Whitehurst, the female police officer from the previous day, who actually arrested Sanger. "The little woman [Sanger] was at first taken aback," reported a Brooklyn newspaper, "but in an instant she was in a towering rage. 'You dirty thing,' she shrieked [at Whitehurst]. 'You are not a woman. You are a dog.' 'Tell that to the judge in the morning,' calmly responded Mrs. Whitehurst. 'No. I'll tell it to you, now. You dog, and you have two ears to hear me too!'"

Although she was absent from the clinic at the time of the arrests, Margaret's sister, Ethel Byrne, a registered nurse at New York's Mt. Sinai Hospital, who devoted many of her spare hours to assisting Margaret, was later taken into custody.

Despite being the third person arrested, it was Byrne whose trial came up first on the court calendar, and in January 1917 she was accused of trying "to do away with the Jews" by setting up shop in a Jewish neighborhood and providing both the information and implements for family planning. Observers in the courtroom knew Byrne would be found guilty of something, but were stunned by the actual charge—which was, in plain and horrifying language, genocide. Not for dispensing birth-control advice, but for doing so in the wrong part of town, a neighborhood that Byrne might not even have known was predominantly Jewish. It made no difference. Thirty days in jail, on Blackwell's Island (now Roosevelt Island).

But Sanger and Byrne, disappointed by the verdict while at the same time encouraged by the favorable publicity they were receiving in newspapers covering the trial, decided on a course to guarantee even more publicity. Byrne would go on a hunger strike. After dining one night on large portions of turkey and ice cream, Byrne went to bed and awoke determined to eat no more, to "die, if need be, for my sex."

After four days without Byrne's accepting so much as a drop of sustenance, and the newspapers savaging the authorities for allowing this to happen over so trivial a matter as a thirty-day jail term, the New York City Corrections Commissioner announced that, for the first time in American penal history, a prisoner would be force-fed through a tube inserted into her esophagus. "[T]he national wire services literally went wild," Chesler writes. "Even the normally sensation-shy *New York Times* carried the story on its front page for four days in a row, alternating with reports from prison officials that Mrs. Byrne's response was 'passive' to her thrice-daily feeding of a mixture of milk, brandy, and eggs, with overstated claims from Sanger that her sister could not resist because she was extremely weak and near death."

A group called the National Birth Control League, made up primarily of women whose pedigrees were impressive or whose marriages had elevated their social standing, formed a Committee of 100, which was able to end the nonsense at the women's facility on Blackwell's Island by negotiating a pardon for Byrne—but only if she promised never to break the law, any law, again. Speaking for her sister, who could by this time barely utter a sound, Margaret turned down the offer. But only until a few more days had passed, by which time Ethel Byrne really *was* near death. At that point, Margaret accepted the pardon on her sister's behalf and her sister began to feed herself, just like in the old days, without an esophageal tube. Margaret's insistence on the hunger strike, and its duration, called into question her character, even among many who continued to count themselves among her supporters.

NEXT CAME THE TRIALS FOR Sanger and Mindell, the two women arrested at the clinic. Mindell, accused of selling *What Every Girl Should Know* to customers, was found guilty of obscenity and fined $50, which was paid by Gertrude Pinchot, a member of the National Birth Control League. That quickly, Mindell was free.

Now it was Sanger's turn—and that of the tabloid press. The courthouse that day in January 1917 was mobbed with reporters, raucous and edgy and certain of scoops. Front pages in New York and even some other cities had been cleared; journalists would have all the space they wanted to tell of Sanger's duel with the prosecution. Also in attendance were people who believed that Sanger was doing the Lord's work, and their opposition, those who were certain she was the bride of Satan. The atmosphere in the room was incendiary, awaiting only a flame to light the fuse. Sanger alone, it seemed, was peaceful, at rest in the eye of the storm. "Regardless of the outcome," she had previously said, "I shall continue my work, supported by thousands of men and women throughout the country."

Of course, Sanger had already admitted her guilt on the same charge that resulted in Byrne's imprisonment; she, too, was apparently genocidal.

But the charge upon which Sanger would actually be tried was whether she had gone "beyond verbal instruction to actually fit her clients with cervical devices. To the prosecutor this seemed an even more heinous crime."

But he could never establish Sanger's guilt beyond a reasonable doubt. Which is another way of saying that he could never find a woman willing to testify either that she had been fitted with a birth-control apparatus or had witnessed someone else being fitted. The beneficiaries of Sanger's services, grateful for what they had received and eager for more of her services when necessary, were not about to turn on her.

And the members of the jury, constantly sizing her up at the defense table, found it difficult to believe her guilty of anything. Once again, as was the case when she previously appeared in the courtroom, Sanger adopted a demeanor that was dignified, respectful, even meek at times. She was quiet, attentive, and, at least so far as anyone could hear, referred to no one, either in or out of uniform, as a dog.

Also working in her favor, ironically, was the youth, inexperience, and ineptitude of her counsel. The young man, a public defender who seemed never to have tried a case before, and to be only vaguely familiar with courtroom procedures, was caught off guard time after time by the opposition, unable to serve his client's interests not because he was unprepared, but because his manner was timid, his inexperience obvious, and his notes a heap of disorganization. He stuttered when he spoke, gulped almost audibly.

The prosecution, on the other hand, having finally gotten its opportunity to put Sanger away, was so well staffed, so fortified with detail, and so loudly, overbearingly repetitive in its presentation that it seemed to be harassing the defense counsel more than merely reciting evidence. It constantly interrupted the young man, denounced him. He could not help blushing. It was David versus Goliath, except that this time David didn't have a slingshot.

That, at least, was how it seemed to many members of the press, and they managed to work that viewpoint into each day's coverage.

The judge, however, did not read the papers and would not have been influenced if he had. Obviously more severe than Byrne's judge, he gave Sanger the choice of paying a $5,000 fine or serving thirty days in the workhouse. Sanger showed no displeasure. She calmly chose the latter and, realizing that the publicity value of a hunger strike had been exhausted by her sister's effort, she decided to eat all the meals served to her behind bars. In fact, she decided not to make a fuss of any sort. Almost. She not only played the role of model prisoner for a month, but afterward claimed to have enjoyed the opportunity "to rest and be alone, and told her supporters in a published letter that their 'loving thoughts pouring in to her' protected her from sadness."

She performed her prison activities without complaint. They included mopping the floors and reading to her fellow inmates, many of whom were illiterate and gathered around her attentively during their free time. Despite the complaints of the matron in charge of her corridor, some of Sanger's reading came from an issue of *Family Limitation* that a supporter had smuggled into her cell. Taking advantage of the fortuitous circumstance, she lectured virtually the entire cellblock on birth control and related matters, wanting them to be better able to govern their bodies when they were free again. The matron fumed. She could be excused for wondering how a woman could be found guilty of a crime outside of a state institution, and then commit the same crime with impunity once within its walls.

But was it really a crime now? Or was it just chit-chat among some gals who had nothing better to do, or the kind of talk one might hear among the regulars at a tavern after their second rounds—and thus was no more subject to regulation by authorities than, say, obscene language? Which, of course, in the view of authorities, was the definition of Sanger's kind of conversation. Still, for a change, she was able to provide birth-control advice without breaking the law. She was delighted with the opportunity, and no less so with the irony. She was breaking the law. The law was providing the venue. No less was it providing the audience. The judge had outwitted himself, and fumed no less than the matron when he learned what was going on in the cellblock.

Finally Sanger's month was over and, as she was freed, a group of supporters representing a variety of social classes greeted her outside the gate of Blackwell's Island prison. The moment they saw her, they began to sing the French "national anthem," the *Marseillaise*, a tune to which Allied troops frequently marched in Europe. As Chesler points out, however, it "made a curious refrain of welcome for a woman of Socialist and pacifist convictions." When the singing stopped, the hugging began, and Sanger was swallowed up in the crowd of well-wishers.

A FEW YEARS LATER, IN 1920, came what was in a sense the most important twelve months in Margaret Sanger's life, even though her name was absent from the press. It was, rather, a year of preparation for the project to which all of her life so far had been leading, the work to which the rest of her life would be devoted.

By night, she worked alone, sketching floor plans, compiling lists of supplies and services, using the notes she had taken in the Netherlands to help her decide on the number of employees she would need, what training would be required of them, and what their precise duties would be. She had had no legal training, but she skimmed law books, trying to decide what limits would be placed on her vision by the police. She was determined to miss no details. She might not be able to stay within the law, but that was the law's fault, not hers. Still, she would observe its boundaries as closely as possible.

During the day, she and her colleagues undertook a project no less important, searching the streets of Brooklyn for a place to house an enterprise more ambitious than a mere birth-control clinic. They had very specific needs: size of building, size of rooms, space for overstuffed chairs and other comfortable furniture in the waiting room, sufficient storage space, a welcoming atmosphere. When they found an office that was conveniently located and large enough for them to refurbish to suit their needs, they signed a lease and eagerly went to work.

Without any professional assistance, the women remodeled and redecorated, cleaned and painted, keeping the windows open to air out their stuffy new home, even though the air that drifted into it was hot and seldom provided a breeze. They filled the shelves and bookcases with all manner of printed material, including a complete collection of *Family Limitation* issues. In the cupboards, some of which they had to build themselves, were a variety of contraceptive devices; diagrams to demonstrate the proper means of insertion were attached to the walls. The search for the proper personnel began in earnest. The number of volunteers was overwhelming.

The group behind the facility, founded by Margaret Sanger, was the American Birth Control League. It would eventually be known as Planned Parenthood.

SANGER WAS A CONTROVERSIAL FIGURE, not only for her own time but for all time. It was more than just her deliberately provocative writings, more than just her support of anarchists like the notorious Emma Goldman and her part-time lover Alexander Berkman, the latter of whom tried to kill robber baron Henry Clay Frick during the notorious Homestead, Pennsylvania, steel strike of 1892. She proudly regarded both as friends, even though Goldman would never speak publicly about birth control. Unlike Sanger, she found the topic too controversial, too likely to attract the authorities, and, in her case, too much of an invitation for deportation hearings. It was, almost surely, the only topic about which Goldman felt such reticence.

But even more inflammatory was the fact that Sanger's study of the various means of birth control led her, in time, to embrace the eugenics movement. She and her fellow supporters

> sought to prevent the propagation of the genetically "unfit," meaning the mentally retarded and chronically criminal. Influenced by these ideas, many states had enacted compulsory sterilization laws that fell mainly on the impoverished and racial minorities. Upholding a Tennessee law, Justice Oliver Wendell Holmes, speaking for eight members of the Supreme Court, supported sterilization in the 1927 case of *Buck v. Bell* with the declaration that "three generations of imbeciles are enough."

There was, and remains, a certain logic in trying to dissuade the genetically unfit from reproducing themselves, especially in large numbers and, as Justice Holmes said, over too many generations. But it is the most delicate of issues, and must be addressed with forethought aplenty and much care and gentleness. The young educator Harry H. Laughlin, however, found the matter more simple than I have stated. It was, to Laughlin, simply "[t]o purify the breeding stock of the [human] race at all costs." And then there was the physician W. Duncan McKim, whose book *Heredity and Human Progress* found that those of impure breeding stock were guilty of a capital offense. McKim, in what he deemed to be an expression of tenderness of his own variety, suggested that "the surest, the simplest, the kindest, the most humane means for preventing reproduction among those whom we deem unworthy of the high privilege, is a gentle, painless death."

It did Sanger no good to be publicly associated with people like this.

YET HER CONTRIBUTIONS TO THE freedom of women to enjoy sex without risk of motherhood, combined with the Nineteenth Amendment, brought a sense of empowerment to half of the American population that had never known such a feeling before. Especially to poor women, those who had never had access to, or even knowledge of, birth control previously, Margaret Sanger became something of a saint.

The office of the American Birth Control League opened to the public in 1921. The first women to enter did so warily. A few others trailed behind, just as wary, looking around for policemen or other government officials. These officials had decided, though, that although they could shut down the place temporarily, it would soon open again. It would close but then open, close and open—eventually, the law would come down on the side of the women; and their efforts, which would be time-consuming and expensive, would be for naught.

Before long, the initial entrants on that first day were followed by dozens more, a floodtide of feminine humanity desperate for services available to them for the first time ever. Among them, at the top of the social ladder, were members of the National Birth Control League, the Committee of 100. They were joined by garment-makers and seamstresses, housewives and store clerks, government employees and secretaries, spinsters and schoolteachers, maids and washerwomen, and even a few men, many of them immigrants, accompanying their wives or girlfriends, providing support, all of them amazed that a place like this existed and was willing to change their lives free of charge.

Sanger did not work at the office that first day. Rather, she stood at the door and watched, a proud witness to what she had done so much to create. She was surprised at the number of people who had turned out, surprised at their courage as they sat or stood in lines before virtually every desk in the office from opening to closing. There were no arrests, not a law officer anywhere in sight, not even Mrs. Whitehurst.

In one way or another, all who had availed themselves of the American Birth Control League's counsel and merchandise expressed their gratitude to Sanger as they left, for so heavy a burden finally lifted. She nodded, smiled—more in relief, it seemed to many, than gratitude. "The real hope of the world," she had said on one occasion, "lies in putting as painstaking thought into the business of mating as we do into other big businesses."

She had done just that; and as a result her own business, small and controversial when it started, would grow unceasingly in its size and impact on society as the years went by. Eventually, the cause to which Sanger, Mindell, and Byrne had devoted their lives would prove well worth their commitment. One day a crime; a later day the cultural norm.

CHAPTER TEN

The End of Ponzi's Scheme

C HARLES PONZI WOULD CELEBRATE THE Fourth of July in 1920 in a grander fashion that he had ever, in the most avariciously luxurious of his dreams, imagined.

His wife, however, was not as enthusiastic. Rose Ponzi, her husband's one and only and ever, "was tiny, at four foot eleven just the right size for him, with rounded curves that defied the stick-figure fashions of the day. She had luxurious brown hair, lively dark eyes, and skin as smooth as Gianduja cream [chocolate with thirty percent hazelnut]." Several weeks earlier, perhaps feeling that the end was approaching and he wanted to leave something tangible behind, Ponzi announced he would build a castle for his Rose, and not one of his castles in the air. She declined; like him, she came from a poor village in Italy, and it was the simple things of life that made her comfortable. He insisted; it was the expensive things of life that made him salivate, the luxuries of the American promise so long deferred. Again she said no. He begged her to let him show his love in his way, and finally they agreed to compromise; the result, however, favored the husband much more than the wife.

The Ponzis bought a house already erected in Lexington, Massachusetts—less than a castle, certainly, but Charles immediately began to add on and rebuild. Employing dozens of workmen seven days a week, Ponzi supervised construction of a living room so large that it took several seconds to notice the grand piano in a corner. Neither of them played. Behind it was the entrance to a sunroom and, directly opposite, a fireplace with a bearskin rug in front. Persian and Oriental rugs covered the rest of the hardwood floors; chairs and sofas upholstered in damask and velour bordered the rugs; and a $5,000 kitchen, which was more than the cost of many entire dwellings at the time, was powered by gas, a rarity for the era. Tending to the Ponzis' needs were a gardener, a butler, and a cook, although Rose, unhappy about the latter, gave her a lot of nights off. She would peel her own vegetables, thank you. She would prepare her own pastas and stews, clean up her own messes, supervise her own shopping.

In truth, Rose was unhappy about much in her new home. It was like a museum, one that few people visited, and she was one of the items on display, one that few people ever saw. She did not complain; she knew that her husband was bathing her in materialism because he loved her, but she could not understand what had happened. So unexpected was Charles's sudden wealth, so excessive—where had it come from? Surely two people didn't need so much. Unlike most of her countrymen, she had just found the American dream come true, but to an extreme that left her shaken and confused. Shouldn't the dreams of more Americans come true instead of those of just one couple, a couple now so drowning in excess that they had bought a piano simply as decoration?

What had happened to her sweet Charles? She was puzzled by his behavior; he seemed so unlike the man who had courted her and won her heart.

Then again, maybe they would one day have a couple of children who could play the piano. They certainly tried enough times. They did not need the services of Margaret Sanger and associates; they needed the opposite.

As Michael E. Parrish relates, "By July 4, 1920, according to some estimates, Ponzi's company was raking in a cool $1 million each week. . . . Ponzi was mentioned in the same breath with Columbus, Michelangelo, and Marconi."

ACCORDING TO *THE AMERICAN CHRONICLE: Six Decades in American Life, 1920–1980*, twelve new words or phrases were added to the English language in 1920. One of them was "profiteer." It is perhaps fair to say that Ponzi was as responsible for its inclusion as anyone else.

He did not, however, remain a profiteer for nearly as long as he had anticipated. He was sued twice in 1920 for dubious business practices; and although he won both cases, one of them a libel judgment that provided him with a whopping award that started out, before appeals, at $500,000, the more cautious among his investors were becoming more cautious still. They began to pull their money out of the Securities Exchange Company, or at least some of it, fearing that Ponzi was not as legitimate as he seemed. Yes, they reasoned, he had been legally vindicated in the two cases, but where there's smoke. . . . Sometimes it just takes a little longer to see the fire, and during that time, as the flames ignite beneath the surface, a great deal of damage can be done.

Fortunately, Ponzi had more than enough revenue on hand to cover the small number of defecting clients, and his ability to pay them, promptly and profitably, reassured his remaining investors. All seemed well. Actually, all seemed better than well, as the July 24, 1920 issue of the *Boston Post* printed a favorable article on Ponzi's firm, and the result was even more clients than there had been before the two lawsuits, the most ever.

But despite the *Post*'s history of favorable coverage, there were doubters on the paper's staff, and they occupied prominent positions. Both assistant editor/publisher Richard Grozier and city editor Eddie Dunn believed that, what seemed too good to be true was in fact too good to be true, and this was never more accurate than in the world of finance. It was time, they decided, to look more deeply into the Securities Exchange Company than the paper had ever done before. On July 26, just two days after the latest encomium, the *Post* published an article by Clarence Walker Barron, "recognized internationally as among the foremost financial authorities of the world." Under a headline that ran . . .

QUESTIONS THE MOTIVE BEHIND PONZI SCHEME
Barron Says Reply Coupon Plan Can Be Worked Only in Small Way

. . . Barron wrote, "If Mr. Rockefeller, the richest man in the world, should offer even 50 percent for money and be found to be putting his own money into 5 percent bonds, there would not be much money offered to him by financial people." In other words, if Rockefeller couldn't deliver a fifty-percent return, no one could. Barron, after whom the highly respected financial newspaper would be named by family members the following year, continued his article by declaring that even if it were possible to continue to pay the kinds of returns Ponzi was providing, it would be "'immoral' because it would be profiting at the expense of a government. 'When a man gets money from the government without performing a service, it is just the same as when a man takes money from an individual without performing a service for that money.'"

Something was wrong somewhere with Ponzi's offering; it was just a matter of discovering where. And, as unlikely as it seemed, it was the *Post* that would soon take on the mission.

In part because of Barron's reputation, and in part because of the carefully reasoned critique he had offered—he had been poring over records of Ponzi's dealings for weeks—the Commonwealth of Massachusetts had also begun to look into the dapper financier's affairs; and as if he hadn't a care in the world, which might truly have been his attitude, Ponzi volunteered to help. Without being forced, or even asked, he announced that he would stop accepting investments during the period of the commonwealth's inquiry. He had more than enough money on which to live for an indefinite time, and by showing his cooperation with the investigators, both public and private, he would, ipso facto, be showing his confidence in SEC. In the long run, he thought he just might attract more investors because of his amenability. In the long run, it would be good business.

So, at his own expense and with a broad smile for reporters who asked him about the matter, Ponzi took out an ad in the *Post*:

PUBLIC NOTICE

I have made a personal agreement with District Attorney Pelletier to cease receiving funds from the public for investment with the
SECURITIES EXCHANGE CO.
27 School St., Boston,
and all branches, until after an official audit is made to determine my solvency and satisfy him that my methods of financial operation are thoroughly legitimate. Meantime, I shall pay all maturing obligations as fast as presented. Further, during the auditing of the books any persons holding unmatured notes can receive back their original investment, without interest, if they desire.
Signed, Charles Ponzi.

Ponzi was convinced that the self-imposed suspension would be a brief one, and that the investigation would reveal his methods to be without flaw. How he could have been certain of either is a mystery whose only solution seems to be self-delusion. A later examination of Ponzi's books revealed some of the shoddiest record-keeping the auditors had ever encountered, shoddy enough to raise questions not just about paperwork, but about the ethical basis of the entire company.

The reasons for the criticism of the original Ponzi scheme are complicated, to the point of being beyond the scope of this book. Or, at least, this author. Suffice it to say, in the simplest possible terms, that, as has been the case with later Ponzi schemes of a simpler nature, Charles did not have enough money available to him to pay for a run by investors. This was not illegal at the time, only dubious; after all, runs by investors are most uncommon occurrences in normal-to-better economic times. And had newspapers, starting with the *Boston Post*, not created doubt in the public mind, and, more important, had the Universal Postal Union not changed its regulations concerning International Reply Coupons, Ponzi would have made a lot more money for a lot more people for a lot longer period. Himself notably included.

But the Union was finally catching on to what Ponzi and Old Colony and others were doing; and although it might have been slow to do so, its actions were quick and decisive once they came. There was no way, the Union decided, that it was going to allow its coupons to be used for a free-money swindle in the United States. It tightened its definition of terms so there was not as great a difference in the cash value between one country's stamps and another's. Then, shortly afterward, determining that any difference at all could lead to some kind of fraud, it took the wiser course of eliminating the International Reply Coupons altogether. The result was far more complexity than before in mailing items from one country to another, but far less opportunity for fraud.

It was at this point that any company doing business like SEC or Old Colony went from being dubious to being illegal, from being unethical to being fraudulent—and in fact most such firms went quickly out of business. But foolishly, even though he was accepting no more money for the time being, Ponzi stayed in business and, because of the new rules, quickly found his cash on hand shrinking in comparison to cash owed investors. The new rules were about to cause that dreaded run on SEC; after a brief hiatus, Ponzi was about to become a full-fledged crook yet again.

On July 30, with his firm still under voluntary suspension, the *Post* ran a headline that he might long have been fearing, even with his kindergarten-ish bookkeeping methods:

EXTRA

COUPON PLAN

IS EXPLODED

New York Postmaster Says Not Enough in Whole World to
Make Fortune Ponzi Claims

Ironically, the next story about Ponzi in the *Post*, and the final nail in the coffin of the Securities Exchange Company, was written not by Barron or by Richard Grozier or Eddie Dunn, but by a man Ponzi had himself hired to do publicity for him, a shill who, in effect, turned state's evidence.

William McMasters was one of the few upstanding practitioners in a field full of carnival barkers and con men with the newly proliferating typewriting machines. Having signed onto the SEC payroll several weeks before the previous headline spread across the *Post*'s front page, McMasters was eager to rescue the company's reputation, just as his employer wanted. But he quickly became suspicious, as he heard his boss say one thing in one meeting with potential investors, then contradict himself in the next session with those he was hustling. So sincere in manner and enthusiastic in presentation was Ponzi that McMasters thought he might simply have gotten carried away, becoming so excited about the prospect of new business that he didn't know what he was saying. Either that, or he had forgotten McMasters's presence and didn't realize he was being overheard; or perhaps he had just gotten to the point at which he didn't care anymore one way or the other. In which case he would have looked at McMasters as less a name on the payroll than an accomplice. It was not to be.

McMasters began after-hours searches of Ponzi's office to verify his doubts, and was amazed at what he found. Incriminating information did not just exist, but lay right out in the open—on top of the desk, in unlocked drawers, even in stacks of papers in the corners of the sofa. How the Commonwealth of Massachusetts could have missed this evidence—or, more likely, not understood its significance—is baffling. But just as baffling is the fact that, since the commonwealth's investigation had begun, Ponzi had apparently gotten even sloppier in his methods. Actually, he did not even have methods; he simply had clutter.

McMasters, however, proved himself expert at sorting through it. He collected the most damning evidence, organized it, wrote an introductory summary to it, and then went to Grozier. The summary was all Grozier needed to hear. He told McMasters to stop talking and begin writing. The headline was the worst news yet for the ambitious Italian.

DECLARES PONZI IS NOW HOPELESSLY INSOLVENT

In the following article, McMasters claimed that Ponzi was at least two million dollars in debt; had never earned so much as a penny from outside the United States, as he had claimed; had once bribed a policeman for a gun permit; and had paid thugs to intimidate, either verbally or physically, reporters primed to publish exposés. McMasters quoted banker Simon

Swig, a leader of Boston's Jewish community, as questioning Ponzi's sanity, and further denounced Wall Street officials for not having looked more carefully, if at all, into Ponzi's procedures and his impossibly unheard-of returns.

It is not certain that all of McMasters's charges are true; some seem exaggerated, even for a man of Ponzi's moral shortcomings. It also speaks ill of McMasters, and the *Boston Post*, that the publicist, despite being on SEC's payroll, received the "fabulous sum" of $5,000 from the newspaper. It is one thing to sit on both sides of the fence, quite another to be paid by both.

A disclaimer, which would have explained McMasters's supposed dual allegiances, is a staple of today's journalism. Or, at least, is supposed to be. It would have protected McMasters from later charges of manipulating the truth for financial gain.

One thing, though, was certain from his article: Ponzi had for quite a while now been paying off old investors with money he had taken in from newcomers. Soon both he and his later investors would be broke, and even a giddy self-deceiver like Ponzi must have felt the pressure of living on borrowed time. The famous—although not yet named—"Ponzi scheme" had been in operation now for several months, and its life span was inherently a short one—eight months, in fact, from the first sale to Ponzi's arrest.

The predictable happened as soon as the McMasters edition of the *Post* rolled off the presses. The scheme's lifespan was over. Virtually all of the investors in SEC demanded their money back, and at the promised 50-percent yield. The first few to get to Ponzi made a profit, although less than they had expected. For the rest of the SEC investors, the vast majority of them, it was already too late when the *Post* was delivered to homes and newsstands. The most that an individual in this group of Ponzie's patsies could retrieve from his life savings was twelve cents on the dollar. Not enough to send the butcher Ettore Giberti's children to college. Not even enough to clothe them, or his wife, in such a way that he could be proud.

No longer was Charles Ponzi being mentioned in the same breath as Michelangelo and Columbus.

PONZI SPENT MUCH OF THE Roaring Twenties, ostensibly America's golden decade, in jail. His Lexington home was gone. His dazzling wardrobe was gone. Most crushingly, his dreams were gone. So vivid had they been, so deeply had he immersed himself in them, that he was barely able to speak when addressed in the courtroom for his first of several sentencings. Writes biographer Mitchell Zuckoff, "The clerk persisted, asking Ponzi if he wanted to plead guilty or not guilty. Again [Ponzi's attorney Daniel] Coakley prompted him, 'Guilty.'

"Ponzi seemed startled. But in a timorous voice, he said the word: 'Guilty.'" When a sentence of five years was announced, Rose fainted briefly, then regained consciousness and began to sob. She had to be helped out of the courtroom by friends who were equally morose.

It was F. Scott Fitzgerald who said, foolishly and yet somehow enduringly, "There are no second acts in American lives," a statement proven false far more often than true. Yet if the five-year sentence was the end of Ponzi's first act in America, there would indeed be no second act in *his* case. He was too notorious, too well known, and too widely distrusted ever again to regain a position of prominence.

Zuckoff deserves to be quoted in detail about the aftermath of Charles Ponzi's appearance in court:

> A few days after Ponzi's guilty plea, a *New York Times* editorial offered a remarkably balanced epitaph on the affair. First, it poured on the condemnation, decrying him as "an egregious falsifier and a wholesale betrayer of simple confidences." But the *Times* recognized that there was more to Ponzi. "There was something picturesque, something suggestive of the gallant about him, and it is almost possible, though not quite, to believe he was as credulous as his victims and deceived himself as much as he did them," the *Times* mused. "Perhaps the disinclination for being harsh in characterizing Ponzi is due to lack of any sympathy for those whom he robbed. . . . They showed only greed—the eagerness to get much for nothing—and they had not one of Ponzi's redeeming graces."

When New Yorkers went to the polls a few weeks later, election officials came across the names of two unexpected write-in candidates for state treasurer: John D. Rockefeller and Charles Ponzi. It was the company he had always hoped to keep.

BY THE TIME HE HAD managed to repay the last of his creditors, it was December 1930, and he still had more than three years to spend in jail on one of the numerous charges that had been filed against him. Released in February 1934, Ponzi, who had never become a U.S. citizen, which had been one of his dreams, was deported back to Italy. According to biographer Donald H. Dunn,

> The deportation scene, despite its tragic overtones, in many ways resembled a farewell party for a successful industrialist. Accompanied by seven uniformed immigration inspectors, several of whom carried his luggage, Ponzi was ferried by government motor launch to the cruise liner in Boston Harbor. Dressed immaculately and waving his cap in salute, he came aboard while newsreel cameras whirred and flash bulbs exploded all about him. In a press conference held in one of the ship's larger suites, he settled his rotund figure into a velvet-covered armchair and explained that friends had provided ninety-five dollars in addition to the $105 paid by the government for a third-class ticket, so that he might travel to Italy first class.

But there would be no more first class for Charles Ponzi after that. He would never know the good life again. In fact, he was about to sink into a gloom more profound than any he had ever known—and, despite his "redeeming graces," as the *Times* called them, would never rise out of it.

The "tragic overtones" of the deportation scene to which Dunn refers are in part a reference to the fact that Ponzi could not afford either to take Rose with him or, as things worked out, to send for her later or even to support her in their native land if she had been able to come. That, at least, was the story most often told. But it might be that Rose, although still loving her failed financier in her way, had had enough of the corrupt life, and was simply unwilling to return to Italy as the handmaiden of a criminal. It may be that, although he was broken-hearted and began missing her terribly the moment she departed, she was less affected, having grown weary of her husband's jolly deviousness.

Two years passed. Two endless years for Charles without his Rose. They wrote to each other often during that time, Ponzi assuring her as he closed each missive that he would see her before long. Then, suddenly, the theory about Rose's disenchantment turned into fact. It was a blow that Ponzi should have expected but didn't; and one from which he would never recover. "When he was down, when he was in trouble, when he was in prison, I stuck to him," Rose told a reporter from the *Boston Post*. "When he had millions, when he had a mansion, when he had cars, I stuck with him. And now I feel that I have provided my loyalty through thick and thin, and I intend to secure a quiet divorce."

Divorce. His soul mate Rose, the only woman he had ever loved, wanted to end her union with him. It is not certain how Ponzi found out about the *Post* article; but that his love for Rose was genuine, surely the most honest feeling he had ever known, cannot be denied. Although the two of them did not realize it at the time, they would never see each other again. They "corresponded with some regularity and with obvious affection"; unfortunately, they also corresponded at great distance, one that would never become closer. Rose kept their correspondence secret from her new husband.

The two of them stayed in the Boston area, with Rose supporting herself as a bookkeeper at a nightclub owned, in part, by the lawyer who had secured her divorce. The nightclub was the famed Cocoanut Grove, most famous because one night in 1942 a fire suddenly erupted inside, a blaze that, with frightening speed, engulfed the club, killing 492 patrons, all of them screaming and wrestling with each other to get out of the inferno.

The terrible irony is that most of them could have made it; there were nine doors on the first floor of the Cocoanut Grove, but virtually none of the night-lifers knew about eight of them, which remained unused during the untamed exodus. They knew only the one through which they had entered, and it was at this door that they piled themselves up into a ghastly mound of charred human rubble.

Ponzi was frantic when he heard about the tragedy. News that Rose had survived was slow in reaching him, but when Charles finally heard it, he was so relieved that it seemed as if he expected to see her prancing down the gangplank of the next ship from America, right back into his arms. He did not, of course, go to meet the vessel; she, of course, was not on board.

By this time, after having worked for several years as an interpreter at hotels in Rome and Venice, Charles had moved to Brazil, where he was employed by an Italian airline. He expected to make more money than he had in Italy. He hoped to see his Rose again. Something in him, though, feared it wouldn't happen, that good fortune, once having deserted him, would never return. Nor did it. Money in Brazil did not go as far as it did in Italy in those days, and Ponzi, as had been the case ever since his prison terms, was unable to put anything away, unable to earn anything more than it took to keep him alive from week to week. No second act.

In one of his letters after the fire, Ponzi wrote to his ex-wife, "Perhaps I made a mess of your life, but it was not for lack of the necessary sentiment. Here I am, past sixty-one, thousands of miles away from you, physically separated from you these past nine years, legally a stranger to you, and yet feeling toward you the same as I did that night in June when I took you home from the first movies we saw together in Somerville Avenue."

If Ponzi's love for Rose never waned, neither did his love for the quick buck. On one occasion, even though still in Brazil, he tried to get Rose to be his accomplice. She couldn't believe it. She read the letter in which he outlined his scam, and, stunned, a dozen different thoughts running through her head, she reminded him that she was married. He told her there were ways around any obstacle. She reminded him that his schemes always failed. To this charge there was no defense, and in fact, the plan that Ponzi had in mind had fallen apart before Rose's letter about his failed schemes even reached him. It seems that Charles, to his unaccountable surprise, was unable to raise the necessary "down payment." Rose feared that, had he had time, he might likely have asked her and her husband for some of the money. What was she to make of this man, her first lover, and in some ways still her one and only, her reprised wedding vows notwithstanding?

His emotional state at this time was as perilous as his finances were, and he could not hold on to his airline job, which had been arranged by a cousin, of whom he seemed to have plenty all over the world. By 1942, after a short period of unemployment, Ponzi was again supporting himself, Zuckoff relates, though just barely, "by running a small rooming house in Rio de Janeiro and teaching English in a private school. Soon the momentary millionaire, with the rise and fall of his scheme, the entire life span of Ponzi's public story taking place in but a few months in 1920, was living on seventy-five dollars a month, though he optimistically called it 'quite a tidy sum here.' His eyesight and his health began to fail, and he remained weakened from a heart attack that had struck him seven years to the day after his deportation." Not wanting Rose to worry, he had never told her about it.

Actually, Ponzi would soon be in even worse straits, as his rooming house was closed by Brazilian authorities after complaints that most of the rooms were occupied by prostitutes, thumping mattresses and fleecing customers throughout the night. Ponzi claimed not to have known—and given his ever-worsening eyesight and fragile health, he might well have been telling the truth. Or he might have thought that what a paying customer did was his or her or their own business. They had, after all, put down the money for the room.

In 1948, so frail as to be unrecognizable as the sport he had once been, and almost completely blind, he could no longer work at any job. His home now was the charity ward of a Rio hospital, which he would never leave. When an Associated Press reporter found him there, a shell of himself in a shell of a building, Ponzi's spirits again brightened, delighting in the attention. He told the reporter that "I hit the American people where it hurts—in the pocketbook. Those were confused money-mad days. Everybody wanted to make a killing. I was in it plenty deep, rolling in other people's money."

Later in the same year, 1948, Ponzi dictated his last letter to Rose, his hand so unsteady that a hospital employee had to transcribe his sentiments for him. "I am doing fairly well," he told his great love, "and in fact am getting better every day and I expect to go back home for Christmas." But where was his home? He had none. He had no one waiting for him.

It didn't matter anyhow. As Zuckoff clarifies, "It was false hope, but that had always been his strength. Deep within the impoverished old man in the hospital bed remained the optimistic young dandy of 1920." But in his even younger days, as a troublemaker about to be exiled from his native Italy, he had had his mother beside him, and his thoughts went back to her now: stroking his cheeks, bragging to the neighbors. He had not been in touch with her for several years; his shame was too great. She, of course, could not write to him as his address kept changing, and he would see to it that she never knew his final addresses—the different jails, the cheap apartments from which he had to keep moving because he could not pay his rent, the flophouse for hookers, the charity ward. No, his mother would never learn of these dwellings, not if he could help it. And as he moved ever closer to death, he was haunted by thoughts that his mother had preceded him, never having heard from her boy about his great American success. Apparently he could no longer force himself to raise her spirits with another batch of lies. And for Ponzi, no more lies meant nothing to say to the second great love of his life.

The year after his last letter to Rose, the story ended. Or seemed to. On January 17, 1949, Ponzi died of a blood clot on the brain. Rose had hoped to have his body returned to Boston for a service and burial but, even with her husband willing to contribute, she didn't have enough money to bring him back to the United States.

PONZI'S OBITUARIES APPEARED WITHIN A day or two in all the Boston papers, and many papers elsewhere, nationally and internationally. The most appropriate mention, though, was longer in coming. It was the inclusion of Ponzi's name in dictionaries, a claim to immortality that few people can make. In the volume that I have used for more than two decades, *The Random House Dictionary of the English Language, Second Edition*, the name "Ponzi" appears between "pony truss" and "poobah," and the definition reads as follows: "a swindle in which a quick return, made up of money from new investors, on an initial investment lures the victim into much bigger risks. Also called **Pon-zi game. Ponzi-scheme.** (after Charles *Ponzi* (died 1949), the organizer of such a scheme in the U.S., 1919–1920)."

FORGOTTEN FOR MANY DECADES, PONZI burst back into public notice early in the twenty-first century, when a man named Bernie Madoff, whose methods, if not his charisma, could have led one to think he was Charles's grandson, committed the biggest fraud in American financial history, a textbook example of the Ponzi scheme that bilked Americans out of the almost inconceivable sum of $65 billion, so great an amount that it threw the nation's entire economy into a tailspin. In fact, the phrase "Ponzi scheme" has probably been written and spoken more in the current century than the previous one.

On a day in 2008, when Madoff and Ponzi were sharing the headlines, the *New York Times* once again decided to analyze the latter, contrasting him with the former, and doing so succinctly. "Ponzi was a great equalizer," the *Times* wrote, "tapped into the desires of the masses, while for Madoff, the brilliance there, if the allegations are true, is that he tapped into the desires of the elite. They weren't looking for the big score—they were looking for great returns and brilliant access."

Since 1920, scores of people have invented new and ever more ingenious forms of swindling the innocent through alleged investment opportunities. But as Madoff so venally proved, it was Carlo Pietro Giovanni Gugliemo Tebaldo Ponzi, an Italian immigrant who came to the United States more than a hundred years ago, who stood as a beacon for them all. Which made him, in his own way, as much a robber baron as those more commonly associated with the term.

CHAPTER ELEVEN

The Closed Door in the White House

I T WAS PONZI WHO MADE headlines late in the summer of 1920, but there was a much more important story in Washington, D.C. at the time, a story of which few people were aware, a crisis that affected not only the manner in which government was conducted but perhaps the decisions that it made—there is no way to know. It was a kind of crisis that had never existed before and will never exist again.

Thomas Woodrow Wilson, who as a boy had been called Tommie by his family and friends, was the son, grandson, and nephew of Presbyterian ministers. As a result, Tommie could not help but inherit a certain stiff-necked, churchified rectitude, an image that he carried into adulthood, when he was known by his middle name.

But the Wilsons were not nearly as strict in their religion as their fellow followers of Calvin. Tommie's father, for example, known to all as Dr. Wilson, smoked, had an occasional drink, played billiards, and enjoyed vacationing at fancy resorts, even when his leisure activities prohibited him from a strict observance of the Sabbath. He also enjoyed tutoring his son; "they talked like master and scholar of classical times," writes Wilson's biographer Arthur Walworth, "the father giving the boy in digestible doses what he had learned of the world, of literature, the sciences and theology—imparting it all with humor and fancy."

However it was imparted, though, theology was probably the most important part not just of Tommie's lineage, but of his life. Dr. Wilson might not have been a strict Presbyterian, but of the fact that he was a true believer there is no doubt. He displayed it to his son most often when the two of them were alone together on Sunday afternoons.

> There were readings . . . in the big leather-bound Bible. The doctor penciled notes in the margins that interpreted the text in the language of the day. His religion had no cant and was suffused with a love of mankind that often overflowed sectarian bounds.
>
> Young Tommie was exposed to the best that Augusta (Georgia) offered in religious education. In the Sunday school, of which Uncle James Bones was superintendent, the boy memorized the Shorter Catechism. To his roving mind this was as painful as formal schooling, and he did not remember the work permanently.
>
> Yet Tommie . . . [o]ften rode in his father's buggy when the preacher made parish calls. His favorite playground was the shady churchyard. . . . Even as he lay in bed on summer evenings the strains of the organ soothed him. Music affected his emotions; he would sometimes weep at the communion service when moving hymns were sung.

This was Tommie Wilson's foundation for maturity, and if it seems more appropriate for a minister than for a politician, that is exactly what it should do, for it indicates the kind of elected official Wilson would eventually become. He was sure of the dictates of proper morality and determined to follow them, regardless of storms of disapproval, both public and legislative. It was this certitude that probably killed him.

At the start, though, it seemed that Wilson would reside in the academe. It was there that the Holy Grail of tenure awaited him; and of the first forty-six years of his life, he would spend almost half as a Princeton faculty member, devout as ever in his faith but teaching primarily jurisprudence and political economy.

In 1902, to the surprise of many, even Wilson himself, he was appointed the university's president. His goals, he decided, once regaining his composure, were twofold, and both extremely ambitious. "First," says historian John Milton Cooper, Jr., "he wanted to make Princeton the nation's top university. Second, he sought to quash the pseudo-rebellious student hedonism that already held sway in the clubs and was making headway in colleges across the country. His symbolic antagonist was a boy who did not enter Princeton until three years after Wilson left—F. Scott Fitzgerald."

While pursuing these goals, Wilson lost a good number of battles with various faculty and alumni committees—not on merit, but because he was unskilled at the fine points of campus politics. Taking on men who believed that Princeton was too noble an institution to require alteration, as well as insufficiently endowed to meet requests for expansion of both the curriculum and the campus, Wilson found himself being continually struck down in his attempts at reform. As a result, he started to think seriously not just about campus politics, which he eventually began to master, but about politics in the larger world of national government and whether that might be a more suitable place for him than an academic cloister. In 1904, establishing his credentials as a conservative Democrat, he spoke publicly and often against the liberal presidential candidate, Democrat William Jennings Bryan, as well as the eventual winner, Republican Theodore Roosevelt.

In 1906, when U.S. senators were still elected by state legislatures, Wilson received a few votes as a minority Democratic nominee. In another two years, there was talk of him as a vice-presidential candidate and even, in some quarters, as a presidential contender, although Wilson does not seem to have encouraged support for either position. He was still observing, still learning, his heart still committed to Princeton. But wavering. In fact, two years later, in 1910, believing he had learned all that Princeton had to teach him about politics, Wilson decided he was ready for a big leap forward and entered the contest for the New Jersey governorship.

Running on a platform that denounced the state's political bosses and promising that he would not be their tool once in office, which was just what the electorate wanted to hear, the scholar conquered the State House, perhaps surprising himself again by entering the world of government in such a prominent position.

And although campaign promises are seldom able to be kept, especially one of this magnitude, Wilson in fact turned out *not* to be a tool of the bosses, refusing to divide the spoils according to the old-time politicos' whims, at times even refusing to grant them appointments to plead for their whims in person. The growth and prosperity of the state, he believed, depended on the best-qualified men, not the best-connected. In fact, once Wilson proved victorious in a hard-fought battle against the Senate and Assembly to institute a system of state primaries, the political bosses of New Jersey had little left to boss. Wilson was right. Princeton had taught him well. He knew how to play the game now, and would play it for high stakes, but with a beacon of morality to guide him.

AFTER SERVING AS GOVERNOR FOR another two-year term, Wilson accepted the pleas of national Democratic leaders and ran for president. His reputation for independence, his introduction of workers' compensation to New Jersey, and his restructuring of the state's decayed, inefficient public utilities commission attracted so much attention that, despite continuing to appear like a cleric and act, occasionally, in the prissy manner of a schoolmaster, he was elected to the nation's highest office in 1912.

Actually, the White House was a gift to Wilson from Theodore Roosevelt. Republicans got 1.3 million more votes than Democrats that year, but the problem was that there were two Republicans in the race, and the bull-headed Bull-Moose rebel, former president Roosevelt, despite knowing that his candidacy would split the GOP vote with his enemy and successor, William Howard Taft, ignored the advice of virtually everyone who offered it and ran anyhow, seeing to it that the opposing party, the minority party, achieved the nation's highest elective office.

Nonetheless, Wilson set out superbly. In his first term, he was one of the most productive chief executives the United States had ever had. His accomplishments included the Federal Reserve Act, antitrust legislation that actually worked, low-interest loans for farmers, unreserved support for woman's suffrage, and the dubious but necessary introduction of a federal income tax.

His second term, however, started out poorly and then began to worsen, finally ending divisively and disastrously, although the reasons were not entirely of the president's making. Wilson ran in 1916 under the banner "He kept us out of war"—and he did, longer than he should have in the opinion of many. Eventually, though, he had to enter the European conflict, and he seems never to have forgiven himself for going back on his word. He believed, however, that he had no choice, and believed further that he would atone for his broken campaign promise by taking steps to make the Great War the last one in which the United States ever participated, perhaps the last war ever to be fought anywhere, by anyone. Woodrow Wilson the idealist now became Woodrow Wilson the fantasist. Unfortunately for him, he also became a preacher to a an assembly of atheists.

In a speech to a joint session of Congress on January 8, 1918, the president introduced his Fourteen Points, known derisively by those incapable of tolerating Wilson's self-righteousness as the Ten Commandments. They were a detailed plan for a postwar world in which armed conflict would no longer have a place. Among other things, the points stressed open diplomacy rather than secret treaties, free trade, freedom of the seas, worldwide disarmament, and the rebuilding or restoration of France, Belgium, Russia, Austria-Hungary, Poland, the Ottoman Empire, and the Balkan states. It was a program of totally unrealistic breadth. It sounded wonderful.

It was because of such humanitarian goals that, when Wilson went to Paris to take part in negotiations for the Treaty of Versailles in 1919, he was hailed by the French as no American since Benjamin Franklin had been hailed. In the words of historian Gene Smith,

> It seemed the whole of France stood in the streets. From the Madeleine to the Bois de Boulogne not a square foot of space was clear. Stools and tables were put out by the concierges of

houses along the parade route, with places on them selling for ten, twenty or fifty francs, depending on the affluence of the customer. Carpenter horses and boards were arranged into improvised grandstands, and men and boys clung to the very tops of the chestnut trees. The housetops were covered with people . . . [who] had gathered hours before [Wilson's] train was due in Paris and stood waiting and looking down toward the station, a tiny bandbox on the edge of the Bois reserved for official arrivals of visiting royalty.

In practical terms, the Fourteen Points ended up serving as the first draft for the constitution of the League of Nations, forerunner of the United Nations. The delegates to Versailles, many of whom had initially supported both the war and the complex web of treaties that led to its outbreak, needed something to atone for their sin, a penance for the fatalities and ruination caused by their earlier bellicosity. Their war-battered constituents demanded it. More important, they needed something hopeful to take home with them, something promising, optimistic. Given Wilson's overwhelming reception in Paris, support for the League, the delegates reasoned, would be just what their nations wanted to hear. They would return home not just with a treaty, as expected, but with a treaty that would eliminate the need for treaties in the future. The League's Covenant began as follows:

THE HIGH CONTRACTING PARTIES,
In order to promote international co-operation and to achieve international peace and security
    by the acceptance of obligations not to resort to war,
    by the prescription of open, just and honourable relations between nations,
    by the firm establishment of the understandings of international law as the actual rule of conduct among Governments, and
    by the maintenance of justice and a scrupulous respect for all treaty obligations in the dealings of organised peoples with one another,
Agree to this Covenant of the League of Nations.

Forty-two countries assented to the League. The United States was not one of them. Wilson was stunned. That his own nation, a nation whose citizens had elected him president twice, the second time without a bifurcated Republican vote, would reject so nobly intended a peace proposal, one that was certain to go down in history and make every man who signed it a hero to posterity, was the greatest embarrassment of Woodrow Wilson's life.

WILSON HAD BEEN AS SHATTERED by the brutality overseas as the soldiers who had returned from it, soldiers who would form the core of the "lost generation." Never again, Wilson vowed, never again such pointless carnage. But was the League of Nations the solution? The majority of Americans seemed to agree not with their president about the League, but with Congress, led by Senate Republican Henry Cabot Lodge of Massachusetts. He, too, shared the president's revulsion to the Great War. All Americans shared it. But Lodge, among many other members of the House and Senate, thought a return to the battleground would be *more* likely, not less, if the United States were part of an association of European countries, thus allowing its actions to be governed by diplomatic ties that were made abroad and allowing the League to call America to arms again if its members couldn't play together nicely. Lodge believed in his own country's law, not "acceptance of obligations," as the Covenant put it, imposed by others. And he did not believe in a "respect for all treaty obligations," only those into which the United States had entered of its own will, without having been reduced to a single voice among a chorus of nations, its vote a mere one forty-second of the final decision.

After all, the United States had already achieved world hegemony in many ways—and it continued to increase its production of railroads, automobiles, and airplanes; continued to manufacture steel and literally thousands of products made of steel; dominated trade with other nations; controlled sea lanes with its management of the Panama Canal; provided weaponry for a small but dynamic military; and created wealth as it had never been created before. Why should America be a team player when it already owned the entire sporting franchise?

To Wilson, these arguments made no sense; they were not rebuttals so much as evidence of "narrow, selfish, provincial purposes," a destructively competitive nature, and that is what he told Lodge and his followers. After which he issued a warning: "I have fighting blood in me and it is sometimes a delight to let it have scope, but if it is challenged on this occasion it will be an indulgence." And fight he did, pushing himself well beyond the limits that his frail body could tolerate in pursuit of the unattainable.

At first, the League was voted down. In fact, two versions of it were voted down in rapid succession. With Lodge leading the way, the Senate rejected President Wilson's plea for League membership, 53–38; and then it turned its attention to another bill, full of amendments added by Lodge and his followers to frustrate what he believed were the president's attempts to yield American sovereignty. This diluted version of the League of Nations, which should have had a better chance of passing, since it satisfied many of the opposition's objections, also lost, this time by the almost identical margin of 55–39. The Senate, apparently, wanted nothing to do with a foreign alliance of any kind.

Wilson surely expected defeat, but that is not the same thing as accepting it. He considered himself a man of principle as well as one of faith, and as long as there was an ounce of energy left in him he would do what he believed was right. There would be one more congressional vote on the League, and perhaps, Wilson deluded himself into believing, if he simply worked hard enough, and explained the League's purposes clearly and eloquently enough, even more clearly and passionately than he had done numerous times before, the American people would pressure their representatives to do the right thing, to ensure peace for all time. How, he asked himself time and again, could the United States not cast a vote for a purpose so noble?

Refusing to heed the pleas of doctors, staff members, and friends, the president set out on a journey all the way across the country to the western states, where opposition to the League seemed to be at its greatest. He would confront the beast in its own lair.

One night in Pueblo, Colorado, an occasion when the crowd was even more restless than usual, seemingly more dubious about what it was hearing, a night when Wilson told his fellow Americans they would lead others "into pastures of quietness and peace such as the world never dreamed of before," the pains he had been feeling throughout his body for more than a week seemed to explode into his head. Finishing his talk to but scattered applause, he turned and tried to step back to his seat. He could not. He lost his balance, stumbling from the podium into the arms of his traveling companions, who had sprung up from their own seats. Those in the audience who saw the president fall assumed he had just tripped over something. Instead, they had just seen the last speech of Woodrow Wilson's life.

LIKE WAYNE WHEELER, WHOM HE somewhat resembled, Wilson wore wire-rim glasses over a will of steel. But the rest of the western tour had to be canceled; and on October 2, 1919, once again in the White House after a virtually sleepless journey back east, the president's will joined his body in breaking down. He awoke that morning with no feeling in his left hand. His doctor, Cary Grayson, was summoned immediately; but by the time he arrived, Wilson was on the floor of his bedroom, his body curled into a semicircle, barely breathing. He wanted a glass of water, but his struggle to form the words was ineffective; he had to motion with his hand.

Previously having contracted arteriosclerosis and possibly influenza, the latter probably a souvenir of Paris, Wilson had now suffered a stroke. Or so it was initially reported. More precisely, what had struck him was thrombosis, a clot in a blood vessel. Not only was the left side of his body paralyzed; he had been blinded in the left eye and suffered brain damage to an extent never made public and still not known. "It was," says historian John Morton Blum, "a wonder and a tragedy that he lived." The president was down now to that final ounce.

There was no provision for anything like this in the Constitution, a president almost totally incapacitated yet with more than a year left in his term. And so it was that Mrs. Edith Bolling Galt Wilson, the widowed president's second wife, made history of which only a few people knew at the time, becoming the first woman, however unofficially, to assume the duties of the presidency of the United States.

She was not totally unprepared. Her husband had discussed politics and diplomacy with her often. Eventually, he began to think of her as his top adviser in a number of matters: she was, after all, an intelligent woman, a woman who listened carefully when the president talked, who asked intelligent questions and remembered the answers, whom Wilson could trust without reservation. In fact, after only a year as First Lady, the *Louisville Courier-Journal* commented on how intimately involved she seemed to be in her husband's decision-making, in affairs both domestic and international. Although she already had two middle names, "Omnipotence," the paper suggested, might well be a third.

Senator Albert Fall of New Mexico was not impressed. Despite the secrecy so quickly and rigidly imposed by the White House, he knew what was happening there. "We have petticoat government!" thundered the fiery Republican, who would later make ignominious history of his own. "Mrs. Wilson is President!"

Women might have gained the vote in August 1920 but, unknown to virtually all of them, they had gained the Executive Mansion the previous October.

For most of the nearly year and a half that remained of her husband's term, which included all of 1920, Wilson was an invalid at best, little more than a rumor at worst. Most of the time, he stayed in his bedroom with the door locked and the shades drawn, secreted in a perpetual night that was virtually all he could bear. No light, no noise, no ability to understand the labyrinth of governmental actions and decisions swirling around him.

"So began my stewardship," Mrs. Wilson is quoted by Phyllis Lee Levin, the author of a book on the White House:

> I studied every paper, sent from the different Secretaries or Senators and tried to digest and present in tabloid form the things that, despite my vigilance, had to go to the president. I, myself, never made a single decision, regarding the disposition of public affairs. The only decision that was mine was what was important and what was not, and the *very* important decision of when to present matters to my husband.

It was Mrs. Wilson who controlled access to her husband, and she permitted few into his quarters. To some, especially those who supported the League of Nations, Mrs. Wilson's restrictive control was destructive, both to the League and the republic. As Levin says:

It has been written that Edith Wilson, "in her quiet, ignorant, misguided way did much damage at Paris, and even more at Washington," where Wilson, disabled and isolated, rendered the Senate's ratification of the league impossible through his absolute refusal to compromise on what the British economist John Maynard Keynes regarded as the "disastrous blots on the Covenant." In that hour, when [former Wilson adviser Edward M.] House's talents for conciliation were supremely required, his efforts were frustrated by the first lady. One wonders today at her disregard of that counsel; [French Prime Minister Georges] Clemenceau was only one of many European leaders who lauded the "super-civilized" [House] "who sees everything, who understands everything," and whose "keen, enlightened intelligence" was of "such assistance."

When Mrs. Wilson allowed someone to speak to her husband, she made certain that the person came and went swiftly, and on the way out reported to her. How did the president seem? The answer was usually not encouraging, although it was always difficult for such a judgment to be made to the First Lady. But there were times when Wilson could not speak a coherent sentence, nor avoid repetition of a few phrases that seemed to stick in what remained of his memory. Seldom could he hold eye contact with his visitor. His wife had to be told.

On his better days, when he *was* able to speak coherently for a time, he "was petulant, irascible, unreceptive to advice. Furthermore, Mrs. Wilson, fearful that pessimistic communications might cause a setback in the President's health, maintained her close surveillance over his correspondence and routine. To many of those who had pressing affairs of state to review with the chief executive, she seemed also to be jealous of the power she had inadvertently acquired."

Consulting with the president in 1920 was a habit, protocol; it was not an effective means of governing.

More often than receiving guests, the president received a note. A staff member of a senator or congressman, or perhaps a junior aide at a diplomatic mission, would tap lightly on the door of Wilson's quarters and his wife would emerge. She would take the note, close the door behind her, and read the note to her husband, trying to help him comprehend. If he could comment sensibly, he did; otherwise she advised him on what he would probably believe to be the best course of action, then waited for a sound or motion that indicated approval. In many cases, when he was simply not up to the complexities of a rider to an already complex bill, she made the decision herself, always as she thought he would have done. Then she wrapped his hand around a pen and helped him write a response, the handwriting a scrawl that could not be recognized as belonging to either of them. She returned the note to the messenger at the door and, if necessary, translated it for him. At another time, the marks on the paper might have been regarded as scratches on pieces of White House stationery. Now they were official U.S. policy.

Still, there were no calls for Vice President Thomas Marshall, "a completely discounted factor," to assume Wilson's duties. Nor did Marshall evince any desire to do so. "What this country needs," he is known for having said once, "is a really good five-cent cigar," and that is easily the most famous policy statement he ever made.

A few times near the end of the president's term, after he had shown slight signs of recovery, and after making certain there were no photographers lurking about, Mrs. Wilson led him by the hand to cabinet meetings. It was a mistake. Wilson could not contribute. Instead, he sat quietly, seldom moving, and when he did his head tended to bob as if it had been attached too loosely to his neck. His occasional comments were uttered in a voice not recognizable as Wilson's previous voice; they were sounds, more than sense. Something was probably getting through to him, but not enough so that he could form actual sentences about it, utter those sentences coherently—this man who had been among the most brilliant and literate ever to reign as chief executive.

It was, of course, not just Washington insiders who knew of the president's condition. The word could not help but spread in government circles. Jules Jusserand, the French ambassador to the United States, told his superiors at home that it no longer mattered what the great Wilson thought; the real ruler of the United States was "Mme. President."

Most Americans did not know the depth of the president's incapacitation. Not wanting to alarm the populace, almost all newspapers referred to his condition in a kind of code—and of necessity; not being able to see Wilson, they were not aware themselves of the state to which he had been reduced. Far fewer papers had Washington bureaus in 1920 than do today; those outlets had to rely on other sources for their news, meaning that they were getting their information second-hand; thus they were even more leery of reporting that the president had broken down and his wife had taken over many of his duties, made most of his decisions.

But was she the real ruler of the United States in 1920? The question cannot easily be answered. It is reasonable to assume that she made the decisions she believed her husband would have made, and therefore it was, in effect, as if Woodrow Wilson were still President of the United States. It is likely that he would have approved the second Palmer raids, and that she did so on his behalf; likely that he as much as she supported California's efforts to limit Japanese real estate holdings; likely that he as much as she approved the tariff treaty between the United States and China. And, Phyllis Lee Levin's opinion notwithstanding, it is unlikely that a healthy Wilson would have allowed Colonel House to persuade him to compromise on the League of Nations. The president had been too hell-bent on self-ruin. He would live or die according to the vote on the League, and perhaps always sensed what the outcome would be.

Besides, in a peacetime democracy, the president's power is limited, diluted by its having to be approved by majorities of the—at that time—400 members in the House and 96 in the Senate. There was never a complaint from the legislative branch, however, that Mrs. Wilson even tried to take a position contrary to one the president would have been expected to take. Both House and Senate seemed to think all was proceeding, if not in all cases well, at least in the vast majority of cases as the president would have wanted.

Only one potentially troublesome aspect of "petticoat government" remains: it cannot be known, must always remain speculation, precisely what issues Mrs. Wilson brought before her husband. Did she deem all the notes she allowed to have read to him of equal importance? Or did she not even present them all; did she simply make a few scribbles of her own at the bottom of some of the missives, then tell the errand boy that the matter was one the president did not wish to consider more thoroughly at present? Mrs. Wilson might have consulted with her spouse, as well as she could, about topics of more interest to herself than to him, and thus, in setting the agenda for his decisions, could perhaps have left a different mark on the country than her husband would have, despite their shared viewpoints. As she herself admitted, according to Levin, "The only decision that was mine was what was important and what was not." But this was, without question, as big a decision as any.

Exactly what happened behind the closed door at the White House will forever remain a mystery to historians. It seems a safe assumption, though, that Mrs. Wilson's influence was of minor import, and that that was precisely what she intended it to be.

THE SECOND TIME THE SENATE voted on the League of Nations, there was no Lodge version, only Wilson's. It was rejected by a vote of 49–35. The *New York Times* declared "senators of both parties united in declaring that in their opinion the treaty was now dead to stay dead." In the words of historian Jackson Lears, Wilson's "grandiose dreams of global redemption went unfulfilled."

It was the First Lady's opinion too, but she did not quite know what to do with it. Should she tell her husband right away that the greatest hope of his life would never be realized? Or should she delay the information? If so, for how long, and to what end? Perhaps one of his rare visitors would let word of the death knell slip—and then what? It was his wife from whom Wilson should hear of what she believed to be the Senate's perfidy, and just as she had performed her previous duties as president, so would she carry out this one.

"Edith withheld the news from the president until the following morning," Kristie Miller learned, and he was able to react—and his reaction was to be expected. In her book *Ellen and Edith: Woodrow Wilson's First Ladies* [the former having passed away in 1914], "Wilson was 'blue and depressed.' He told his doctor, 'I feel like going to bed and staying there.'" He was tucked under the covers and closed his eyes on the future.

Edith Wilson, Miller continues,

has been criticized for shielding her husband from important advisers who might have persuaded him to compromise [on the League of Nations, thereby ensuring its passage—an impossibility]. She and Grayson—he consulted with other doctors but was very much the primary care physician—did indeed limit Wilson's visitors. But they were following conventional medical wisdom of the time. Although the modern view is that stimulation is beneficial for stroke victims, it was not the view in Wilson's day. On March 16, 1920, Dr. [Francis X.] Dercum [who had treated Wilson years earlier for hypertension] wrote Dr. Grayson that he was doubtful whether the president should be seeing "a larger number of persons." He warned Grayson, "If his contact with other persons is increased, it should . . . be only with close personal friends." If this was his opinion nearly six months after Wilson's stroke, on the eve of the second treaty vote, Dercum would certainly have discouraged Edith from allowing her husband to be seen by more than a handful of people during the months the treaty was debated.

For creating the League of Nations, which was affirmed by most of the rest of the world and would last from 1920 to 1946, eventually enlisting 63 countries, Woodrow Wilson was voted the Nobel Peace Prize for 1919. He was certainly told the good news, but that does not mean he was aware of it, that it ever sank in. If it did, he surely found it poor consolation. He also, of course, found it impossible to accept the award in person. The United States Minister in Norway, Albert G. Schmedeman, received the prize in Oslo on Wilson's behalf, bringing it back to Washington on his next home leave. Mrs. Wilson put it in her husband's bedroom.

On February 3, 1924, Woodrow Wilson succumbed to a stroke at his home in the nation's capital. Dr. Grayson announced the news to reporters. "Mr. Wilson died at eleven-fifteen this morning. His heart action became feebler and feebler and the heart muscle was so fatigued that it refused to act any longer. The end came peacefully." The occasion was one of the most sorrowful in the capital's long history, perhaps surpassed only by the deaths of Franklin Delano Roosevelt and John Fitzgerald Kennedy.

A few days after he died, Wilson became the only president to be buried in Washington, D.C.

Ironically, despite his lengthy illness, Wilson would outlive the man who succeeded him in the White House, a man who seemed so much healthier, yet so much less dedicated to world peace, or perhaps any other issue of the time.

CHAPTER TWELVE

On the Air

O N NOVEMBER SECOND, WOMEN IN all forty-eight states joined men in voting Mrs. Wilson out of office. Most of them didn't know that's what they were doing, but it wouldn't have mattered regardless. Her husband, hanging on to a kind of life, as he would do for a few more years, was not one of the candidates.

Americans selected Warren G. Harding, a former small-town businessman and former U.S. senator from Ohio, as the twenty-ninth president of the United States. Harding attracted 16,144,093 votes, compared to a mere 9,139,661 for the Democrat, James M. Cox. Finishing third, even though he was in jail at the time for his opposition to the Great War—specifically, and ludicrously, for violating the Espionage Act of 1917—was the socialist union leader Eugene V. Debs. It was the fifth time that Debs, an electoral tradition by now, had run for the nation's highest office. He received 913,691 votes, a small number for a presidential candidate but rather a large number as a measure of dissatisfaction with ongoing capitalistic excess, especially war profiteering at the top of the list. In other words, the robber barons, with their services more desperately needed during the war than ever, had figured out ways to make even more money than usual from military demands for materiel.

Carrie Chapman Catt was also on the ballot in 1920, as the vice-presidential candidate of the Commonwealth Land party. It finished fifth, with a mere 5,750 people marking their ballots in its favor.

On the surface, it seemed just another presidential election, with no issues out of the ordinary to be decided, no change in the culture likely to result. Except there was. There was something very different about this election, something that had nothing to do with politics, everything to do with electronics, primitive though it was. For in the long run, the results of the voting in 1920 were not nearly as important as the means by which a small number of Americans learned of them.

For the first time, election returns were broadcast, a word new to the language for a means of communication new to the nation, radio transmission. Signals were sent through the air in the Pittsburgh, Pennsylvania area and, by adjusting knobs on their radio sets, those relatively few people who had them could learn the voters' preferences more quickly than ever before, the same hour as the votes were cast. Radio made the citizenry as much a part of the event as the pollsters counting the votes. It was, for those people able to tune in, an extraordinary sensation, even though the election itself lacked the suspense of a close outcome.

Airplanes and automobiles, women in voting booths and men in picket lines around their places of employment. And now—radio. It was a time like no other in our country, and those of an older generation were dizzied by the changes. It was not something so simple as the world around them gradually taking on a different form; it was as if the world had become a different place, as if a new God had taken command, as if new rules, new possibilities, a completely new atmosphere, had all replaced the old.

The idea for the technology of, in effect, transporting sound came about gradually. And, at the beginning, militarily. Although research on radio had started in earnest late in the nineteenth century, it became a top priority as the Great War began. Even before the United States entered the conflict, the Allies were trying to develop a primitive form of radio technology to help detect the location of enemy vessels at sea. For this purpose, "a central need" was vacuum tubes. Several American companies entered the race to produce the tubes, most notably the Westinghouse Electric and Manufacturing Corporation, which was in the process drawn into the infancy of the new communications medium after the war.

Westinghouse, like the few other corporate entities dabbling in radio, was trying to decide whether the medium could one day become a profitable venture, which is to say, as historian Geoffrey Perrett informs us, it was trying to decide what might be broadcast and whether or not anyone would listen.

> Experimental stations opened in New York, Cliffwood, New Jersey, and Long Beach, California to find out. The Bureau of Standards in Washington began broadcasting music concerts once a week, as did an experimental station created by the *Detroit News*. Another station was opened by Westinghouse in Pittsburgh. No one seemed to have the vaguest idea about what they were doing. They were all optimistic and enthusiastic, however, and it soon became evident that there were thousands, then tens of thousands, of equally zealous amateurs building crystals sets to listen in. At which point it occurred to Westinghouse that broadcasting did have a future after all.

And so, as Perrett points out, several other stations had preceded KDKA in making using of the air waves for commercial enterprise before the historic presidential balloting. Most likely, KDKA is considered the pioneer because it was the only station that provided the results of the voting as they became available. It was covering a news event "live," and nothing like that had ever happened before. Such was the publicity for election-day coverage that radio sales began to soar in its aftermath, and programming henceforth became more frequent, more regularly scheduled.

KDKA was also the first station in the United States to receive a government license, which is to say that it was the first station permitted to attempt to make a business of radio.

But precisely how would the Pittsburgh station go about it? Westinghouse was stumped, but not for long. On September twenty-ninth, a little more than a month before the election, Harry P. Davis, a Westinghouse vice president, saw a newspaper advertisement for a product that Pittsburgh's Joseph Horne department store had begun to sell.

AIR CONCERT "PICKED UP" BY RADIO HERE

Victrola music, played into the air over a wireless telephone, was "picked up" by listeners on the wireless receiving station which was recently installed here for patrons interested in wireless experiments. The concert was heard Thursday night about 10 o'clock, and continued 20 minutes. Two orchestra numbers, a soprano solo—which rang particularly high and clear through the air—and a juvenile "talking piece" constituted the program.

The music was from a Victrola pulled up close to the transmitter of a wireless telephone in the home of [Westinghouse executive] Frank Conrad, Penn and Peebles Avenues, Wilkinsburg [a Pittsburgh suburb]. Mr. Conrad is a wireless enthusiast and "puts on" the wireless concerts periodically for the entertainment of the many people in this district who have wireless sets.

Amateur Wireless Sets, made by the maker of the Set which is in operation in our store, are on sale here $10.00 up.

Something about the ad registered with Davis. He called an executive at Horne's and found out that although the wireless sets were not yet selling well, expectations were high. The store had set aside an entire wall of shelves to display different models of radios. It got him to thinking. "If a retail store saw enough in radio to set up a department to sell goods on the strength [of Frank Conrad's twice-a-week broadcast of his records through a primitive microphone] suppose the technology improved, the entertainment were provided daily, broadcast on greater power, and a variety of features were added?"

The next day, Davis asked Conrad whether he could build a larger and more powerful transmitter, not in his home, but at the Westinghouse factory. If so, the company would broadcast a random variety of events and advertise them all in advance; and, since Davis was that rarity who already thought the future for receiving sets was "limitless," Westinghouse would eventually not only recoup its return on the investment for the transmitter, but create a product line both unique and extremely profitable. Furthermore, it could advertise its products and the products of other companies who would pay for the air time, during its programs.

But Davis had even more in mind. He would jump-start the new Westinghouse service by broadcasting the most exciting event of the year, the presidential election. If, that is, Conrad could finish putting together the transmitter in time.

Conrad said he could. He knew how soon election day was, knew how complicated the task would be, but still said yes. And, with but a few days to spare, he succeeded.

"On the roof of one of the taller buildings of the East Pittsburgh Westinghouse works," writes media historian Erik Barnouw, "a shack was built, and a 100-watt transmitter assembled. The antenna ran from a steel pole on the roof to one of the powerhouse smokestacks. . . . On October 16, Westinghouse applied to the Department of Commerce for a special license to launch a broadcasting service. A week or so later, by telephone, the Department assigned the amateur call letters 8ZZ for use in case the license did not arrive in time. On October 27 the Department assigned the letters KDKA—commercial shore-station call letters—and authorized use of 360 meters, a channel away from amateurs and comparatively free of interference."

It was close, nerve-rackingly so, for Westinghouse executives; but with less than a week to go, KDKA was in position to make history on the first Tuesday night in November, 1920 by broadcasting, through a persistent—and persistently increasing—rainfall, the results of the Harding-Cox election.

It happened like this: The latest returns were phoned in to the so-called radio station from the editorial room of the Pittsburgh *Post*. The KDKA announcer was the vocally untrained Leo H. Rosenberg, who worked in the Westinghouse publicity department. Whenever he received a bulletin from the *Post*, he repeated the numbers into his microphone. He might have been playing music at the time, reading a commercial, chatting with the audience about the weather—it didn't matter. He immediately interrupted the proceedings to give the latest news from the nation's polling places. In fact, after a while, the shack began to receive phone calls not just from the *Post* newsroom, but from Westinghouse officials tuning in. More election news, they demanded, less music. It was the returns, not the crooners, who brought the unprecedented sense of immediacy and history to the air that night. And when there were no returns coming in at the moment, Rosenberg was to make a plea for the first "ratings" in media history. "Will anyone hearing this broadcast communicate with us," he kept saying, over and over, "as we are anxious to know how far the broadcast is reaching and how it is being received."

KDKA also posted the returns on a bulletin board outside the shack, "while . . . crowds stood in a driving rain."

Rosenberg was one of five men in the KDKA shack that night. There were two others answering the phone calls from the *Post* newsroom, jotting down the latest figures, and slipping them to Rosenberg; and two more men—engineers, we should call them—in charge of keeping the makeshift operation on the air and functioning properly. All did their jobs as well as the technology permitted, and to listen to Rosenberg, as is possible to do thanks to a recording of "KDKA's 65th Anniversary Special," which aired on the station on November 2, 1985, is to marvel at the sound quality the new medium had already achieved.

"And so it seems, ladies and gentlemen, that—just a minute, just a minute here, I've received some new numbers from our newsroom, and here they are for you. . . ." Every word distinct. Slightly echoing, perhaps, but easily comprehensible.

Hundreds upon hundreds followed along with Rosenberg, "many of whom were Westinghouse employees who had been given sets for the occasion," and numerous others who were friends, huddled around the radios with them, ears as close to the announcer's voice as they could squeeze them, listening intently as Harding's margin mounted through the night.

But these were not the only people following along with Rosenberg on that historic occasion. "To increase audience," says an undated and unattributed "KDKA History of Broadcasting and KDKA Radio" found in the archives of Pittsburgh's Carnegie Library, the first of such institutions to be endowed by the late philanthropist, "Dr. L. W. Chubb—then manager of the Radio Engineering Department and one of the little band of pioneers—was delegated to install a receiver and loudspeaker system, using two horns borrowed for the occasion from the Navy, in the main ballroom of the Edgewood Club, a suburban Pittsburgh community center where many Westinghouse people and other local residents gathered."

According to some reports, there were times that night when the American election results shot through the air as far as Canada.

Harding, expecting victory, had already written his acceptance speech. He provided a copy of it to KDKA, which did not yet have the technological ability to broadcast Harding's actually reading it—and so it was "read on the air [by Rosenberg] while the new President was speaking in Washington."

AS HARDING PREPARED TO TAKE over for Edith Wilson's ailing husband, radios began to overflow the shelves of stores, all kinds of stores, and just as quickly to vanish until a new shipment came in. Immediately recognizing the power of the new medium, Harding believed that the government should assume control of it, and he and Secretary of Commerce Herbert Hoover and a few others met informally to draw up regulations and assign frequencies. Broadcasters were called to Washington for meetings; if they wanted a frequency, they accepted the government regulations, most of which were technical in nature, only a few of which had to do with content.

In a matter of months, the talking box, as some were now calling it, would revolutionize the way Americans spent their time—creating new patterns of family life; new styles in everything from music to conversation to attires; new hobbies and diversions; new attitudes toward the events of the world, which were now announced by radio more quickly than newspapers could print them; new strategies in political campaigning and decision-making; new tastes in entertainment and, in the process, the creation of new kinds of celebrities, from announcers and singers to faddists like marathon-dancers and flagpole-sitters.

The talking box would more seriously and enduringly influence society than any invention before it. By 1922, 576 radio stations were broadcasting in the United States, and most of their listeners had earphones clamped to their heads, as speakers were not yet in general use.

But radios were. Or at least they were on their way. Americans bought about 100,000 of them in 1922. The following year, the number leaped to 500,000; and the year after that, in 1924, a third of all money spent for furniture in the United States went for the purchase of radios. After another two years, in 1926, the number of radio stations had surpassed 700, virtually covering the nation with their signals—think of them as invisible tracks—as, some years before, railroads had covered the nation with their visible tracks. As the latter had monopolized transportation in their heyday, so had the former begun to monopolize communication.

As for KDKA, having gotten off to such a good start with the Harding-Cox Show, it went on to achieve an overwhelming number of firsts. Among them:

> The first regularly broadcast church services and the necessary remote pickup.
> The first regular broadcast of baseball scores, first play-by-play baseball and football, first blow-by-blow boxing, first heavy-weight championship and first World Series.
> The first market reports from which grew the first complete farm service and, later, the first barn dance.
> The future for barn dancing on radio seemed unpromising from the start, and in fact it was not long before KDKA dropped the program, one of American broadcasting's first ratings casualties.

NO OTHER EVENT OF 1920 would have more of an effect on the future than the birth of radio, which was in turn the birth of American mass media. No other invention would lead to more other inventions, such as television, that had similar effects, only to a more powerful degree. No other product of the era could possibly be called "the electronic equivalent of the Model T," one that "middle-class consumers could afford and that would eventually transform society."

Nor could those relatively few people who listened to the election returns on what they thought of as something of a toy, a device for those who had ten dollars of discretionary income with which to play, have imagined what lay ahead for the country as Harding, his victory assured, began to think about the henchmen with whom he would surround himself for what, surprisingly, would be less than a single term in office. During that time, Harding's cronies became the least savory bunch of Americans ever to occupy the country's most prestigious address.

CHAPTER THIRTEEN

The Ohio Gangsters

R EPUBLICANS, AND EVEN SOME DEMOCRATS, believed that Harding might well have been the most presidential-looking man ever to inhabit the White House. He was also one of the most likable—short on ego, long on cheerfulness, a friend of those on both sides of the aisle as a member of the United States Senate, in which he served but a single undistinguished term before becoming the nation's chief executive. Gray-haired, stern-visaged, clear-eyed, stiff-chinned, ruggedly constructed, almost always attired in a three-piece suit of modest hue and equally modest tie, Harding was the first American head of state for the media age, in which, of course, he played a starring role. As has often been said, he was the chief executive from central casting. It was not meant as a compliment.

The problem was that his reality did not match his appearance. "In the end," writes biographer Robert K. Murray, "it was the quality of Harding's mind, as much as any personal habits or character traits, which limited his effectiveness as president. . . . Actually, Harding had a good mind but he simply made little use of it."

He certainly gave it the day off when he wrote his Inaugural Address. One of the least memorable ever recited, it began with an attempt at eloquence that left careful listeners shaking their heads.

"When one surveys the world around him after a great storm, noting the marks of destruction and yet rejoicing in the ruggedness of the things which withstood it, if he is an American he breathes the clarified atmosphere with a strange mingling of regret and new hope. . . . In the beginning the Old World scoffed at our experiment; today our foundations of political and social belief stand unshaken, a precious inheritance to ourselves, an inspiring example of freedom and civilization to all mankind. Let us express renewed and strengthened devotion, in grateful reverence for the immortal beginning, and utter our confidence in the supreme fulfillment."

One thing was certain, though, Harding told his fellow Americans: there would be no more incidents like the Wall Street explosion of September 16. Or, if there were, the culprits, the Reds or anarchists, would have been caught and sentenced by this time, with no mercy shown.

The applause, like the speech itself, was tepid.

Among the journalists listening to the new chief executive was the most uniquely readable of his breed that our country has ever produced. "He writes the worst English I have ever encountered," said Henry Louis Mencken, of Harding. "It reminds me of a string of wet sponges. . . . It is so bad that a sort of grandeur creeps in."

According to a poll of scholars conducted by Harvard College in 1948, Harding was the worst president the United States had ever had up to that point, twenty-ninth in a field of twenty-nine. By 2010, in a survey from New York's Siena College Research Institute, Harding's reputation had shot up to forty-first out of forty-three chief executives, with James Buchanan, America's only bachelor president, and Andrew Johnson, Lincoln's successor and the first president to be impeached, having fallen behind him. According to scholars Eugene P. Trani and David L. Wilson, Harding

did not provide moral leadership; he did not have much understanding of forces at work in the United States after the World
War; he was not willing to use the federal government to ease
adjustment after the war. . . . He sought to avoid controversy,
even if it meant avoiding real problems. . . . [He] was an ineffective leader, who suffered both personal and political scandal. It
is not surprising that historians rate Harding a poor president.

Perhaps, influenced by the right cabinet members and other advisers,
Harding would have performed more admirably, exercised his mind more
often. Instead, he surrounded himself with a horde of hard-drinking,
cigar-smoking, poker-playing, perpetually scheming banditos known as
the Ohio Gang. They were certainly not the first presidential associates to
combine personal and political misbehavior, but they were without question the first to combine them to such extremes. The political misdeeds
were mainly the doing of Harding's pals from back home, who reacted to
the election returns like kids who found that the door to the candy store
had been left unlocked and the cop on the beat was home sick tonight.
They smoked, they drank, they chewed tobacco, and at least twice a
week they played poker, with Florence Harding, the unattractive, barely
sociable, and normally straitlaced wife of the president often sitting in
herself. Poker, she admitted reluctantly, was her weakness.

Secretary of Commerce Herbert Hoover was dubious of the Ohio Gang
before they even had time to break their first law, and the more he saw of
them, as Harding filled important government posts with one after another
late in 1920, the more apprehensive he became. Hoover liked Harding,
respected him for a variety of reasons. But, he believed, the president

> had another side which was not good. His political associ-
> ates had been men of the type of Albert B. Fall, whom he
> appointed Secretary of the Interior; [Harry M.] Daugherty,
> whom he appointed Attorney General; [Charles] Forbes, whom
> he appointed head of the Veteran's Bureau; Thomas W. Miller,
> whom he appointed Alien Property Custodian, and Jesse
> Smith, who had office room in the Department of Justice.

[Harding] enjoyed the company of these men and his old Ohio associates in and out of the government. Weekly White House poker games were his greatest relaxation. The stakes were not large, but the play lasted most of the night. . . . I had lived too long on the frontiers of the world to have strong emotions against people playing poker for money if they liked it, but it irked me to see it in the White House.

THE OHIO GANG'S FIRST CRIMINAL deed was to be expected. It was the almost mandatory act of violating the Eighteenth Amendment. It didn't have to. It could have set an example of compliance to the law, or at least could have non-complied behind closed doors. Instead, the White House made no secret of its malfeasance, the edifice being stocked with more liquor than a city block of high-toned speakeasies, with shipments arriving in unmarked trucks under cover of darkness almost every night of the week. The Ohio Gang bought, or was given by shady friends who would later have favors to ask, only the best of alcoholic beverages.

Other than that, the first of the administration's scandals was the only one *not* involving a member of the Ohio Gang. But as a close friend of the president, Charles Forbes might well have been an honorary member. He knew well the members of the gang; he was also a close friend of the first lady, with whom he may have been the only male in Washington to grit his teeth and flirt at the same time. His reward for this proximity, and feigned affection, was being appointed head of the Veterans' Bureau.

He was a strange choice. As Murray writes, although he won the Congressional Medal of Honor in the Great War, "Forbes nonetheless had earlier once deserted the army and been arrested although never brought to trial. . . . Forbes's personal reputation among Republicans was unsavory. Neither [Republican National Committee Chairman Will] Hays nor Daugherty, the two men most responsible for party patronage, endorsed Forbes's appointment to the Veterans' Bureau. Daugherty told the president at the time that it was a mistake." The attorney general would later turn out to be a mistake himself. As for Harding, he refused to be dissuaded, and eventually Forbes assumed his new duties.

Because of the Great War, veterans' hospitals were facing severe shortages of supplies, more than they had at any time since the Civil War. It was up to Forbes to refill the warehouses. It was, in fact, the first set of duties he faced upon taking office. Instead, he did just the opposite, not restocking the storage areas but temporarily emptying them. Declaring as "worthless" all manner of items that were actually invaluable to the care of his patients, Forbes sold them to accomplices at bargain-basement rates. Then he bought them back from dummy corporations for much more than they were worth, with Forbes and his allies pocketing the difference. As Harding biographer John Dean writes, "Forbes was indeed selling surplus supplies (sheets, towels, soap, gauze, winter pajamas, and the like), and at absurdly low prices, to private contractors in private deals." Other goods that went straight from Veterans' Bureau storage to the black market were drugs, moleskin, medicinal liquor, "and even hardware and some trucks."

In addition, Forbes and his most trusted companion in wrongdoing, the Bureau's chief counsel Charles F. Cramer, knowing that more hospitals were going to be built to house the afflicted, purchased the land for them at grossly inflated prices. Two examples will suffice: The Veterans' Bureau paid $90,000 for a site worth $35,000, and $105,000 for a site worth a mere $19,000. Once again, a large portion of the overpayment went into the private caches of Forbes, Cramer, and the other crooks in charge of health care for veterans, so much so that critics charged there was not enough money left over for the state-of-the-art medical treatment that had been planned. And, in fact, there wasn't.

It has been estimated that the Veterans' Bureau lost at least $200 million because of Forbes's chicanery, a total made all the more appalling when one considers that it was amassed by adding to the pain of men who were already suffering the wounds of the world's most technologically excruciating war. The normally functioning human conscience reels at such heartlessness.

It did not take long for the Justice Department to learn of Forbes's activities and begin an investigation. Nor did the investigation itself take long. When Attorney General Daugherty reached the point at which he was certain of the truth, he told Harding what was happening and provided documents backing up his charges. The president summoned the Veterans'

Bureau chief immediately. It took a lot to arouse Harding's ire. This was a lot. Daugherty resisted the impulse to tell the Chief Executive "I told you so."

But Forbes was ready for the confrontation. Perhaps believing that his relationship with the Hardings would protect him from outsiders, he decided to be casual instead of contrite. Instead of admitting his transgressions, he claimed that the materials being sold truly *were* worthless, and that the cost of storing them was more than half a million dollars a year. The government, Forbes insisted, could simply not afford to spend that much money for that inconsequential a reason.

Harding did not believe him, looking at him with disappointment more than disgust. He had been prepared with too much paperwork by Daugherty, paperwork that seemed at first glance to be irrefutable proof, but later seemed too hastily gathered and thoughtlessly organized. Still, the president's friend was a crook, a thief, the openness with which he committed his crimes an insult that Harding could not help but take personally. That was on the one hand.

On the other was the fact that for many years the man *had* been a friend of the Hardings, had gone out of his way to do favors for them, had offered gifts, hospitality and more—and Harding simply did not have the heart to fire him. His weaknesses toward those close to him, already legendary and soon to be put to further, even more egregious trials, interceded on Forbes's behalf. Instead of firing his Veterans' Bureau head, Harding simply ordered him to stop his illegal practices immediately. Forbes agreed in writing that, thenceforth, he would put no more surplus government goods on the market. The meeting ended with accord, but one of which the president was dubious.

As he should have been. Forbes wasted no time in returning to work—i.e., continuing to peddle government property and stash away the gains. Harding, however, not trusting him, had assigned government agents to monitor Veterans' Bureau activities, and Forbes was ordered to pay a return visit to the president's office, where he foolishly tried to bend the truth again. This time, Harding would have none of it. This time, the friendship didn't matter. According to one witness, Harding grabbed Forbes by the shoulders and shook him while shouting in his face, "You yellow rat! You double-crossing bastard."

Harding told Forbes to submit his letter of resignation immediately. Forbes agreed. Sort of. He gave Harding his usually worthless word that he would give up his position, but begged to be permitted to flee to Europe first. He would write the letter from across the Atlantic. It would be his first action once safely abroad; he swore it.

On the surface, it sounded preposterous, chutzpah without so much as a shred of justification behind it. But the more Harding thought about it, the more he liked the idea. The effects of the scandal would be muted if Forbes were out of the country when the story broke, and since he would be unavailable to reporters, his criminal activities would drop from the front pages much more quickly than they would if he were nearby and available to the press. The president would seem, as was true, the victim of a duplicitous colleague rather than a miscreant himself. That he had waited too long to fire that colleague might not even be known. Harding told Forbes to get out of his sight and start packing. And not to forget his stationery.

To the surprise of many, Forbes's word was good on this occasion, and the White House received the letter of resignation within a month. The scandal was big news for a few days, but, as expected, Harding had been portrayed sympathetically, the victim of a trusted appointee who had turned on him once placed in a position of trust. When the press got tired of the story, as it did more quickly than it should have, the unconscionable behavior of Charles Forbes and company disappeared from public view, never to be seen in print again.

Nonetheless, it seemed to some in the Fourth Estate and many in Congress that the president had acted irresponsibly by not insisting that Forbes be brought back to the United States to face prosecution. "Years later," however, "historian Robert H. Ferrell confirmed, with regard to the criminal activities at the Veterans' Bureau, that Harding acted quite appropriately and that those who criticized Harding for letting Forbes slip off to Europe to resign ignored the fact that Harding did not have any evidence of Forbes's criminal activity, only his insubordination. Ferrell also notes that Harding immediately appointed a new director for the Veterans' Bureau, who quickly cleaned up the mess Forbes had made and proved an able administrator."

But Ferrell was writing about the immediate aftermath of the crime, defending Harding's original impulses. Eventually, Daugherty and the Justice Department were able to dig up even more proof of their charges against Forbes, this time presenting it more professionally, as a result of which his guilt was established beyond doubt—and it went far beyond just insubordination. Forbes was extradited from his overseas redoubt and tried in an American courtroom. The verdict was a fine of $10,000 and two years in a federal prison. Given the outrageousness of what he had done, and given what the victims of his chicanery had been through for their country, the punishment was not nearly severe enough for the crime. No one, however, seemed to complain, although from the vantage point of the present it is impossible to understand why. Certainly these days the punishment would have more closely suited the misdeeds.

About two weeks after the Senate began a hearing on the matter, Charles Cramer became the first of two suicides resulting from the Harding scandals. Cramer knew that, with Forbes being disposed of, he would be the next Veterans' Bureau figure called to the stand, and knew just as well he could not bear to be humiliated in a forum so public. Instead, he opted for holding a .45 pistol to the side of his head and, standing in front of a bathroom mirror, squeezing the trigger. The scene was too grisly for even the most tasteless of tabloids to publish. Cramer was removed from his house on a stretcher, covered by as many sheets as emergency workers carried. Even so, patches of blood seeped through and were visible to the onlookers who had formed a path from the front door of his house to the back door of the ambulance.

"In an ironic twist," John Dean points out, "Cramer had purchased the Harding home on Wyoming Avenue."

JESSE W. "JESS" SMITH WAS the informal head of the Ohio Gang. It was through his connections that the White House was able to ignore the Eighteenth Amendment and keep its officials lubricated. Smith procured the finest distilled beverages available north of the Canadian border, had them shipped across the Detroit River from Windsor, Ontario, to Detroit, then transported by rail to Washington, D.C.

It was as the members of the Gang sipped, swigged, and dealt out the cards that they began to turn their attention to more overtly illegal deeds. Soon they were buying votes, selling votes, forging presidential approvals, granting other unscrupulous favors, making financial demands of those who sought the favors, and in other more subtle ways enriching their bank accounts at the expense of the American people. They were careful about it. Individually, none of their crimes approached the scale of Forbes's. But they made up for the lack of quality with what amounted to a surfeit of quantity. Charles Ponzi was in jail by this time, and surely never knew what was happening at the White House, but how he would have admired the Ohio Gang, how he would have pleaded for membership!

Smith, for example, unofficially the top aide to Attorney General Harry Daugherty, who had taken over for A. Mitchell Palmer after the election, managed to pocket $200,000 out of $441,000 that had been a bribe in the first place, disguised as a settlement for wrongdoing in a stock transaction during the war.

Smith's primary contribution to the Harding administration's historical rating, however, was his liquor purchases—not the liquor he bought for his mates and himself to drink at the poker table, but the liquor he purchased as a middleman and then sold to others; Smith was reputed to be a principal supplier of bonded liquor to Washington-area bootleggers. As such, of course, he was an important figure in the District of Columbia's world of organized crime, and his ties to the White House made him feel impervious to either discovery or punishment. They also made the White House into a depot for illegal activity.

Smith and Daugherty were from the same small town in Ohio, Washington Court House; and despite Daugherty's being eleven years older, the two had been friends since Smith's early years, when Daugherty acted as a kind of big brother to the younger, less-civilized lad. Daugherty had helped Smith get started in the department store business in Washington Court House, and during the 1920 presidential campaign, in which Daugherty served as Harding's campaign manager, Smith repaid the favor by working without pay as his assistant. "Given the fact that Daugherty's wife was ill and forced to remain in Columbus [Ohio]," writes John Dean, "Jesse Smith set up house for Daugherty in Washington and made himself so valuable to the new Attorney General that Daugherty gave him an office near his on the sixth floor of the Department of Justice, although Smith was never on the government payroll."

It was rumored, in fact, that Smith went further than just making Daugherty comfy in his new home, that his divorce from a beautiful redhead was due, at least in part, to his lack of suitable performances with her between the sheets, that he was much better when partnered with a member of his own sex—say, his roommate in Washington. No evidence supports the rumor, but Washington, D.C., then as now, was a city of whispers as well as bombast, and once Daugherty and Smith moved in together late in 1920, their relationship inspired all manner of whispers.

More to the point, the two men were close enough to make it a reasonable assumption that the nation's top law enforcer knew his friend was acting illegally by flouting the Eighteenth Amendment and dealing with bootleggers. No less reasonable an assumption is it that Daugherty was raking in his own share of the transactions, just as he raked in a healthy percentage of what Smith referred to as a $200,000 "fine." After Daugherty, he was "without doubt the most controversial appointment made by Harding," says Robert K. Murray, and later revelations that Smith was the prince of Capitol Hill bootleggers did nothing to dispel the charge. Murray is wrong in referring to Smith as an "appointment," however, as he held no position to which he could have been appointed; he was simply the unofficial aide-de-camp, or tagalong, to the attorney general.

As for Harding, it was reported that he "definitely knew about some of Jesse Smith's actions and attempted to scare him away from Washington in order to forestall his arrest and imprisonment. [No one] will ever know how many specific details Harding uncovered about the house on K Street [where Daugherty and Smith lived], but it was enough to make him realize Smith's culpability."

Nonetheless, Smith managed to hang on to his position at the Justice Department—whatever it was—until 1923, when Harding was planning a trip to Alaska from which he would never return. Daugherty prepared a list of people who would accompany the president on the journey, and Harding read it over in the attorney general's presence. He noticed that Smith's name was on it. Harding ordered it struck off, and furthermore, having heard enough gossip about Smith in the past few years, most recently that he was running around Washington with "a gay crowd," told Daugherty he wanted him out of the nation's capital as soon as possible. (The word "gay" did not then have its present connotation.)

The attorney general had no choice other than to agree but was frightened of the possible consequences. And not just to himself. Smith had been depressed after an operation on his appendix failed to heal as well as expected, and was further upset because the diabetes with which he had been plagued for several years was worsening. His exclusion from the Alaska trip would be yet another blow, proof that he was suddenly an outsider in a town where respects were paid only to insiders. His removal from the White House altogether, which Daugherty decided he would not tell Smith about until later, would be less a dismissal than an exile. Nonetheless, Daugherty assured Harding that he would deal with Smith as the president desired, but he did so with trepidation.

In fact, it might have been the most difficult thing ever asked of him. Both Daugherty and Smith's ex-wife were afraid that Smith might harm himself if left alone, might perhaps even follow Charles Cramer in taking his own life. So, after finally breaking the news to Smith that he was no longer on the Alaska list, that it wasn't so bad, that he could tend to other "business" more freely with the president and his retinue having departed, Daugherty asked his special assistant, Warren F. Martin, to start spending his nights with Smith. Pay close attention to him, his actions, and his mood, Daugherty cautioned.

Martin agreed. The attention he paid, however, was not close enough. At nine o'clock on the first night of his assignment, which was the day Smith learned he wasn't going to Alaska, Martin said goodnight to his temporary roommate, who claimed he was tired despite the early hour. Martin said Smith did not seem distracted, did not seem depressed, only tired. He went to his room, closed the door, and Martin stood against it listening for several minutes. He heard only the sounds he expected to hear: a man undressing, a bed being unmade, teeth being brushed, a desk light being turned out. For the first time that day, Martin relaxed. He went to an adjoining room where he would spend the night. It passed without incident.

The next morning, May 30, Martin was awakened suddenly by a sharp, familiar noise. He was foggy and initially could not place it; then, in an instant, he did. He had heard similar bangs all too many times before. He told police that he dashed through the doorway into Smith's room and found the body. Still in his pajamas, Smith had fallen with his head in a wastebasket, a revolver in his hand, a bullet hole in his head.

"Mystery had surrounded Smith's death," says Dean, "because there was no autopsy, and he had burned all of his personal papers just before his death." And, of course, mystery meant even more whispers in Washington, a roar of them. Had he *really* killed himself? To those who knew of Smith's fading status in the Harding administration, his health problems, and the crimes he had committed, crimes that might be revealed at any moment, the answer was a resounding yes.

By committing suicide, however, he had created repercussions at the highest levels of government, making his superiors fear that their own crimes might soon be revealed. The cover story, quickly decided upon, is reviewed by Robert K. Murray: "Although Jess Smith's suicide was more eloquent than words in indicating the creeping malaise affecting the administration, both Harding and Daugherty pretended that nothing serious was wrong. They turned aside queries about the rumors of corruption by claiming that Smith's death was due to a mentally unbalanced condition brought on by diabetes, and nothing more."

It seemed to play. The papers went along with it and the populace thought it was a shame that Smith had been afflicted with a disease so terrible that he could no longer live with its torments.

THE LAST TWO MAJOR FELONIES during Harding's administration were not discovered until after he had passed away. Both were examples not only of scandalous activity but, given the person involved in one, and the audacity on display in the other, which could easily have compromised national security, they were the most surprising of all the criminal acts in which the federal government engaged early in the twentieth century.

After weeks of speculation that most Washingtonians found hard to believe, despite the eagerness with which they repeated it, Attorney General Harry Daugherty was indicted on charges of fraud. Listed on the indictment with him was Colonel Thomas W. Miller, a former war hero and former congressman. The two men were accused of having been "illegally transferring a German-owned American subsidiary of American Metal Company to a syndicate that paid [Miller] $50,000 and Jesse Smith $224,000, of which $50,000 ended up in a joint account belonging to both Smith and Daugherty. When government investigators tried to get the records for the account, Daugherty saw to it that they couldn't."

Miller was fined $5,000, meaning, one supposes, that he came out $45,000 ahead, and sentenced to a year and a half in jail, meaning that he came out eighteen months behind. About Daugherty, the jury could not make up its mind, in large part because of the blustering sanctimoniousness of his denials and the eminence of his office. In addition, his claim that he could not take the stand because he was protecting the memory of the late President Harding was a master stroke of public relations—if not of logic—making him seem, at least to some, more honorable than evasive. Through his attorney, he "maintained that he had been unaware of Smith's activities until shortly before the suicide and that the 'Reds' were after him." Another good idea; when in doubt, blame the Bolshies. It was as effective a defense in the twenties as it was during the heyday of the Cold War.

Only access to Daugherty's bank records could prove or disprove the charges against him, but the attorney general claimed that to grant access would be a breach of privacy. He was standing on principle, he claimed, not hiding his guilt. Initially, the court ruled in his favor.

But the prosecutors refused to give up. They finally convinced the judge that, given the crucial role Daugherty played in the American criminal justice system, the records should be made available to them. If they were, prosecutors declared, the case against Daugherty would be proven, one way or another, beyond doubt; the American people, they concluded, had a right to know whether a serious breach of faith had been committed by the nation's foremost guardian of the law.

Finally the judge agreed. But it didn't matter. The records, it turned out, were missing. No one could offer an explanation, certainly not Daugherty, not even anyone at the bank—but they had vanished. Without them, the prosecution's case crumbled. Charges against the attorney general were dropped; but that he was responsible for the absent records few people doubted, and his reputation, as a consequence, plummeted.

He remained Harding's friend, though, perhaps his best friend among members of the Ohio Gang. He stayed on as head of the Justice Department whose standards he had been mocking since his first day in office.

He did not, however, go gentle into the controversy that engulfed him. His response to those suspicious of his actions was a combination of vitriol and arrogance. For the rest of his life, whenever he was asked about the charges against him and the conveniently missing bank records, he put the glibness of public relations behind him. "If anybody does not like my position," he wrote to a friend, recapitulating his attitude toward one and all, "you can tell them to go to hell."

EVEN STUDENTS WHO HAVE SAT through the kind of high-school history classes so tedious that they end up making it impossible for a historian to find a place on the best-seller lists have heard of Teapot Dome. But for most of them, the knowledge doesn't go much further than the name. Some people know that whatever it was happened during the Harding administration. Fewer know it had something to do with oil, specifically the illegal sale of leases. And fewer still know the cabinet officer who made it all happen. Still, the odd phrase "Teapot Dome" has a resonance to it that transcends the absence of meaning, the ignorance of details. For what many people *do* know is that the words refer to what a majority would consider the second most outrageous scandal in the history of American politics.

Three oil reserves in the western United States had been set aside for future use by the military, especially the Navy. Two of them were in California, at Elk Hills and Buena Vista, and the third lay under a rock formation in Salt Creek, Wyoming, shaped somewhat like a teapot resting atop a dome—in this case, a dome covering a huge underground pool of oil, its quantity virtually unmeasurable. With the shadow of the Great War still draped over the nation, the reserves were considered vital to the country's defense, indispensable in the event of future hostilities. They were certainly not to be treated with the same cavalier disrespect as supplies in a Veterans' Bureau storehouse.

But one more member of the Ohio Gang had a different idea, finding in the oil an opportunity for self-enrichment that was simply too good to overlook. Albert B. Fall, another good friend of President Harding who, as a United States Senator from New Mexico, was a well-known critic of the previous petticoat government, "was regarded as above suspicion by friend and foe alike. The only opposition to him," according to Eugene P. Trani and David L. Wilson, "came from those who opposed his conservation views, not his morals. A few rabid conservationists, such as Gifford Pinchot, maintained a drumfire of criticism against the Fall appointment, but they were not a large enough group to matter. From everybody else's point of view, the appointment was perfectly logical."

The appointment was for Fall to be secretary of the interior, and the nomination passed both houses of Congress easily. After which, one of Fall's first acts was to arrange to have two of the three oil reserves transferred to his department from the Department of the Navy. The move should have seemed a suspicious one; instead it seemed a change of heart. It appeared as if Fall wanted to atone for past environmental indifferences by deciding to protect the oil reserves now, keep an eye on them himself. It was the perfect con, yet another of the many that stained this period in American history.

But it gets worse. As it turned out, it was not the Department of the Interior that would oversee the reserves—for after they were under Fall's jurisdiction, he promptly sold their leases to private investors, an act of criminal irresponsibility under any circumstances, but all the more egregious because the leases were sold without being put up for public bid. Of course, had Fall announced that he was opening the bidding, he would have been admitting that he was up to no good. Even Harding would have had to step in and tell him he couldn't do something like that. For this reason, the bidding was *so* private that there was really no bidding at all. The cards had been cut the moment Fall acquired the leases.

Buena Vista, the smallest of the three reserves, remained under control of the Navy. The Elk Hills lease went to a longtime friend of Fall named Edward Doheny, a respected and experienced figure in his field, the president of the Pan American Petroleum & Transport Company. Teapot Dome went to another well-qualified executive, the president of Sinclair Consolidated Oil, Harry F. Sinclair.

Both Doheny and Sinclair had dealt with drainage problems in the past, and both had the know-how and equipment to do so in the future. It was for this reason, Fall claimed, that he wanted oilmen, not government or military officials, to oversee the reserves, to make sure the oil would not seep beyond the bounds of public ownership and onto private property, where it would not only be wasted, but, if it did damage to the water supply on an adjoining ranch, might subject the government to legal action. Doheny and Sinclair would not let that happen, Fall confidently announced as he granted the leases. The oil was safe. From everything but greed.

Some accepted Fall's explanation at face value. Others, however, saw the risk immediately. The oil, United States Navy oil, was henceforth no longer under the Navy's control, but rather was the property of private, profit-making enterprises. Conservationists were enraged and insisted on hearings before the transfer could be finalized. Reluctantly, the Senate agreed. "When the hearings commenced," John Dean reveals, "there was so little interest that [Thomas J.] Walsh [chairman of the hearings] initially had trouble mustering a quorum of his committee."

That was soon to change. Walsh proved a relentless interrogator, especially when it was finally Fall's turn to testify, and before long the outlines of Teapot Dome, not as a rock formation but as a scam of greater than Ponzian proportions, began to emerge.

The interior secretary, Americans were about to learn, was still not a friend of the environment. Neither, unfortunately, was he an honest man. Unlike the case with Daugherty, Fall's bank records were readily available, and they showed that a man who had just suffered through "a decade of financial difficulties," and whose annual salary as a cabinet member was $12,000, suddenly had a net worth of almost $125,000. It seems that the arrangements he had made with Doheny and Sinclair had less to do with oil drainage than they did with personal gain. And not just for Fall. In addition to stipulating that his two friends do all they could to prevent the oil from oozing beyond its boundaries, Fall allowed them to drill for profit, to keep for themselves vast amounts of black gold and then selling it to consumers through their companies on the open market. Doheny and Sinclair had kicked back more than

$100,000 for the favor—and much more money might await Fall if the profits were greater than expected.

The arrangement was breathtaking in its contempt for the public good, not only because it would have allowed Doheny and Sinclair to keep most of the money they made from drilling into the oil reserves, which could easily have been tens of millions of dollars, but because sufficient amounts of oil might no longer be there when the Navy, or other government agencies, needed it for military purposes. Who knew when that might happen? Who knew what kind of catastrophe might have resulted with depleted energy supplies? Up to this time, no other American scandal, with the behavior of Benedict Arnold and Aaron Burr excepted, had involved the sale of national security.

To be fair, if almost irrelevant, the deals did include a few crumbs for the government. Sinclair's lease, which was to last for a minimum of twenty years, required that he pay a sixteen-percent royalty into federal coffers on all oil drilled at Teapot Dome. As for Doheny, he too had to compensate the government for his lease, by building a pipeline, a refinery, and oil storage tanks in Hawaii at Pearl Harbor. It should not be necessary to point out that the amount of money the oilmen were supposed to spend was considerably less than what they stood to earn once they started selling the underground bounty that used to belong to Uncle Sam.

It did not take long for the real motives of Fall's transactions to become public, and when he was convicted for issuing the drilling permits, he became the first Cabinet officer in American history to suffer the indignities of arrest and imprisonment. He served nine months of a paltry one-year sentence but, although fined $100,000, never paid the money, claiming he did not have that much. In other words, he kept the entire bribe from Sinclair and Doheny. As for those two, for some reason neither of them even stood trial for their offense. Nor was a fine levied on them. The prime beneficiaries of Teapot Dome, they were, and it was as if they had had nothing to do with the subterranean dealings.

In fact, the entire episode, and indeed all the preceding criminal activities of the Harding administration, were treated by the courts as much less important matters than they really were, the fines and jail terms for those involved amounting to little more than scoldings, their knuckles being rapped by a wooden ruler. Thus, although it never seems to be viewed this way in any study I have read, the scandals of the Ohio gang and cohorts were scandals for the judicial system as well, which minimized the punishments it handed down almost to a point of being ludicrous—perhaps because the criminals had previously held such high positions of trust, perhaps for more devious reasons that can only be guessed at. It is far too late at this point to discover the truth behind Teapot Dome, but there is more to it than meets the history books, this offense not just against an individual or a federal bureau but against an entire nation.

IRONICALLY, ON THE DAY THAT Fall went to prison, Doheny secured the mortgage on Fall's ranch for $168,250. Several years later, when Fall was out of prison and living there, back in the home he had come to love so much—Doheny foreclosed him. Fall had to give up the ill-gotten residence bestowed upon him by Teapot Dome. He pleaded with the court that had granted the foreclosure to reconsider its verdict. It would not. This time, having spent a great deal of money in the interim, most of it on legal fees, Fall could not raise nearly enough to pay off his mortgage and keep his residence. He raged at his former friend, cursed him, threatened him. Doheny was unmoved. If Fall didn't have the money, he was evicted; it was as simple, and ruthless, as that. Business, just business. There was no honor, apparently, among disgraced Cabinet members and their companions in crime.

ONCE AGAIN, IT IS BELIEVED that the affable but dense Harding, even more inept at choosing colleagues than he was at governing, knew little of the illegal activities swirling around him in the three and a half years of his administration. Or knew of them in general terms but was not aware of their extent. Or suspected them but believed that his old friends, some of whom had been with him since childhood, were simply not capable of turning into criminals when he turned into the president.

Finally, though, there came a time when Harding could no longer remain ignorant of the Ohio Gang's actions; and when it did, this man, fundamentally decent in a number of ways, was hurt more than angered. "My god, this is a hell of a job!" he said to the Kansas newspaper editor and author William Allen White. "I have no trouble with my enemies;

I can take care of my enemies all right. But my damn friends keep me walking the floor nights!"

Perhaps. But Harding's performance as a practitioner of marital infidelity was worth some dusk-to-dawn pacing too. After the election of 1920, he said good-bye to a lengthy dalliance with Carrie Phillips, "the most beautiful woman in Marion [Ohio]," and moved on to other affairs in the nation's capital, where the selection of beauties was much greater. According to an article in the *Washington Post*, Harding had extramarital sex with at least four women once he took up residence in the White House. Two of them were friends of Mrs. Harding. The third was Harding's aide in the Senate. The fourth, Nan Britton, claimed that the president was the father of her daughter. Harding neither affirmed nor denied any of the charges.

Although Britton later wrote *The President's Daughter*, which is considered the first "kiss-and-tell" book of American politics, a lot more than kissing made its way onto the pages.

> The latter part of February, 1919, I knew for a certainty that I was to become the mother of Warren Harding's child. I remember one morning in the subway train I felt so queer and faint that I was obliged to ask someone for a seat. Too, I had faint spells from nausea.

When Britton sent a letter to Harding to tell him the news, "he wrote to tell me that this trouble was not so very serious and could be handled." Which Harding did, it is believed, by regularly sending checks to his mistress for the child's care. It was a long time before Florence Harding was able to engage in small talk at the poker table again.

BY THE START OF THE fourth year of his presidency, not only was Harding's administration showing signs of strain, but so was Harding. Most Americans seemed not to notice, seemed to think of him as the same hearty fellow who had won the first election ever broadcast on radio. But most Americans were in no position to see the man closely.

Larger than average to begin with, Harding had gained weight, up to 240 pounds, and lost the healthy glow to his skin, which had been replaced with a pallor that his friends had never seen before. "The flu attack which felled Harding in mid-January 1923 unquestionably was the triggering factor in the subsequent rapid deterioration in his health," according to some opinions. Then again: "One medical expert later claimed that the flu attack was actually accompanied by an undiagnosed coronary thrombosis followed by myocardial infarction." But according to yet another suppos-edly informed opinion, Harding was struck by a cerebral hemorrhage. There were also reports that attributed the president's lack of vigor to congestive heart failure. Whatever the cause, a few days before he died, Harding collapsed and had to be lifted into bed by several aides. Although no one knew it at the time, in 1920 one terminally president was followed into office by another who would be terminally ill long before his time.

Afraid that journalists would find out about Harding's collapse and make too much of it, the White House issued a press release announcing that the president had simply been the victim of food poisoning and the culprit was a tainted crab. It was an interesting story, but a little too imaginative. According to several reports, Harding had not eaten any kind of seafood, much less shellfish, in recent days.

When he died, on August 2, 1923, doctors listed the cause of death as apoplexy, and so it has been proclaimed for posterity on his death certificate. There is no particular reason to believe it; then again, there is no particular reason not to. So vigorous in appearance when he first took office, he had lost his hardiness quickly and in a number of ways, so many that the real cause of death, which was perhaps a combination of maladies, will never be known.

From Plymouth Notch, Vermont, "Silent Cal" Coolidge, probably the least verbose man ever to occupy the White House, sped to Washington to be sworn in to his new duties. Before he left, he spoke his first words upon learning of Harding's death. As if sending a telegram and paying by the word, he was typically terse.

I believe I can swing it.

Later, though, in a eulogy broadcast on radio, the first such sorrowful event on the nation's airwaves, Coolidge was more expansive.

Some will say that such a sweet and gentle nature could only
have found its setting and its opportunity for service in a strange
and peculiar time. Yet he came to the world's stage in an hour
when it seemed set for other characters. The captains and the
kings, the armies and the navies, the men who would have war,
and the men who would not have peace, had long dominated the
scene. Where among them could place [be] made, could place be
found, for this kindly, gentle, gracious soul?

It seemed that the longer Coolidge spoke, the less sense he made. His
brevity, all of a sudden, began to seem his most effective method of
communication.

POOR WARREN HARDING COULD NOT even die without scandal, or at least intima-
tions of it. One of them was that the various differences in opinion about
what had actually ended the president's life were part of a conspiracy to
keep the real reason a secret. For what purpose, though, no one could say.
Nor could any of the conspirators declare what that real reason was, or who
was behind it, or what was to be gained by the president's death. In fact,
there wasn't even anyone who could say who the conspirators actually *were*.

Another rumor had it that, because he knew his health was failing and
was certain that more scandals were about to attach themselves to his
administration, Harding had committed suicide, like Cramer and Smith.
But his 1924 campaign for the White House was already under way, and
Harding had taken an active role in the planning, one of several reasons
that his having taken his own life seems unlikely.

In a related vein, there was the rumor that hundreds of thousands
of Americans read or heard about. A book called *The Strange Death
of President Harding* was written by an equally strange fellow named
Gaston B. Means, a part-time gangster, part-time FBI operative. In jail
on publication day, serving time for perjury, Means strongly hinted that
Harding's wife killed him because of Nan Britton's forthcoming revela-
tions of his extramarital scandals. It was not anger; it was benevolence:
Means believed Florence Harding wanted to spare her husband the ignominy of the charges she knew were on the way.

And then there was the tale that seemed most to intrigue the public, that Mrs. Harding, who was not a popular figure with the Washington press, had in fact murdered her husband, poisoned him—anger this time, *not* benevolence. The First Lady did not want to save Harding from shame, but to punish him for his serial affairs. The fact that she refused to allow an autopsy was one source for this suspicion. Another was that she had gathered and burned all of the former president's papers in a White House fireplace. The new First Couple, the Coolidges, stood by watching the flames, the three of them united in their approval.

But Mrs. Harding wasn't done with her little book of matches. When she returned to Marion, she ordered that her husband's personal papers meet the same fate as his presidential papers. Those documents that, for some reason, escaped a fiery end are stored at the Harding Memorial Association in Marion—but for what reason one can only guess. Mrs. Harding insisted that the public have no access to the papers. The public didn't, still doesn't, and, according to Mrs. Harding's instructions, never will. That being the case, why not ignite those artifacts as well?

When asked about all the fires she had been setting lately, the former first lady struggled with a reply. Finally, she said she had destroyed her husband's documents to preserve his legacy, which, of course, suggests that what had since been consigned to ashes revealed nefarious behavior of one sort or another, even more than exists on the historical record. This might not have been what Mrs. Harding meant by her comment; but, unfortunately, she died the year after her husband without explaining further—and no one else ever can.

It was certainly not what she had expected on November 2, 1920, when her husband, having won the presidency of the United States, was the most admired man in the country, and she was no less admired as the woman at his side. Nor was it what the men of America had expected on that day in 1920 when they were joined in the voting booth for the first time by women. Neither sex, it seemed, cast a very wise vote. The White House was a blackened institution for the next three and a half years.

PART FOUR

CHAPTER FOURTEEN

The Investigation

A MONTH AFTER THE ELECTION OF 1920, Christmas decorations began to appear in homes and on the streets of business districts. Santa was scheduled to make appearances in a number of civic venues; manger scenes had been erected in front of churches without controversy. Jingling bells could sometimes be heard from a distance. Bundled up against the weather with heavy coats, scarves, and mittens, mothers and fathers took it all in, holding children's hands, the children changing their minds about their favorite toys with each store they passed.

But the holiday was the furthest thing from the minds of the federal investigators and members of their staffs who were looking into the explosion that had killed more than forty people and injured more than 140 others in front of the Morgan Bank more than three months before. They had made no progress. The tips they received had all been dead ends. Barring something miraculous, it seemed certain that all of their stockings would be filled with coal this year.

Their difficulties were numerous. The first was caused, inadvertently, by the board of governors of the New York Stock Exchange, and the damage was not only serious, but irreparable. Wanting to demonstrate their courage, their resilience, their unwillingness to be intimidated by whoever was responsible for the bomb, they met within hours of the blast and decided they would open for business the following morning. They would defy the Bolshies, the anarchists, the cowards of whatever name who had murdered so many Americans and then vanished somewhere into a late summer day. They would not be daunted. Whether the Justice Department's Bureau of Investigation had approved the board's decision or, with too many other things on its mind, simply did not realize what the money men were planning, is not known. But they could not have sabotaged the investigation more effectively if they had been paid accomplices.

So that the immediate neighborhood of the Stock Exchange would look welcoming, open for business on the day after, the board hired cleanup crews. They began working late on the afternoon of the blast. They kept at their labors all the way to dawn, sweeping and washing the streets, sidewalks, and benches and trimming patches of greenery. They picked up scraps of paper and other debris. There was nothing they could do about the thousands of panes of glass that had imploded; but outside the buildings, they worked with more than usual efficiency, picking up stray shards, rubbing away patches of dirt on exterior walls. It was not easy, especially when the sun went down and they had to rely on candles and gaslight to see what they were doing. But they did their job as well as it could be done, and by the time the Stock Exchange sounded its opening bell on September seventeenth, it appeared almost as if nothing extraordinary had happened the day before.

Which was precisely the problem. Members of the Bureau of Investigation looked around that morning at what no one would have believed had been, less than twenty-four hours earlier, the site of the first terrorist attack ever on American soil, and suddenly understood the problem. What the BOI had allowed might have been the end of the investigation before it even began. Who could say what clues might have been mixed in with the trash and thrown away, unable now to be retrieved? What personal possessions might have been discarded? Documents of identification, items of clothing? Even body parts? Who could say what other clues had been washed down city drains? None of the BOI agents, nor any of the New York City policemen who had been the first to descend on Wall Street the day before, had begun a careful examination of the scene before the janitorial services arrived and virtually remade the area. As the first full day of inquiries and planning got under way, the answer to the questions of guilt and motive might already have been lost, hauled to the dock and buried irretrievably somewhere in the midst of a barge full of trash, soon to be towed out to sea.

As for the biggest clue, at least in terms of size, it had also been eliminated. The horse, according to the *New York Call*, had been "sent off to Barren Island and ground into paste." The *Call* then went on to ask the unfortunately reasonable question, "Are the authorities investigating the Wall Street explosion deliberately destroying evidence, or are they just stupid?"

It was the latter. The BOI could not have been more inept in its initial reaction to the bomb. It did not even consider the possibility that it had been the work of terrorists. It believed that too many innocent men and women had been killed in the blast for it to be the expression of a specific, politically oriented grievance; this was not, after all, like the small explosives that had been sent several months previously to the various big-city mayors and judges, or to the home of A. Mitchell Palmer. In fact, as far as anyone knew, virtually all the victims of the explosion were free from governmental affiliation.

More likely, the BOI decided, the bomb had been set off accidentally. There were several possibilities. The horse might have dragged the cart over a bump in the street in just such a way that it jangled the dynamite to life. Someone might have walked behind the cart and, after lighting a cigar, flipped the match in precisely the wrong place. The cart might have been too hot inside, somehow bringing its deadly contents to life. Or the horse and cart might not have had anything to do with the blast; the explosion might have been the result of dynamite stored elsewhere to clear space for new construction somewhere on Wall Street.

Bolsheviks, socialists, and even a number of anarchist groups agreed with the diagnosis of holocaust without intent and began sending out letters to that effect as soon as they heard about the blast. They wrote to law-enforcement agencies, local and federal, and swore their disavowal of the deed. On the morning of the seventeenth, the *Call*, a socialist newspaper, and the communist journal *World Tomorrow*, opined in favor of the accident theory, as did the Yiddish *Forverts* and the Hungarian *Lore*. But these papers were read by few and influenced even fewer. The only endorsement of the horrible mishap theory from a reliable source came from the perpetual presidential candidate, socialist, and union leader Eugene V. Debs, who should have known better.

The BOI should have known better too; and on the day after the explosion, it came to its senses. What had blown apart the lower Manhattan neighborhood, investigators determined, was a well-constructed bomb that had ignited precisely where and when it was intended to. True, the Bureau had had no experience with terrorism, not on this scale at least; but, preliminarily, common sense was just as valuable a tool in discarding the "accident" theory. How many loads of dynamite were rattling along the streets of New York on any given day? What were the odds that one of them would erupt on Wall Street, in front of the country's most glitteringly wealthy bank, where it had no business to transact? Further, what were the odds that the blast would occur just as the empty streets and sidewalks of late morning began to fill, the number of potential victims at its height? Taken all together, there were simply too many implausibilities.

Besides, as should have been obvious from the start, the murder of innocent people did not eliminate terrorists from consideration; rather, it fit the definition of the word perfectly. Terrorism: indiscriminate slaughter, the more victims the better. And the location of the bomb, in the midst of New York's financial district, also pointed to terrorism, an act symbolic of capitalism's destruction, the goal of all radical groups.

THE OFFICIAL END OF THE accidental-explosion theory came early on the afternoon of the seventeenth. A few hours earlier, the Sons of the American Revolution had gone ahead as planned with their celebration of Constitution Day. Like the governors of the New York Stock Exchange, they wanted to demonstrate their refusal to be intimidated by the catastrophe. They even kept their originally planned starting time, twelve noon—"the murder hour," as the *New York Times* referred to it.

But it turned out to be even more of a celebration than the Sons had envisioned. As they sang their songs and made their speeches, five to ten thousand New Yorkers crowded onto Wall Street, many of them telling reporters that they, too, wanted to show that they would not be intimidated. And when the Sons began singing "The Star-Spangled Banner," much of the crowd joined in, resulting in an enthusiastic version of the national anthem, with arms pumping in the air, legs marching in place, exuberant yet solemn. Others, less carried away, admitted they were merely curious and, feeling safe with so many policemen and BOI officers patrolling the area, wanted merely to mill around the scene where the destruction had occurred, just as people had taken in the sight yesterday: terrorism's grim aftermath as a tourist attraction.

It was a few hours after the crowd had dispersed that the Bureau released a packet of flyers found in a Wall Street post office box. They had been written by hand, rather than being printed, which might have led authorities to the press that had turned out the messages. The paper was yellow; the ink, from a stamp, red. The message, obviously threatening, was nonetheless imprecise in its meaning.

Remember
We will not tolerate
any longer

Free the political
prisoners or it will be
sure death for all of you.

The flyers were signed "American Anarchist Fighters." The name was supposed to mean anarchists who fight Americans, but reads as if it refers to the opposite, Americans who fight anarchists. It is hard to be confusing in just three words; the terrorists managed it.

Postal authorities told federal officials that the flyers had been placed in the box shortly before yesterday's explosion, between the 11:30 collection and the next one only twenty-eight minutes later. Other than that, they knew nothing about the crudely written documents which, for some reason, they had held on to overnight and all morning without a public announcement. According to some reports, there were five pieces of paper, all communicating the same threat, and all had been placed in a single box near Wall Street, at the edge of the blast's range, where they were unlikely to be damaged, sure to be found.

No one in the BOI had ever heard of a group called the American Anarchist Fighters. Still, the flyers provided the Bureau with its first clue, helping it to see a pattern. The barrage of bombs released in late 1919, those that precipitated the first series of Palmer raids, had been signed "The Anarchist Fighters." The same group, then, seemed responsible for all the acts of violence, probably even those that had precipitated the second series of Palmer raids.

But who *were* these guys? For the first time, the Bureau realized it had truly formidable and persistent foes with which to deal. And, shrouded in mystery as they were, and having had ample time to escape after Wall Street erupted, they would be almost impossible to catch.

AMONG THE FIRST PEOPLE INTERVIEWED by the BOI were men named "Carusso, Abato, Ferro, Luigio, and DeFillipos," whose nationality alone was enough to make them suspects. Unfortunately for the Bureau, all these Italians had alibis.

The first person who legitimately stirred the Bureau's interest, at least for a few days, was an anomaly, a fascinating character, a man who "fit nobody's picture of a bomb-throwing anarchist." Still, he was the most promising of the lot for a time, and some agents, try though they might, could never quite get him out of their minds, no matter how long the investigation dragged on. True, he was "neither a Sicilian, a Jew, a Scot, an East Side peddler, nor a greasy fellow, but a middle-class professional man of Anglo-Saxon lineage with friends high in Wall Street"—but his story was unlike any other that law-enforcement officials had ever heard.

The man in question was the red-white-and-blue-named Edwin P. Fisher (whose name is spelled "Fischer" in at least one prominent source, but "Fisher" more often), formerly employed at a respected Manhattan brokerage house. He was also an athlete of sufficient skill to have been ranked ninth in the country by the United States Lawn Tennis Association in 1901.

However, despite his background, he had long pronounced himself an enemy of all those who lived on unearned wealth, and moved even further to the left by becoming exposed to the anarchist Emma Goldman and finding many of her ideas worthy of support. But even more than his admiration for Goldman, it was a proclaimed ability by Fisher to see into the future that brought him to the attention of authorities. He might have been a patient in New York mental hospitals on two occasions, but there was something close to clairvoyance in utterances he made in September 1920. As Susan Gage writes:

> In the week before the explosion, Fisher had sent at least three notes to friends in the financial district alerting them, in a variety of phrasings, that a "Bolshevist professor" had instructed him to "[s]tay away from Wall Street this Wednesday afternoon." His warnings were off by a day, and his correspondents assured the Bureau that "no conspirators, after talking with Fischer [sic] for ten minutes, would consider letting him into a plot with them."

Prior to that, "a passenger in a Hudson Tube train had encountered a stranger who was carrying a tennis racquet and whose description tallied with Fischer's, and who abruptly leaned forward and said, 'Keep away from Wall Street until after the sixteenth. They have sixty thousand pounds of explosives and are going to blow it up.'"

No one has ever offered a satisfactory explanation for these statements by Fisher. Had he dropped into a meeting of subversives one night and overheard them? Had he actually been one of those who planned the blast, or a friend of a planner who confided the imminent terror to him? Was he, then, a material witness? Or, as he insisted, was he possessed of psychic powers? "I know when anything bad is going to happen," he said, and the BOI could not help but wonder. However, there was no evidence that linked him to violent anti-Americans, other than a few utterances that might have revealed "mental derangement" more than prescience.

Despite his background of dubious psychological health, Fisher was one of the first men arrested by the Bureau. He was north of the border when the Bureau cabled Canadian officials to return him to the United States. They agreed, and found the total assets on his person at the time of his apprehension to be seven cents. What he was doing in Canada, no one knew, and Fisher could not satisfactorily explain. When his brother-in-law was alerted to Fisher's extradition, he reacted as if he were hearing the same old song one time too many, urging the Bureau to turn him over to the "Lunacy Commission" as soon as he arrived back in New York. No such organization existed, but the name gives the right idea of the brother-in-law's attitude.

Fisher was apprehended in Niagara Falls. Before that, in the Toronto hotel from which he had sent the postcards warning his three friends about the danger ahead on Wall Street (the "notes" Gage refers to), he is said to have been heard muttering about "millionaires who ought to be killed."

When federal agents got their first look at Fisher in New York's Grand Central Terminal, they glanced at one another in disbelief. Their suspect departed from his train clad in "a lopsided gray cap, a wrinkled gray suit, and a silk scarf around his waist. Later, he explained that the suit was the outermost of three full sets of clothes. Wearing multiple layers helped to keep him cool, he said, and meant he didn't have to carry baggage." Among his first statements in the presence of the men from BOI were that he had received information about the Wall Street explosion from God via air waves, which had also informed him that it was time for farmers to tend to their harvest, and that money would cease to have any value soon; labor would be the new American unit of commercial exchange.

It took a while for the investigators to regain their composure after Fisher's bizarrely attired monologue; when they did, they handcuffed him, and he offered no resistance as he was escorted to police headquarters.

After a few days of interrogation that was sometimes comprehensible, sometimes not, he was released, and he disappears from the historical record immediately afterward. No one seems to know where he went, what he did, or whether, other than his apparently unsympathetic brother-in-law, he had a family to look after him. The BOI was certain it had done the right thing in setting Fisher free; but some of the comments he made, the few that were close to the truth of September 16, were hard to dismiss. How did he *know*? The man was obviously unbalanced, but so was the act committed in front of the Morgan Bank. Could there possibly be a connection? Should the BOI have had Fisher examined by a psychiatrist? Might such an examination have revealed that Fisher possessed the kind of extrasensory perception that none of the lawmen believed in? Fisher had been officially discounted as a suspect, but he lingered in the minds of investigators for years to come.

AS THE YEAR WOUND DOWN, the BOI was making more accusations than progress. It was inevitable. "With just a handful of agents assigned to radical affairs," writes Gage, "the Bureau's New York office could not handle the Wall Street case alone." So it reassigned some of its men from other locations and matters of lesser import—such as enforcement of Prohibition, which had never been a priority among those in law enforcement and was already regarded by many as the biggest mistake the Constitution had ever made. Almost all of America, in fact, gaped in unison when the commissioner of Internal Revenue, David H. Blair, in a public address, "recommended that all American bootleggers be lined up in front of a firing squad and shot to death. The site of the speech was a Presbyterian church in Philadelphia." That proposal not gaining any traction, "Blair had the government print leaflets urging drys to spy on their wet neighbors and report their intelligence anonymously, using telephones outside their neighborhoods so they would not be seen or overheard."

The Anti-Saloon League supported both proposals, and was virtually alone in doing so.

It might have been a coincidence, but a week or so after the increase of manpower on the bombing investigation, Gage tells us, some provocative, if muddled, clues began to appear. "A chauffeur named Hiram David had told detectives that he was driving east on Wall Street behind a 'red explosives wagon' when he saw a flash and a concussion of air rip the roof from his car. He distinctly recalled that the wagon bore the name of the DuPont Powder Works. It also flew a red flag, he said, the required legal warning for dynamite."

A bond salesman in approximately the same place at the same time also remembered the wagon, as well as the DuPont sign.

Joseph Kindman, an electrical engineer, said he saw a red wagon in the area of the blast and that he clearly read "DuPont Powder Company" on the side. He also saw the word "Danger" in large white letters, and a red flag jutting out from the end of the wagon.

Rebecca Epstein, a stenographer at a nearby brokerage house, was even more specific than Kindman in her timing. "She told police that she had seen a 'reddish' wagon pull up alongside the Morgan bank just before the explosion. The wagon . . . flew a telltale red flag. The front of the wagon bore faded impressions of the three letters *D, N,* and *T.* The letters were separated by odd spaces, she said, as if they had once formed a word like 'DuPont' or 'Dynamite.'"

And at least two other people remembered a vehicle of some sort with the word "DuPont" or something like it written on the side. But these people did not agree with the others that the cart was red. They did not remember the color, but were certain it was something other than red.

Was all of this as suspicious as it sounds, all these fingers pointing to DuPont? Almost certainly not. Earlier in the day, according to the *New York Times,* "It was revealed that a permit had been issued to the du Pont de Nemours Powder Company . . . to unload explosives from their pier at West Forty-Eighth Street and the North [i.e., Hudson] River."

Whether or not this particular vehicle was in the vicinity of Wall Street at noon on the sixteenth is not clear, although it does not seem to fit the vehicle's schedule. Another vehicle with the name DuPont on it had parked on Wall Street at the approximate time of the bombing, but was several blocks away from the Morgan Bank. In addition, it was a truck, not a van, and its cargo was paint pigments, not dynamite.

Besides, as everyone, at the Bureau and elsewhere, knew, DuPont was far too respectable a company, too fervently capitalistic, to be involved in the Wall Street bombing. Could someone have stolen one of its carts? The company reported none missing. Why, then, did the firm's name keep popping up in the investigation? There had to be *some* reason. Was it just that so many Americans associated the name DuPont with explosives that a few of them saw a picture in their minds that did not, in truth, exist? Perhaps someone had painted the name DuPont on the side of a cart that had nothing to do with the company, a ploy to throw investigators off the scent. So many possibilities, nothing that constituted proof.

Most of the preceding reports, interestingly, came from legwork done not by the BOI or any other law-enforcement agency, but by the *New York Call*. Desperate to protect the reputation of socialists and other foes of what they perceived to be American greed, they assigned a higher percentage of their employees to the Wall Street investigation than did the BOI. They were to be commended. And nothing that the *Call* printed, despite its being such a tiny paper, was ever contradicted by the people whose names appeared in the articles.

YET ANOTHER THEORY CAME FROM Attorney General A. Mitchell Palmer, an avowed Democrat. His notion did not concern responsibility for the bomb, for he was as usual certain that foreign radicals of one stripe or another were responsible; rather, his theory concerned the timing of the event.

In the spring of 1920, the Republican-controlled House of Representatives had sliced the Justice Department's budget for Red-hunting from $2.5 million to a mere $2 million. The $500,000 that the Department had gained before the Palmer raids was gone—a punishment directed personally at himself, Palmer thought, although without good reason—and he was furious. He and J. Edgar Hoover had implored lawmakers to change their minds, to restore the money and even add to the sum, but without success. The result was that numerous agents had been laid off, and even with the added personnel from the Prohibition forces, the BOI was operating under what Palmer believed to be a severe handicap. The cops from the booze beat were hardly in the same class of crime-solvers as longstanding BOI agents. Thus, Palmer believed, the best law-enforcement agency in the United States was vulnerable—perhaps, all things considered, more vulnerable to radical deeds than ever before.

> [Palmer] suggested . . . that the proximity of these two events—the budget cuts and the bombing—was no mere coincidence, speculating that the bombers might have known about the cuts and therefore felt emboldened to attempt what before they would not have dared. "Acquiescing in the

direction of the Republican-controlled Congress," Robert
T. Scott, his private secretary, explained to the *New York
Times*, "this department reduced its operating forces to meet
the amount of money provided. Inevitably this cut became
public. Three weeks after it became actually effective this
outrage was perpetrated in New York City."

The day of the explosion was also election day in New York, and all five
Socialist assemblymen won their races by substantial margins and would
remain in the state assembly. To Palmer, it was all of a piece, proof that
subversives were gaining ground in mainstream America, and that efforts
to vanquish them must be increased, with more substantial budgets to
support the efforts.

TAKEN INDIVIDUALLY, SOME OF THE preceding information was, to one degree
or another, promising. Looked at all together, it was a hash of hastily
formed impressions—some items seeming to verify others, others to
contradict, the mass of them leading officials nowhere except to further
confusion. The clues they needed, if in fact they had ever existed, were
by this time either water-logged in Davy Jones's locker or made into an
equine-based paste long since put to use.

It was at this point, suddenly, that a new investigative avenue opened.
As John Brooks says, it was the horse, despite its dismal fate, who now
stepped to the fore of the BOI's efforts—and stayed there longer than did
any other subject of inquiry.

For a decade and more, the local and federal police went on
conducting one of the most extensive and prolonged inves-
tigations on record. They visited over four thousand stables
up and down the Atlantic seaboard in an effort to establish
ownership of the horse; every blacksmith east of Chicago,
and even the editors of every blacksmith trade journal, in an
effort to identify the horseshoes conclusively; and every sash-
weight manufacturer and dealer in the country in an effort
to trace the source of the iron slugs. These procedures, which

were uniformly fruitless, were mocked from time to time by confessions to the crime, each of which caused a momentary stir until it was shown to be implausible.

On one occasion, William J. Flynn, heading the BOI, led a contingent of men to a stable situated in a neighborhood of New York "notorious for its Italian criminals and for murders." A blacksmith named Gaetano De Grazio, himself of dubious national origin, told agents about a man who had brought in a horse to be shod a few days before September sixteenth. The man was small in stature, about five-foot-five, De Grazia said, maybe weighing 165 pounds. And he spoke with an unmistakable Sicilian accent; having been born in Italy, De Grazia knew what the dialect sounded like. But he had no idea what the man's name was or where he lived; he had just stood by without saying a word as the blacksmith did his work, less than half an hour's worth, and then paid the bill in full and was gone.

Knowledge of the incident led nowhere. De Grazio's customer might well have been the bomber, but there was no way to know, certainly no way to track him down at this point. Some of the investigators realized that the description of the horseman fit that of Mario Buda, but only in general terms, too general to be of any value.

After having visited the four thousand stables, the BOI could come up with no more specific information than this.

The investigation continued. Or, more accurately, it dragged on. And on and on.

CHAPTER FIFTEEN

Uproar in the Arts

I F THE BUREAU OF INVESTIGATION had had time and manpower enough, it would surely have investigated American authors in 1920, although it would have reached its conclusions before a formal inquiry even began. The BOI would have realized that there had been a change, a significant change, just as there had been a change in the relationship between labor and management, just as there had been a change between radicals and law-enforcement officials. The BOI would have noted that, all of a sudden, traitorous or lurid sentiments were bursting from the page for all to see; it would have condemned the fact that filth was replacing literature, perversion replacing tales of proper societal behavior. It would have condemned the writing as un-American and determined that if people were capable of such rebellion in novels, poetry, and drama for the stage, perhaps they were equally capable in real life.

As a result of the Great War, men and women of letters had become preoccupied with politics and social criticism; in the former they leaned more leftward than ever before, and in the latter they were scathing.

There were no terrorists among them, no anarchists or Bolshies, at least not as far as anyone knows, but neither were there Eagle Scouts, Rotarians, Chamber of Commerce boosters, flag-wavers, members of the newly formed American Legion, or any other celebrants of the grand ol' status quo. In many cases, the sympathies of the artists seemed to lie with the groups that threatened the United States more than with those that praised it uncompromisingly. But artistic violence, or at least opposition, whether it be verbal or visual, was not the concern of law-enforcement officials. It was, rather, the product of men and women of thought and careful expression, not propaganda of the deed.

However, it was not just the pessimism of the postwar years that fueled the artists of 1920; it was a desire to explore more profoundly than ever before the hidden corners of human nature. Such European authors as Zola, Flaubert, and Hardy, among others, were already doing that. It was time for American authors to follow their lead, time for more mature and probing work.

With few exceptions, the art that left the greatest impression in 1920, and is still studied today for both its stylistic innovation and cultural hostility, reflected the views of the lost generation: disenfranchisement, it was, set to page and stage and in many cases canvas. Such painters as Picasso, Matisse, and Duchamp, among several others, were taking apart the pieces of humanity and putting them back in different sizes and shapes and even places, creating images that startled, captivated, and appalled. Conventional notions of composition and shape, of color, placement, and conveyance of meaning, were ignored, even destroyed, forcing Americans to look differently at what they saw both in the museum and on the street outside. The revolution in painterly vision left more destruction of tradition in its path than a tornado leaves after it rips through a trailer park.

AROUND THE TIME THAT HARDING defeated Cox, copies of Sinclair Lewis's *Main Street* were being delivered to America's bookstores. It was an appropriate coincidence. The novel could easily have been set in Harding's hometown of Marion, Ohio. Instead, according to historian Nathan Miller, *Main Street* satirized Gopher Prairie, a thinly-disguised portrait of Sauk Center, [Lewis's] hometown in Minnesota, where "dullness is made God." . . . the lodge members in their comic regalia, and the women of the uplift societies—were skewered for what Lewis saw as provincialism, emotional poverty, and lack of spiritual values. The publication of *Main Street* ranks with that of *Uncle Tom's Cabin* as one of the few literary events with a profound political or social fallout, for it established a new way of looking at small-town America.

Relating the wistful thoughts of the novel's heroine, Carol Milford, Lewis wrote, "The days of pioneering, of lassies in sunbonnets, and bears killed with axes in piney clearings, are deader now than Camelot." Carol was a student at Blodgett College, "a bulwark of sound religion. It is still combating the recent heresies of Voltaire, Darwin and Robert Ingersoll. Pious families in Minnesota, Iowa, Wisconsin, the Dakotas send their children thither, and Blodgett protects them from the wickedness of the universities."

What was so blasphemous about *Main Street* was that it had been standard practice at the time, and for generations preceding, to idealize small-town America. It was viewed as a fortress that housed old-fashioned morality, older-fashioned values, and the principles that, at least on paper, had been the foundation of the United States ever since those papers, the Declaration of Independence and the Constitution, had been written.

But the fortress had been penetrated. *Main Street* left no axiom unexamined, no bromide unshattered. To Lewis, places like his hometown taught conformity in their schools more effectively than they did any academic subject. The accumulation of material goods was venerated; the striving after intellectual goals was looked at suspiciously, a goal of socialists, that kind of person. And as for one's so-called friends, the trustworthy, rock-steady, benevolent men and women of Gopher Prairie, the people who made it such a cheerful place to live, Lewis warned against turning one's back to them, warned that they would cheat and lie about their neighbors at the slightest prospect of gain for themselves. Even for the simple joy of gossiping, reveling in the power of possessing information unknown to others. Small towns, small minds, and, when opportunities for gain presented themselves, small treacheries. If Lewis's masterpiece could be reduced to a single phrase, this would have been a good candidate.

Critics, on the whole, were not fond of *Main Street*. One New Yorker, Deems Taylor, normally a music critic, said the book "owed much of its success to its offering culturally insecure Americans . . . 'a set of consistently contemptible and uncultured characters to whom [they] superior must feel.'"

And Walter Lippmann, the dean of global-affairs columnists who virtually never wrote about literature either, accused Lewis of merely "inventing stereotypes . . . substituting new prejudices for old . . . marketing useful devices . . . used by millions . . . to express their new, disillusioned sense of America." In addition, critics charged, Lewis's prose tended to ramble; he was less interested in telling a single, unified story than he was in accumulating incidents to make his accusations—piling on, rather than proceeding artfully. And those accusations were more often than not too harsh, his characters more parodies than flesh-and-blood mortals—such was the consensus.

The fact that men who were not normally book reviewers, men of more prestigious rank, raced into print to denounce Lewis is telling, indicative of the threat that *Main Street* posed to the conventional values to which they subscribed. But Taylor was wrong in his specifics. Lippmann was wrong. Their condemnations were publicity for the book, their judgments more suitable to the days of "lassies in sunbonnets" than to the present. For what Lewis was doing was writing a new kind of fiction, helping to create a new literature, one of the purposes of which was to stir emotions, examine motives beneath the surface, and reinforce the newly forming biases that were the basis of the lost generation.

After a slow start, *Main Street* had sold 200,000 copies before 1920 ended. Within a few years, the total was up to three million, and the book has not stopped selling, or being studied in both high school and college, ever since. A spokesperson for the publisher whom I contacted claimed not to know how many copies of *Main Street* are being sold these days, a patently and inexplicably false statement, but the number is surely in the tens of thousands, if not the hundreds.

Former small-town newspaper publisher Warren G. Harding could have lived on *Main Street.* He looked the part, espoused the cautious means of proceeding from day to day. "What is the greatest thing in life?" he once asked; then answered for himself: "Happiness. And there is more happiness in the American small village than in any place on earth." He could have taken the physician Will Kennicott's place at the side of his contrarian wife, one-time Blodgett student Carol Milford, whom he married later in the story.

Carol Milford Kennicott, try though she did, could never make herself comfortable in Gopher Prairie. She had married Will in good faith; but when she could no longer bear the stagnation of her hometown, or her husband's complacency and inability to appreciate art of any kind, she left him for two years of war-related work in Washington, D.C. She returned to her husband and others she knew in Gopher Prairie not so much because she wanted to, but because there was nowhere else to go. As the 46-year-old poet Robert Frost had written five years earlier, "Home is the place where, when you have to go there, they have to take you in." Gopher Prairie welcomed her back, but she was not feeling what she had hoped to feel; there were times, in fact, when she seemed more discouraged than she had been before her out-of-town sabbatical.

Less than a year after leaving Washington, when the Kennicotts' first child, a little girl, was born, Carol led husband Will to the hospital nursery and

> pointed at the fuzzy brown head of her daughter. "Do you see that object on the pillow? Do you know what it is? It's a bomb to blow up smugness. If you Tories were wise, you would arrest anarchists; you'd arrest all these children while they're asleep in their cribs. Think what that baby will see and meddle with before she dies in the year 2000! She may see an industrial union of the whole world, she may see aeroplanes going to Mars."

Her husband might have agreed with her, or perhaps did not. After all these years of marriage, his disputes with Carol had become lifeless. "Yump, probably be changes all right," he yawned. And that was the end of the conversation.

ERNEST HEMINGWAY WAS JUST BEGINNING to make a name for himself as a short-story writer, but his first novel, *The Sun Also Rises*, full of the angst and emptiness of the lost generation, was still six years away. It might not have been published at all, however, had it not been for the urging of F. Scott Fitzgerald—impressed by Hemingway, then later dominated and ridiculed by him, the beggar turning vindictively on his benefactor, Fitzgerald pleaded with his editor at Scribner's, the famed Maxwell Perkins, to take his friend as a client. Perkins was dubious at first, but began reading Hemingway's short stories in 1920 and finally, in 1925, published a collection of them, called *In Our Time*.

Then, the next year, Scribner's published *The Sun Also Rises*, a tale of tedious people that is among the most tedious of twentieth-century classics. The book became the first of a shelf-load of successes for Hemingway that included, among others, *A Farewell to Arms*, *For Whom the Bell Tolls*, *The Old Man and the Sea*, and *A Moveable Feast*—all with vastly different plots, yet most featuring at least a few characters from the lost generation. "This is a hell of a dull talk," says a woman in *The Sun Also Rises*, accurately summing up the conversation Hemingway has presented in the book. "How about some of that champagne," she says, just as accurately summing up the hobby of choice—virtually a vocation—for all the characters. If it weren't for abuse of bulls in the ring in Pamplona, Spain, nothing would have happened in Hemingway's volume at all. It is difficult to write purposeful books about purposeless people.

His entire body of work enabled Hemingway to join Lewis in winning the Nobel Prize. Lewis won it in 1930 but refused to accept; Hemingway accepted his own trophy twenty-four years later. "For a true writer," he said in his speech in Oslo that, in a way, described the literature that had changed so drastically in the twenties,

> each book should be a new beginning, where he tries again
> for something that is beyond attainment. He should always
> try for something that has never been done, or that others
> have tried and failed. Then, sometimes, with good luck, he
> will succeed. . . . It is because we have had such great writers

in the past, that a writer is driven far out, past where he can go, out where no one can help him.

AS A NOVELIST, FITZGERALD GOT the jump on his friend, publishing *This Side of Paradise* in 1920, one of only four full-length books, not counting short-story compilations, that he would manage to finish. The book's protagonist, Amory Blaine, is, like the author, a Minnesotan with a high opinion of his own abilities. He attends Princeton to have his opinion confirmed; then, according to plan, he will become a successful author.

In brief, *This Side of Paradise* is the story of two of Blaine's love affairs, one in Minneapolis with Isabelle, which ends with his returning to college at Princeton; and the other, which begins at Princeton and ends with his beloved Rosalind deciding to marry a far wealthier man than he. He develops a crush on another young lady, and then another, but neither lasts nor means nearly as much to him as the first two relationships.

The result of it all is a distraught, and surprised, protagonist.

> Women—of whom he had expected so much; whose beauty he had hoped to transmute into modes of art; whose unfathomable instincts, marvelously incoherent and inarticulate, he had thought to perpetuate in terms of experience—had become merely consecrations to their own posterity. Isabelle, Clara, Rosalind, Eleanor, were all removed by their very beauty, around which men had swarmed, from the possibility of contributing anything but a sick heart and a page of puzzled words to write.

At the novel's end, Blaine's summary of his life to date is a sad one, despite being uttered to himself under "the crystalline, radiant sky. 'I know myself,' he cries, 'but that is all.'"

This Side of Paradise was the biggest seller of Fitzgerald's lifetime. Unfortunately, he was deluded by the book's success into thinking that all of his work would be so profitable, and that he was, therefore, capable of the same kind of wealthy lifestyle of which he wrote. But it was just that: a delusion. And it was not just literary profits that misled him. A movie producer optioned *This Side of Paradise* for $3,000. But the movie was not made and the money not paid, the producer forfeiting on the project and the story remaining between the covers of the book version. Still, Fitzgerald continued to believe that financial woes, which would in fact worsen for him, were a thing of the past.

Nineteen-twenty was probably the apogee of Fitzgerald's life, both professionally and personally. In addition to *This Side of Paradise*, Scribner's also published *Flappers and Philosophers*, Fitzgerald's first book of short stories; and then later in the year, seven months to the day after his novel was released, he married Zelda Sayre, the free-wheeling, universally pursued but deadly addled, nonsensically poetic belle of Montgomery, Alabama. Somehow, he believed he could lead a stable life with her. Another delusion.

Actually, the year before they wed, Zelda's biographer Nancy Milford tells us, "she wrote to him that if he felt he had lost his feeling for her, if he'd be happier without their marrying, she would release him from whatever promises had once been made." It was an offer he should not have refused.

> And she added: "Somehow 'When love has turned to kind-ness' doesn't horrify me like it used to—It has such a peaceful sound—like something to come back to and rest—and some-times I'm glad we're not exactly like we used to be—and I can't help feeling that it would all come back again."

After years of alcoholism, which fueled the couple's frantic, argumentative, high-volume, bar-hopping, glass-smashing, fountain-bathing mirth, Scott died in the arms of another woman, his Hollywood mistress, in 1940. He was forty-four years old.

Years earlier, Zelda had decided to revive a passion of her youth—although one to which she had not given so much as a thought since she was a little girl—and become a ballet dancer. Never mind that she had reached the over-the-hill age of twenty-eight, she would make up in dedi-cation what she lacked in adolescent suppleness. And she tried, oh how she tried, with a maniacal, pointless energy, working at her exercises with the zeal of her younger self, as all the while Scott ridiculed her with the zeal of a committed drunk. She "practiced in front of the great ornate mirror," Milford says, "sweating profusely, stopping only for water, which she kept beside the Victrola, and ignoring Scott's remarks as he watched her leap and bend. He hated the large glass that reflected her, doubling the portraits of angst. He called it their 'Whorehouse Mirror.'"

Every muscle in her body ached throughout every day of her attempted comeback, and the harder she attempted to execute her moves, the more she realized that she was no longer capable of them, no longer capable of her dreams. But what else was there for her to do? Scott had no answers, and so she kept at it, sometimes screaming at what her body would no longer permit of her. But it was not just her body that had lost its ability to do as she pleased; her mind, which had long been slipping away from her, began to accelerate its pace, until finally she lost it altogether and was committed to a mental hospital. She lived there in a state of dull, medicated felicity until 1948, eight years after her husband died. Then, for reasons unknown, a fire broke out in the kitchen. "There was no automatic fire alarm system in the old stone and frame building and no sprinkler system." Medical personnel saved a few of the patients, but Zelda was not one of them. The hospital was consumed in flames and burned to the ground so quickly, it might have not been there in the first place.

Engraved on Zelda Sayre Fitzgerald's tombstone are the famous words that bring to a close Scott's shortest but most enduring novel, *The Great Gatsby*. "So we beat on, boats against the current, borne back ceaselessly into the past."

BEFORE THE FITZGERALDS CRASHED, THEY had become the embodiments of the wild side of the twenties, the sin-without-atonement, drunkenness-without-hangovers, war-without-emotional-reckoning side. To look at the photographs of them, so fashionably and expensively attired, is to think of mansions on Long Island, hotel suites overlooking Central Park, villas in the south of France. It is to think of deep blue water in swimming pools, perfectly mown grass on private tennis courts and on gently sloping lawns that reached from the front porticoes of mansions to the edge of Long

Island Sound. It was an image that the Fitzgeralds, Scott in particular, did much to encourage.

But a careful reading of his work reveals that he knew, even accepted, the phrase that Gertrude Stein had coined and passed along to Hemingway. He knew, when he was sober, that he was lost. He knew that his wife was lost. Sobriety, then, was the curse of unbearable knowledge to them both. Never once in 1920 did he use the phrase "lost generation" in his public writing, but in his first novel he didn't have to.

"Here was a new generation," Fitzgerald mused in *This Side of Paradise*, showing remarkable insight for a man of twenty-four, "shouting the old cries, learning the old creeds, through a revery [*sic*] of long days and nights; destined finally to go out into that dirty gray turmoil to follow love and pride: a new generation dedicated more than the last to the fear of poverty and the worship of success; grown up to find all the gods dead, all wars fought, all faiths in man shaken."

It proved the epitaph for an era, written by one of the first men to realize that the era would require one.

THE FRENCH WERE ONE OF the two countries battered most in the war. More than a quarter of a generation was lost. "1,315,000 [men] had been killed in action—27 percent of all men between the ages of eighteen and twenty-seven, a figure that does not include the wounded: those left blind, or legless, or armless, or with no limbs at all."

As for Great Britain, it would mourn the passing of what it referred to as an entire generation; although strictly speaking it was less than that, the death toll was appalling. More than 908,000 men, most of them between their late teens and mid-twenties, gave up their lives on one battlefield or another, while another two million were injured, some seriously and permanently. In his BBC documentary *Voices from the Great War*, Peter Vansittart said that "As a small boy in Southsea, I saw streets disfigured by ragged, unwanted ex-soldiers, medalled, but ill, blind, maimed, selling matches, bootlaces, notepaper, trundling barrel-organs or standing with a melancholy dog or monkey. . . . Their wretchedness suggested that, in overcoming Germany, they had earned some monstrous penalty now being . . . enacted."

In 1914 alone, it has been estimated, more than thirty percent of Englishmen between the ages of twenty and twenty-four were killed. Before the war was over, one out of every eight men of *all* ages who lived in the British Isles would lose his life because of the fighting, either because he was in the midst of it or was too close at the wrong time. Although it is not certain, civilian deaths probably surpassed 100,000.

AMONG THE MOST TROUBLED, AND talented, of those who did not serve in the war was David Herbert Lawrence, more commonly known by the initials of his first and middle names. He was a schoolteacher in his early thirties, and thus old enough to escape conscription, when England first began to fear not merely defeat but annihilation. Given his nook in academe, there was little he could do other than write about the prospect. But he did not do so in a conventional manner. Even though he worked on his book from 1916 through 1918, the most bruising, brutal, battle-wearying years of them all, Lawrence did not write what one would call an anti-war novel, of which, he knew, scores would be produced in the years ahead. Instead, he reached more broadly. In *Women in Love*, the title notwithstanding, his purpose—or one of them—was to vilify the entire nation in which he lived, its values and ideals, its weaknesses and hypocrisies, all of which, in Lawrence's view, made it susceptible to the Great War's needless violence.

A novel offensive to British society in some manner was to be expected from D. H. Lawrence. His previous book, *The Rainbow*, issued in 1915, contained scenes so sexually explicit for its time, although hardly for ours, that it was declared obscene. The author was not sentenced, but his book was punished to the maximum extent of the law. The publisher was ordered to stop manufacturing it, and authorities seized as many copies already in existence as they could retrieve and burned them. One can only imagine Lawrence's reaction to the expense and energy of so trivial a matter as a book-burning a full year after the war had begun.

For more than a decade, a copy of *The Rainbow* could not be legally secured in Great Britain. In New York it was available legally, but in privately published editions, which sold in small numbers and only to those who knew the book existed in the first place. As far as the author was concerned, he was left where he had so long dwelt, on the perilous brink of poverty.

In *The Rainbow*, Ursula Brangwen finds the British educational system to be "sham, spurious"; she rages, with her country on the battlefield, that such "organised fighting" might send the whole universe "tumbling into the bottomless pit"; and decides that "[s]he hated religion, because it lent itself to her confusion. . . . There was then no Jesus, no sentimentality." For good measure, if even more bad publicity, Lawrence threw in a lesbian affair for Ursula and a few hints of heterosexual sodomy.

And then, five years later, in 1920, came *Women in Love*, the sequel to *The Rainbow*. In the main, *Women in Love* is concerned with the affairs between two couples. One is Ursula and a troubled intellectual named Rupert Birkin, whom Lawrence might have based at least partly on himself; the other is Ursula's sister Gudrun and the business tycoon Gerald Crich. As might be expected, the love scenes were even bolder than those published five years earlier. For instance, Ursula and Birkin, in the midst of foreplay:

> She traced with her hands the line of his loins and thighs, at the back, and a living fire ran through her, from him, darkly. It was a dark flood of electric passion she released from him, drew into herself. She had established a rich new circuit, a new current of passional electric energy, between the two of them, released from the darkest poles of the body and established in perfect circuit. It was a dark fire of electricity that rushed from him to her, and flooded them both with rich peace, satisfaction.

Ironically, though, it was the hint of men in love that most upset at least some of the readers of *Women in Love* and almost all of the authorities. At one point in the story, Birkin is ill and Gerald comes to see him. "The two men had a deep, uneasy feeling for each other," Lawrence tells us. And a few lines later:

> Gerald really loved Birkin, though he never quite believed in him. Birkin was too unreal;—clever, whimsical, wonderful, but not practical enough. Gerald felt that his own understanding was much sounder and safer. Birkin was delightful, a wonderful spirit, but after all, not to be taken seriously, not quite to be counted as a man among men.

If it had been Gerald who had traced with his hands the loins and thighs of Birkin, the British Isles would have exploded with indignation. As it was, the book created controversy enough for its time. Most reviews were negative, and even many of those that were positive criticized Lawrence for going too far. Said one commentator, throwing his share of logs onto the furor, "I do not claim to be a literary critic, but I know dirt when I smell it, and here is dirt in heaps—festering, putrid heaps which smell to high Heaven."

As Lawrence wrote *Women in Love*, his apparent bisexuality erupted. All around him young men were dying—lean and strapping, handsome and bold; the criminality of such waste left him unhinged, and would in time go so far as to affect his physical well-being. In 1912, at the age of twenty-seven, he met a married woman named Frieda Weekley, and he would spend the rest of his life with her. They lived in adulterous sin for two years, making Lawrence an even more disdainful figure to many, before marrying, after her divorce became final, in the summer of 1914. That he loved her is undeniable. But Frieda believed that, within a few years of their vows, her husband had had at least one affair with a man, a farmer named William Henry Hocking. Lawrence's discovery of his attraction to men as well as women, which had been building in him for years, left him secretly tortured, painfully ambivalent.

On the one hand, he wrote in a letter to a friend, "I should like to know why nearly every man that approaches greatness tends to homosexuality, whether he admits it or not." And, "I believe the nearest I've come to perfect love was with a young coal miner when I was about 16."

On the other hand, Lawrence professed to despise the men who loved the Brandwens in *Women in Love*, claiming that it was difficult to write about them, as he found their latent homosexuality malodorous and filthy. He dreamed of beetles, he said, when he thought of Crich and Birkin, and would awaken in the black of night disgusted with himself. In an earlier draft of the book, Lawrence was more transparent about homosexuality, writing about two would-be male lovers who engaged in a wrestling match not for the sport of it but for the romance of coupling.

Frieda stayed with him through it all. But just before *Women in Love* was published, their lives took a turn. Frieda did not see it coming; her husband might have surprised himself as well.

Lawrence decided that he could no longer live in a place like England. He pronounced himself an exile, escaping not just the war's terrible aftermath, but the criticism that his books and essays had already aroused and the controversy that he knew lay ahead from *Women in Love*. He and Frieda went first to Italy, but Lawrence soon grew restless and Frieda, ever compliant, was willing to uproot herself before they had even settled. The two of them then began to drift aimlessly, their destinations often determined by the smallness of the sums of money that they could afford. They sailed in steerage to the United States, and from there traipsed on foot into Mexico. Also ahead of them lay Australia, Malta, France, Germany, Monte Cassino, and Ceylon, now Sri Lanka. It was a "savage enough pilgrimage," Lawrence wrote to another friend, one that enabled him to find no peace, no geographical basis for contentment.

He kept writing all the while, but his health began to fail now, and the only book of significance that he produced after 1920 was *Lady Chatterley's Lover*, in 1928, four years after the savagery of his travels had ended and he had returned to England. He managed to squeeze two more novels of uneven merit into the next two years, but in 1930 he died in France, an exhausted and tormented man who looked as if he had lived more of life than his years suggested. He was forty-five, only one year older than Fitzgerald.

Lawrence's was not what people were used to thinking about when they thought of the literary life. It was more the life of an escaped prisoner, one who had managed to extricate himself from his cell but was unable to free himself from the ceaseless punishment meted out by the years in which he lived.

NOT ALL, HOWEVER, WAS BLEAK or lascivious on the world's bookshelves in 1920. As it happened, that was the year when an author who would go on to become an industry, and remains one almost a century later, published her first book. The author, like Lawrence, was a Britisher but had virtually nothing else in common with him, including gender. But although Agatha Christie was a woman, she published her first novel in the voice of a man, Captain Hastings, one of thousands of small-town English police officers.

He was not, however, the story's hero. That distinction belongs to Hercule Poirot, a private investigator from Belgium who would go on to achieve a distinction in the real world that only he, of all the fictional characters ever created, would be able to claim.

He was a charming fellow in his way. Undoubtedly he gave off a whiff of snootiness, an air of superiority—but wasn't he entitled? Nobody could detect the way Poirot detected, and no one was as ingeniously clever in assembling the suspects in a single room of a British mansion in the final chapter of a book and, after a series of false hints about the killer's identity to raise the level of suspense, actually revealing it.

In narrating the first of Poirot's adventures in 1920, Captain Hastings, upon his initial meeting with the unlikely-looking crime-solver, was impressed that, despite the fact of his being but five feet, four inches tall, "his extravagance of personality . . . was sufficiently plausible to stand and survive by himself." Christie biographer Janet Morgan continues with her description of Poirot by relating that he "was clever, and equipped with a pompous character, a luxuriant moustache, and a curious egg-shaped head."

But how was Christie to find the peace she needed to concentrate on her first of Poirot's adventures? She decided, after a time, to write at least part of her novel in a hotel room in a section of England that was "desolate, tranquil, and utterly unique in the nearly spiritual serenity that transcends the vast moorland." Nonetheless, the creative drive demanded by Poirot's investigative methods would tax her physically as much as it did artistically. According to biographer Richard Hack, the ambience "was dreary, yes, and outside, the damp cold weather no doubt furthered that impression as Agatha settled into a daily routine of rising early and writing in longhand for several hours in the morning, until her fingers ached and cramped around her pencil, and the lunch bell finally pealed the call for the dining room."

Christie's fingers did not completely un-cramp for the rest of the day; she was finished writing until tomorrow.

And when she was finished writing her book in its entirety, she did what all unknown authors did in those days before agents—she submitted it, unsolicited, through the mail to a publishing house, hoping that someone who worked there would pluck her envelope from the stacks and stacks of other unsolicited manuscripts and read it. In this case, that is exactly what happened, and it did so, to Christie's ineffable joy and immediate success, at one of England's leading publishers, the Bodley Head.

Stunned when an editor contacted her and told her he had actually read *The Mysterious Affair at Styles*, even more stunned when he asked for a meeting, and stunned yet further after the meeting when he told her the book would be published and then offered her a contract, Christie virtually took flight from his office and "wanted to hug someone, or scream, or do something so wonderfully silly that everyone on the street would stop and stare in her direction."

Hercule Poirot's career was about to begin.

Christie could not, or would not, ever satisfactorily explain the origin of either her hero's name or his Belgian nationality. But his brilliant deductions at Styles made him, virtually overnight, the most famous crime-solver on the planet. Only he, it seems, could have discovered the identity of the murderer of the grande dame of Styles, Emily Cavendish Inglethorp, who was elderly, near death, and had a great deal of money to dispense when her demise finally came.

This first of Christie's books, in Captain Hastings's voice, began as follows:

> The intense interest aroused in the public by what was known at the time as "The Styles Case" has now somehow subsided. Nevertheless, in view of the world-wide notoriety which attended it, I have been asked, both by my friend Poirot and the family themselves, to write an account of the whole story. This, we trust, will effectually silence the sensational rumours which still persist.

However inadvertently, Christie was being coy. She *wanted* the rumors to persist, rumors not only about the possible perpetrator of Dame Inglethorp's slaying, but of the murders by the score she would set to paper in the years ahead, eventually putting aside her pencil and, with fingers straightened, making use of a typewriter.

And, to this very day, the rumors have indeed persisted.

Agatha Mary Clarissa Christie was born in 1890, her parents wealthy but their daughter uninterested in other little girls of her age and similar circumstances. Although she would later describe her childhood as a happy one, Christie preferred to spend her time alone, with her pets, and often with her imaginary friends. One of them was Sue de Verte, and little Agatha was perhaps describing herself as much as her fantasy playmate when she wrote that Sue was "curiously colourless, not only in appearance . . . but also in character."

As she grew older, Agatha turned to books for companionship, and they may have been her truest friends of all in childhood. She began with the works of Maria Louisa Molesworth, who was simply Mrs. Molesworth on her dust jackets and who produced such British childhood classics as *Carrots, The Cuckoo Clock,* and *Tell Me A Story.* Eventually Agatha moved up to the sophisticated, sometimes nonsensical verse of Lewis Carroll and Edward Lear, and in time, too inspired by her reading to resist, she began to write her own works. She began with short stories that were not published, then novels that were not published. But she was becoming a determined young lady and would not be dissuaded by early disappointment.

It is the story of many an author. Years of failure—or, to consider them less depressingly and in some cases more realistically, years of learning her craft—and then finally a breakthrough.

At this point, however, Christie's real-life story, like her fiction, takes an unforeseen twist. *The Mysterious Affair at Styles* becomes an immediate best seller. So does every other book she writes, all of them mysteries, more of them than the number of years remaining in her life. It is reported by her estate that the books of the woman who would eventually become Dame Agatha, a total of sixty-six novels and fifteen short-story collections, rank behind only the Bible and the plays of Shakespeare in sales. She is, thus, with four *billion* of her volumes in print, the most widely read novelist of all time.

And as if that weren't enough, she also succeeded beyond any playwright's dreams on the stage, where her work *The Mousetrap* has for many years been the longest-running play in history. It opened in London's West

End in 1952 and, as of this writing, after more than sixty years, has yet to close. On November 18, 2012, it celebrated its 25,000th performance. It has gone far beyond the status of mere theatrical drama to being one of England's principal tourist attractions, ranking with Big Ben, the Tower of London, and Buckingham Palace.

Even Christie, in her autobiography, admitted her puzzlement at the success of *The Mousetrap*. "Apart from replying with the obvious answer, 'Luck!'—because it is luck, ninety per cent. luck at least," Christie wrote, "I should say . . . it is well constructed. The thing unfolds so that you want to know what happens next, and you can't quite see where the next few minutes will lead you."

At the beginning of the play, with the stage still in darkness, a young woman is murdered. After the killer is finally identified, the person's identity a surprise to almost all, the curtain falls and the audience is asked not to discuss the play's ending with family members, friends, or associates at work, who might thus have the experience of *The Mousetrap* spoiled for them. The assumption is that, eventually, everyone in London, whether resident or tourist, will get around to seeing it. So far, almost everyone has.

Curiously, the world's longest-running play has never had much success in this country. Hundreds of productions have been mounted, but almost all of them in community and regional theatres, and they have been limited by the theatres' schedules to a run of a few weeks, a month at the most. No attempts at a major New York production have been made for decades, and none has ever had more than a tiny fraction of the success of the original.

Still, that original, now an institution, is the great marvel of live drama—certainly in modern times. And Christie's continuing book sales are the great marvel of the publishing world. She is far from being the world's most honored author, often criticized for an inability to create three-dimensional characters, her works accused of being puzzles more than true literary creations. Nonetheless, whatever her shortcomings, Agatha Christie is without question the queen of engaging quantity.

AH, IF ONLY HE COULD have offered his services to the Bureau of Investigation in the United States after the Wall Street bombing. . . .

On August 6, 1975, the *New York Times* ran one of its rare front-page obituaries. It reported the death of Hercule Poirot. But it was a strange kind of passing, and there was far too much to say about it for a single page. The notice of decease continued at greater length on page sixteen.

An article about the death of a man of Poirot's eminence is always accompanied by a picture. However, since no photograph of the decedent could ever be taken, the *Times* article was accompanied by a painting done some fifty years earlier, when Poirot was at the peak of his powers, not to mention the peak of his dandified, even haughty, presence. It looked just like him.

Since his was a death that saddened hundreds of millions of readers the world over, the obituary of this man deserves to be quoted at some length.

> Hercule Poirot, a Belgian detective who became internationally famous, has died in England. His age was unknown.
>
> Mr. Poirot achieved fame as a private investigator after he retired as a member of the Belgian police force in 1904. His career, as chronicled in the novels of Dame Agatha Christie, his creator, was one of the most illustrious in fiction.
>
> At the end of his life, he was arthritic, and had a bad heart. He was in a wheelchair often, and was carried from his bedroom to the public lounge at Styles Court, a nursing home in Essex, wearing a wig and false mustaches to mask the signs of age that offended his vanity. In his active days, he was always impeccably dressed.
>
> Mr. Poirot, who was just 5 feet 4 inches tall, went to England from Belgium during World War I as a refugee. He settled in a little town not far from Styles, then an elaborate country estate, where he took on his first private case. . . .
>
> The news of his death was confirmed by Dodd, Mead, Dame Agatha's [American] publishers, who will put out "Curtain," the novel that chronicles his final days, on Oct. 15.
>
> The Poirot of the final volume is only a shadow of the well-turned out, agile investigator who, with a charming but immense ego and fractured English, solved uncounted

mysteries in the 37 full-length novels and collections of short stories in which he appeared.

Dame Agatha reports in "Curtain" that he managed, in one final gesture, to perform one more act of cerebration that saved an innocent bystander from disaster. "Nothing in his life became him like the leaving it," to quote Shakespeare, whom Poirot frequently misquoted.

It was the first and only obituary of a fictional character that the *New York Times* has ever published.

CHRISTIE WAS THE MAGNIFICENT EXCEPTION of 1920, a traditionalist who succeeded in a radical age of literature, which consisted of verse as well as prose. T. S. Eliot, who had shaken the world of poetry a few years earlier with *The Love Song of J. Alfred Prufrock,* and would startle it again in two years with the modernist classic *The Waste Land,* published his first volume of collected works in 1920, including *Prufrock.* It was the poem's first great showcase. Described as "a drama of literary anguish," *Prufrock's* language was dense and some of its references oddly chosen, but one did not have to understand every word in the epic to feel the aching depression of the title character's life, a life in which there was no love, no music, no hope. Going further, Eliot biographer Craig Raine offers a withering description of Mr. Prufrock, calling him "a thin-skinned sensitive, a dithering compass of cowardice and crippling lack of self-esteem. Prufrock fails to live, fails to declare himself—and is therefore culpable by romantic lights. He does not seize the day." It is, rather, the days that seize him, and do with him what they will.

Eliot, an Englishman who moved to St. Louis as a young man, was another of the year's prominent figures who looked as if he belonged on *Main Street,* although in a position superior to that of Harding—perhaps bank president, perhaps president of the Gopher Prairie Chamber of Commerce, despite appearing a bit reserved for a hale-fellow-well-met crowd. Eliot wore three-piece suits, parted his hair in a wide, straight line and flattened it to his scalp, both of which actions appeared to have been taken ruthlessly. He was a private man. His smile was slight and benign, his mind always appearing to be on something other than the photograph. The frames of his glasses, which he wore in only a few of his pictures, were perfectly round.

Eventually, moving back across the ocean and settling as far as comfort would allow from Gopher Prairie, Eliot became a citizen of Great Britain, as staid in his choice of homeland as he was in his appearance. But devoted to it. When the United States announced it was entering the Great War with little more than a year remaining, Eliot wrote from London to his mother in St. Louis with undisguised bitterness. "You [Americans] will be having all the excitement and bustle of war with none of the horrors and despairs."

For Agatha Christie, the Great War was seldom more than a fact turned up in the background of a suspect by Poirot or her other great detective, the village busybody Miss Jane Marple. It usually meant nothing more than that the individual in question knew how to shoot a gun, or that he might still have walked with a slight limp.

BUT T. S. ELIOT WAS not what he seemed, for he created nothing less than a revolution in verse, an overthrow of conventional themes and rhythms, the end of romance and the beginning of introspection that could lead down alleys so dark that their entrances had not even been visible before. His was the poetry of the disaffected intellectual, the lament of the lost generation set to atonal music. In *The Love Song of J. Alfred Prufrock*, Eliot writes:

> Let us go then, you and I,
> When the evening is spread out against the sky
> Like a patient etherized on a table;
> Let us go, through certain half-deserted streets,
> The muttering retreats
> Of restless nights in one-night cheap hotels
> And sawdust restaurants with oyster shells:
> Streets that follow like a tedious argument
> Of insidious intent
> To lead you to an overwhelming question . . .
> Oh, do not ask, "What is it?"
> Let us go and make our visit.

Prufrock felt the inevitability of time, of its passage and power, and of his inability to do anything other than yield to it, to feel it as a weight upon him, pressing down without surcease. Haunting thoughts they were, that Eliot expressed, but an element of his genius was the small, seemingly irrelevant details out of which he so poignantly related cosmic sorrows.

> And indeed there will be time
> To wonder, "Do I dare?" and, "Do I dare?"
> Time to turn back and descend the stair,
> With a bald spot in the middle of my hair—
> (They will say: "How his hair is growing thin!")
> My morning coat, my collar mounting firmly to the chin,
> My necktie rich and modest, but asserted by a simple pin—
> (They will say: "But how his legs and arms are thin!")
> Do I dare
> Disturb the universe?
> In a minute there is time
> For decision and revisions which a minute will reverse.
> . . .
> I grow old . . . I grow old . . .
> I shall wear the bottoms of my trousers rolled.

Prufrock has heard mermaids singing, somewhere in the distance, but does not believe they will ever sing to him. They will provide no relief from his suffering, none of the contentment he cannot find on land.

> We have lingered in the chambers of the sea
> By sea-girls wreathed with seaweed red and brown
> Till human voices wake us, and we drown.

Eliot knew early in his career that he would not write nearly as much poetry as others, although he did not explain why. It may be that he had already decided that writing for the theatre would take too much of his time; ahead of him still, among others, were such plays as *Murder in the Cathedral*, *The Cocktail Party*, and *Old Possum's Book of Practical Cats*, which provided the lyrics for Andrew Lloyd Webber's late-century musical delight, *Cats*. Or it may be that he realized his poems demanded too much of him, left him psychically enervated. "My reputation in London is built upon one small volume of verse," he conceded once to a friend, "and is kept up by printing two or three more poems in a year. The only thing that matters is that these should be perfect in their kind, so that each should be an event."

Most were. No one had ever made one shudder through his reading of poems like T. S. Eliot. The collection published in 1920 was far from a best seller and, as far as non-existent human beings were concerned, J. Alfred Prufrock could not compare in popularity to Hercule Poirot; but Eliot's anthology was one of the most influential collections that the literary world would ever know—although, for the most part, the influence would not be felt until time had passed and comparisons were more easily made.

THAT POETRY COULD BE TAKEN down yet another untrodden path the same year was a remarkable coincidence. But that is exactly what happened. Between Eliot and an exceedingly different kind of man named Carl Sandburg, the very definition of verse was expanded in 1920, beyond limits that would have been thought possible earlier in the century.

If Eliot was ethereal, Sandburg was gritty, the poet of the working class, of the robber barons' victims, although there are times when Sandburg seems to be exalting in the raw power of industry more than sympathizing with those who have been oppressed by it.

Eliot was for a year a visiting professor at Harvard, and for a longer period the head of the prestigious English publishing firm of Faber and Faber. Sandburg, before landing a reportorial job with the *Chicago Daily News*, worked as a milk-wagon driver, a farm laborer, a bricklayer, a traveling salesman, a coal-heaver, and both a servant and a porter at different hotels. As a young man he undertook "an exploration of the American frontier as part of the vast procession of hoboes, tramps and bums who sought to find or escape work in the wake of the depression of the 1890s." He would come to describe himself as an "Eternal Hobo."

Sandburg attended three colleges, including the United States Military Academy at West Point, but didn't last at any of them for more than a few months, and would never receive a degree.

But he knew life, life as all too many Americans lived it at the time, and he wrote about it in a distinctive manner, his style as extraordinary as his subject matter. In a poem he never published, he wrote "Study the wilderness under your own hat," and it might have been precisely the aphorism that spurred him on.

In 1920, however, his long face already beginning to settle into its often dour expression and his hair to whiten, he published *Smoke and Steel*. It was a vast sampling of his work that could not have been more different, in either sensibility or topic, from Eliot's. But neither could it have been more similar, in its own way, to the concerns of the year, the reports in the newspapers, the explanation of continuing work stoppages.

> Smoke of a brick-red dust
> Winds on a spiral
> Out of the stacks
>
> For a hidden and glimpsing moon.
> This, said the bar-iron shed to the blooming mill,
> This is the slang of coal and steel.
> The day-gang hands it to the night gang,
> The night gang hands it back.
>
> Stammer at the slang of this—
> Let us understand half of it.
>
> In the rolling mills and sheet mills,
> In the harr and boom of the blast fires,
> The smoke changes its shadow
>
> And men change their shadow;
> A nigger, a wop, a bohunk changes.

But Sandburg was a remarkably versatile poet, much more so than he is given credit for, and *Smoke and Steel* is a collection of almost impossible diversity. Biographer Penelope Niven tells us that it included "reflections on the aftermath of war. There were lyrical affirmations of family and home in poems for [his wife] Paula and the children. He wrote of peach blossoms, birds, the landscapes he loved, and of prophecy for his daughters."

One of the latter was called, simply, "Helga."

> The wishes on this child's mouth
> Came like snow on marsh cranberries;
> The tamarack kept something for her;
> The wind is ready to help her shoes.
> The north has loved her; she will be
> A grandmother feeding geese on frosty
> Mornings; she will understand
> Early snow on the cranberries
> Better and better then.

The wilderness under Sandburg's hat was terrain that he alone knew. One wonders how he would react if reached at a séance and told that, among the buildings and institutions named after him posthumously, in addition to schools and a library, archives and a commemorative stamp, there is, in his hometown of Galesburg, Illinois, the Sandburg Mall on W. Carl Sandburg Drive.

Perhaps he would have smiled. "He was hailed as the poet of the future," biographer Niven wrote, "the poet of America," and what could have symbolized so well the American future when Sandburg was at the top of his game than a shopping center?

THE MOST RADICAL OF THE new literature might have been written for the stage, and no one wrote it, either in volume, verbosity, or passion, like Eugene O'Neill. Providing the American theatre with some of its most memorable evenings, he was also responsible for some of its longest. In the latter case, the results affected millions of people, not necessarily theatergoers, and are still affecting them more than eighty years later.

In 1928, O'Neill won one of his four Pulitzer Prizes for *Strange Interlude*, a nine-act epic about abortion and adultery and various other matters that ran for more than four hours. A mere intermission would not do for a play of this duration and emotional intensity; instead, O'Neill provided a dinner break.

Early in the thirties, a troupe of actors performed the play in a space they had recently leased in Quincy, Massachusetts. Across the street was the only place close enough to the new theatre for audience members to dine and still return to their seats in time for the play's later innings. It was "a curious restaurant," William Manchester wrote, "with a bright orange roof and pseudo Colonial architecture," and, with the owner more than $40,000 in debt, was on the verge of bankruptcy when *Strange Interlude* opened. It was the only restaurant the man owned, the only business about which he cared or knew anything. He was panicked when he considered what lay ahead.

The play, however, was an enormous hit, perhaps more than it had been in any previous production, and because of that, so too was the restaurant. It served hundreds of theatergoers for six nights and one matinee a week, and many of them, pleased with the fare and the prices, told their friends. As a result, the restaurant continued to thrive even after the play closed, and with the evenings not so busy, it began to attract a lunch crowd as well. The owner, a man named Howard Johnson, had Eugene O'Neill to thank not only for saving his business in Quincy, but for enabling it to become one of the first successful eatery franchises in the United States. In 1965, HoJo's, as it was called, sold more food than McDonald's, Burger King, and Kentucky Fried Chicken combined. By the late 1970s, the HoJo name was attached to a thousand restaurants and five hundred motor lodges. *Strange Interlude*'s long interlude had created an empire.

BORN IN 1888, HOWARD JOHNSON's inadvertent benefactor was the son of a drug-addicted mother and her husband, James, known primarily for his starring role in second-rate road show productions of *The Count of Monte Cristo*. In fact, for the first seven years of his life, O'Neill was often dragged along with his father, who sometimes played a theatre for a week, sometimes was booked for only a one-night stand. The child and his father and nanny endured "the ceaseless succession of railroad trips and poor hotels. . . . They never stayed anywhere long enough for a little boy to find a playmate." Unlike Christie, he did not develop imaginary friends; rather, he began to store up real grievances.

The playwright's father was an alcoholic, and as O'Neill grew older he began to follow the same path, showing the same instability of character, the same kind of self-destructive thirst. Writes historian Page Smith, O'Neill "was a heavy drinker; he was nicknamed Ego by his Princeton classmates because of his preoccupation with his own states of mind. A few months [after his marriage] he set out on a gold-mining expedition to Honduras. . . . A son was born in his absence. His wife obtained a divorce, and O'Neill never saw his son until the boy was eleven years old."

For no particular reason, O'Neill later took passage on a Norwegian vessel bound for Buenos Aires, where "he worked briefly for the Singer Sewing Machine Company, acquiring, in the process, a lifelong distaste for machines."

Back in the United States, O'Neill continued drinking, reaching new excesses, and at the same time began to absorb the dark new writings of novelists like Jack London and Joseph Conrad. These were the influences for his early plays, which he probably started writing in 1914, at the age of twenty-six. Two years later, supposedly with a trunk full of his work, none of which had ever been performed, he arrived at the Cape Cod theatre of the Provincetown Players. His first play to be produced was also the first one he pulled randomly out of the trunk to be read aloud. The one-act *Bound East for Cardiff* was presented in Provincetown when O'Neill was twenty-eight.

In 1920, two of his plays were staged in New York, to enviable results. *The Emperor Jones*, with an all-black cast, "was based on a story that O'Neill had heard in a bar about a Haitian . . . who, convinced that he could be killed only by a silver bullet, had seized and held power in Haiti for six months." In O'Neill's more mystical version, set in the jungle of an unidentified equatorial nation, the playwright's description of the setting tells all that one needs to know about the mood of the performance. "Only when the eye becomes accustomed to the gloom," O'Neill wrote, "can the outlines of separate trunks of the nearest trees be made out, enormous pillars of deeper blackness. A somber monotone of wind lost in the leaves moans in the air. Yet this sound serves but to intensify the impression of the forest's relentless immobility, to form a background throwing into relief its brooding, implacable silence."

The play is oddly constructed. There are eight scenes, and in all but the first and the last, Emperor Brutus Jones, previously a Pullman porter trying to outrun a murder charge, is the only character who speaks. In the background is the pounding of drums, an ominous sound that Jones interprets as the signal of his impending death.

In the first and last scenes, a white trader named Smithers, a man of dubious probity, is featured. As the play nears an end, Smithers is seen talking to rebels who have set out to kill the emperor. The assassination is accomplished by means of a silver bullet, although it might also be said that Emperor Jones was, in reality, "overthrown by his own fear and madness." O'Neill's play, raved the *New York Times* critic Alexander Woollcott, was a "striking and dramatic study of panic fear." He might also have added racism. Although decidedly not a racist himself, O'Neill portrayed the trait so effectively in some of his characters that actor Charles Gilpin, one of the few black stage stars of his time, was dropped from the London cast for objecting to the play's bigotry of language.

O'Neill's other 1920 opus, produced earlier in the year, was his first full-length work and, in his opinion, "a simon pure uncompromising American tragedy." According to historian Geoffrey Perrett, *Beyond the Horizon* had "little plot, no melodrama, no surprises. It was naturalistic, and starkly tragic." What the play *did* have, however, was a classical denseness of language new to the contemporary stage, its haunting overtones harkening back to the ancient Greeks.

The Mayo brothers are both in love with the same woman, Ruth Atkins. But Robert, the younger brother, is also in love with faraway places and the shipboard journeys necessary to reach them. "Supposing I was to tell you," he says at one point, "that it's just Beauty that's calling me, the beauty of the far off and unknown, the mystery and spell of the East which lures me in the books I've read, the need of the freedom of great wide spaces, the joy of wandering on and on—in quest of the secret which is hidden over there beyond the horizon."

But it was not the beauty of the far-off and unknown that eventually attracted Robert so much as it was Ruth Atkins. In winning her heart, though, he gives up his dream, deciding he will not go to sea after all but, rather, will stay with Ruth on the family farm, which has been driving both brothers to poverty and madness. Under these circumstances, Andrew, the older sibling, decides he can no longer stay with Robert, and it is he, the loser in love, who adopts his brother's dream and becomes the sailor. Later, however, we learn that Ruth has loved Andrew all along, causing Robert to rage at her, calling her, among other things, a "slut," almost surely the first time that word had been heard by a New York theatrical audience.

"In its time," declare Arthur and Barbara Gelb in a biography of O'Neill and his father, *"Beyond the Horizon* was perceived as a play of such tragic sweep and grandeur that it dwarfed the efforts of American playwrights who had come before." Or, as the *Times*'s Woollcott put it, the play was "so full of meat that it makes most of the remaining fare seem like the merest of meringue."

O'Neill was surprised that the reviews were so favorable. He had been dubious. On opening night, he "hid nervously behind a pillar to avoid recognition. The audience was unsure what to make of the play." Yet the play ran for 111 performances, a surprisingly strong showing for so different a theatrical experience.

O'Neill was asked once to explain why he wrote such dramas as *The Emperor Jones* and *Beyond the Horizon* with characters embittered and angry, failing and grasping for rescue from the merest of threads; after all, he was to write more than thirty plays in his career, and only one, *Ah, Wilderness!*, was a comedy. O'Neill's reply was brief, and many thought it perverse; inevitably, it told as much about the man as it did about his art.

> I have an innate feeling of exultance of tragedy. The tragedy of Man is perhaps the only significant thing about him. . . . What I am after is to get an audience to leave the theatre with an exultant feeling from seeing somebody on the stage facing life, fighting against the eternal odds, not conquering, but perhaps inevitably being conquered. The individual life is made significant just by the struggle.

Beyond the Horizon was the first of O'Neill's dramas to win the Pulitzer, and later he and Eliot would also win Nobel prizes. O'Neill was the first American playwright to be so honored, and at the present time he is still the only one.

Anarchy, as it turned out, had more than one form, and it was in 1920 that the written arts gave the term a new definition.

THE MOST SUPERFICIAL LITERATURE OF the decade, and some of the most popular among those who could not bear the ever-spreading gloom of the lost generation in their reading and viewing, was not really literature at all. Yes, the playwright Marc Connelly would win the Pulitzer Prize in 1930; and yes, George S. Kaufman, the Neil Simon of his era, would also win Pulitzers for the stage in 1932 and 1937; and yes, Harold Ross would create the undeniably sophisticated *New Yorker* in 1925. But the ayes do not have it; the more substantive achievements of these men and others of their informal association were too far in the future. For now, they were primarily self-promoters, and had found an ideal forum for the greater renown that awaited.

Starting in late 1919, Connelly, Kaufman, and Ross would lunch daily at the Algonquin Hotel with newspaper and magazine writers Robert Benchley, Alexander Woollcott, Dorothy Parker, Alice Duer Miller, Heywood Broun; newspaper editor Herbert Bayard Swope; actresses Tallulah Bankhead and Margalo Gillmore; and Harpo Marx, who, with his movie career ahead of him at this point, actually spoke as he ate. And there were more; all together, believes Benchley biographer Billy Altman, charter members of the so-called Round Table, or, as they preferred to be known, the Vicious Circle, numbered about two dozen. Their goal was the witticism, the memorable one-liner, the crisply lethal putdown, which another of their group, Franklin Pierce Adams, more commonly known as FPA, would include in Saturday's "Conning Tower," his popular column in the *New York Tribune*. He was thereby "illuminating," wrote Kaufman's frequent collaborator, the playwright Moss Hart, at a later date, "not only the world of the theatre, but the world of wit and laughter as well."

The quips in Adams's column would be discussed as avidly as later generations would discuss Johnny Carson's monologue of the previous night.

And, like the *Tonight Show* bon mots, FPA's collection of Algonquinite quotes bestowed a certain cachet not only on those who uttered them, but on those who knew and could discuss them. Also known as the "Diary of Our Own Samuel Pepys," the column was must-see reading.

By 1920, the jesters of the Algonquin were all the rage in New York. Their verbal riffs seemed especially in tune with the rapid-fire exertions of jazz, as opposed to the complexity in language of such as O'Neill and Eliot, language that was virtually symphonic in presentation if usually desolate in meaning.

According to Kaufman biographer Scott Meredith, the Algonquin lunchers were "nearly all famous members of New York's smart set, even though some of them had not yet written or appeared in anything of prominence—and a few never did." Yet, claims the website Quotes Galore, the Algonquinites were cited more than any other assemblage of Americans in history, with the possible exception of deceased presidents. It sounds dubious to me but may, at least for a brief period in the early twenties, have been true.

To Ben Yagoda, on the other hand, it all makes perfect sense. In his history of *The New Yorker*, published in 2000, he writes that "[*New Yorker* art critic Murdock] Pemberton and [free-lance publicist John Peter] Toohey, would feed the members' quips to columnists for whom there wasn't room at the table, either because the utterers paid them (not likely), or [Algonquin manager] Frank Case paid them (probable), or they just enjoyed placing an item (almost certain). The remarkable result was that this group of several dozen friends and colleagues, none of them at this point outstandingly accomplished, became intimately known to the hundreds of thousands and eventually millions of readers of the public prints."

It was so much in keeping with the nascent values of the celebrity culture. Many of the Round Tablers would, in fact, end up where KDKA's Leo H. Rosenberg had started, on the radio, as panelists on talk shows or humor-based quiz programs. Robert Benchley would even make it to Hollywood, starring in short subjects in which he provided erudite and preposterous discourse on such topics as the sex life of the polyp.

But it was at the large round table in the Algonquin Hotel, the clock having reached the lunch hour, that the jokes first and most prominently

began to fly; that people like Connelly, Kaufman, and Ross sometimes became better known than they would for their more significant
achievements.

For instance . . .

Kaufman, when asked by a press agent how to get the name of his client,
an actress, into the newspapers more often: "Shoot her."

Benchley: "I know I'm drinking myself to a slow death, but then I'm
not in any hurry."

Woollcott: "Every girl should be married to [writer] Charlie MacArthur
at some period of her life."

Parker: "That woman speaks eighteen languages and can't say 'no' in
any of them."

Parker: "I like to have a martini,/Two at the very most./After three
I'm under the table,/After four I'm under my host."

Parker, after aging to the point of becoming bespectacled: "Men seldom
make passes at girls who wear glasses."

It was Dorothy Parker, a married woman who preferred to be called
Mrs. Parker, who emerged as the maven of these carefully scripted, carefully rehearsed ad-libs and spoke what is probably the most famous and
clever Round Table bon mot of them all. It seems that when the Vicious
Circle was playing a game of their own devising called "I Can Give You
a Sentence," someone tossed out the question, "Can anyone use the word
'horticulture' in a sentence?" Parker's reply: "You can lead a horticulture,
but you can't make her think."

Other "I Can Give You a Sentence" classics included Kaufman's "I know
a man who has two daughters, Lizzie and Tillie. Lizzie is all right, but you
have no idea how punctilious." And then there was the modest FPA's own
rare contribution, "We wish you a meretricious and a happy new year."

In her 2013 novel *Farewell, Dorothy Parker*, author Ellen Meister turns
the title character into a modern-day ghost. But Violet Epps, the woman
Mrs. Parker haunts, often finds herself thinking back to the golden days
when the ghost was a creature of flesh and blood and devilish humor. "For
an entire decade," Violet recalls, "the Algonquin Round Table was a pop-
culture phenomenon that came to symbolize the wit and sophistication of
the nation's most cosmopolitan city. And at the center of it was the tiny

woman Tallulah Bankhead had called 'the mistress of the verbal hand grenade,' Dorothy Parker."

The Round Table would not be possible today, would not attract either members or public notice. Perhaps not even a table. But yesterday . . . ah, yesterday, Meister declares, "was a time when Americans were in love with words and enamored of writers."

She is right. In today's post-literate society, though, the word "wit" has lost its cachet. Even in formal settings—between hard covers in bookstores, as feature stories in magazines, on the OpEd pages of prestigious newspapers—wit is often used incorrectly, and true wit is as rare as true perception. Some of the writers in whom at least a number of Americans seem most interested have achieved their status because of the speed with which they can text, tweet, and twitter, two thirds of which I cannot define, much less accomplish.

In 1920, though, the word was not only art in many cases, but was being transformed into a different kind of art from what the world had ever known before—more sarcastic, irreverent, haunting, analytical, mystical, emotionally wrenching, deeply personal. But those who succeeded in their use of the word, those masters of the new art, were changing the definition of the term forever.

THE ALGONQUIN HOTEL REMAINS, AS it has always been, in the center of midtown Manhattan. It has lost its prestige over the decades, but not its business. I passed it on my way to work every Friday morning for ten years, always taking a look inside at what seemed to be cavernous darkness; but seldom was there not someone checking in or out, or at least a bellman or two bustling from reception desk to sidewalk or vice versa, obviously busy at something.

Occasionally I would step into the cavern, the gloominess remaining. I have no idea what the lobby looked like in 1920, but it always felt to me when I stood there as if that could have been the year. The furniture is old-fashioned, the wallpaper and fixtures equally are suggestive of another era, an undercurrent of faint mustiness is noticeable. Or is it just imaginable? But the place is well kept up, and the rooms, like those of other noted New York hotels, rent for hundreds of dollars a night.

The Round Table, however, once placed front and center in the Rose Room by Frank Case, has not been there for a long time. There is a painting, though, that brings back all the memories. The Rose Room is brighter than the lobby, and a large oil painting of the Vicious Circle hangs on the wall with all the prominent people gathered around and enough light to see them with their eyes a-twinkle, eager for their turns to feed the "Conning Tower." First-floor bookcases contain countless volumes by and about Parker, Benchley, Kaufman, and their merry lunchmates. They are covered with glass panes, under lock and key.

Other floors are equally reverential to the past. There are 181 rooms in the hotel, and a one-liner from a long-ago wit has been placed on the door of every one; a guest could as easily say he is in the "horticulture" room as in 322. And each of the hotel's twenty-four suites is named after one of the most famous figures in the Vicious Circle.

Perhaps those who preached a lost generation were right, but the men and women who had been honored with a seat at the Round Table in the twenties chose to ignore such pessimism, believing it served no purpose other than self-indulgence. Let Hemingway write his deliberately stiff and repetitive novels about it. Let Fitzgerald act it out while under the influence. Let O'Neill put it on the stage and send his audiences home draped in morbidity. Those seated at the Round Table didn't care. They would wisecrack their way through the apocalypse. Wit above all.

"The Algonquin Round Table," said Margaret Case Harriman, Frank Case's daughter, "came to the Algonquin Hotel the way lightning strikes a tree, by accident and mutual attraction." But lightning is the briefest of phenomena, and the tree may not long withstand its bolt.

INEVITABLY, THE VICIOUS CIRCLE, BASED on so ephemeral a premise as attaining a few lines in the next day's newspaper, fell apart. Author Edna Ferber, a frequent member and the group's most commercially successful novelist, said that she knew it was over the day she strolled into the hotel after an absence of several months. She expected to sit and chat with her fellow jesters—and instead found a family of tourists at the hallowed table. She asked where they were from. They said "Kansas." Ferber was horrified. *Kansas!* she repeated silently and slunk out of the hotel, hoping not to be recognized. Said Frank Case sadly, "These things don't last forever."

Nor did the friendships formed at the Round Table. With the bond of shared publicity having departed, the jokesters found that they had little to say to one another. They would pass on the street, or in the corridors of *The New Yorker* or some other publication, and nod, say hello, maybe utter a few banalities at each other. Seldom did they rise to the level of repartee. But with few exceptions, the old friends did not snipe at those with whom they used to lunch, did not hold grudges against those whom they believed to be FPA's favorites; they had simply lost their context and, thus, their reason for a deep cordiality. Which, as it turned out, wasn't so deep after all. FPA quickly found other people, other events, to write about, and wrote about them well, in a long and distinguished journalistic career.

YEARS LATER, LONG AFTER DOROTHY Parker had read *Main Street*, seen *Beyond the Horizon*, and heard Aaron Copland, the homosexual Lithuanian Jew, begin to define American classical music with such promising early works as *Keyboard Sonatas 1-3*, the queen of the verbal hand grenade looked back on the Round Table. She could not hide her remorse.

> These were no giants. Think who was writing in those days—Lardner, Fitzgerald, Faulkner and Hemingway. Those were the real giants. The Round Table was just a lot of people telling jokes and telling each other how good they were. Just a bunch of loudmouths showing off, saving their gags for days, waiting for a chance to spring them. There was no truth in anything they said. It was the terrible day of the wisecrack, so there didn't have to be any truth.

But it was also the day, not terrible at all, of the United States, well on its way to becoming a colossus beyond either conjure or compare. In 1900 it had laid 193,000 miles of railroad tracks; by 1920, almost 254,000. In 1900 it had produced 13,200,000 metric tons of pig iron; the 1920 total was 33,500,000. Between 1920 and the Great Depression, which began gradually in 1929, the Gross National Product per capita grew a remarkable 4.2 percent a year, a rate it has never approached since in peacetime. And according to a Voice of America broadcast, "Americans had more steel, food, cloth, and coal than even the richest foreign nations. By 1920, the United States national income was greater than the combined incomes of Britain, France, Germany, Japan, Canada, and seventeen smaller countries. Quite simply, the United States had become the world's greatest economic power."

It had made some of its greatest strides toward that power in 1920, a year when it seemed as if Americans might be returning to the battlefield and that the battlefield might be their own back yards. It had been a year that whimpered as much as it roared, hinting, especially in some of its commodities markets, at the lean era of economic hardship soon to come. It was a year whose most scandalous, violent, and unsettling event, a bomb placed in a wagon hitched to a horse on Wall Street, remained unsolved as the new year approached, its meaning as mysterious as its perpetrators.

Or was it?

CHAPTER SIXTEEN

The "Jass" Age

ATCHMO MIGHT STILL HAVE LIVED in New Orleans, but his music continued to be on the move, as some of his emissaries in Chicago had since departed for New York. They began playing in Greenwich Village. They played in a few places in midtown, which wasn't nearly the wealth-riddled corporate neighborhood it is today. And they played in Harlem, where it seemed the whole world was spinning blissfully off its axis.

Armstrong himself was finally able to spread his new, jazzed-up jazz in 1920, as he took a break from playing his hometown clubs and whorehouses to take lead cornet for the Fate Marable Band on some Mississippi River steamboat excursions. "Fate was a very serious musician," Armstrong later said of the man who taught him how to read music. "He defied anybody to play more difficult than he did. Every musician in New Orleans respected him." Still, the cruises he played with Marable were the first times Armstrong had played so far from home, the boat paddling its way from the Delta to the Mississippi's headwaters in Minnesota. And it was the first time he had played before so many people from different parts of the country.

The boat, the S.S. *Sidney*, rode the currents through ten states, and on quiet nights the music landed on banks where lovers strolled, and wafted inland toward the nearby cities and towns. Sometimes the breezes did not carry that far, but sometimes you could hear it on the outskirts of Minneapolis and next door in St. Paul, where Fitzgerald was writing his short stories that themselves seemed to have a horn wailing in the background. And the Fate Marable Band might have been heard in Dubuque, Iowa; Galena, Illinois; St. Louis; Memphis; and in Natchez and Vicksburg, Mississippi. An ad for the boat advertised the "Best dance music in the United States, 1500 couples can dance on the dance floor at one time."

Armstrong enjoyed his time with Marable, but he knew Chicago was coming, and he was growing impatient. The city on Lake Michigan was for him what the green light at the end of the dock was for Fitzgerald's Jay Gatsby.

He tried not to let his eagerness get the better of him and for the most part succeeded. He knew, as many people told him, that he was too good to be playing in whorehouses and on riverboats, even if Fate Marable was the bandleader. But why make a fuss? This was the way things happened, not only in music but in America's big corporations: Andrew Carnegie, after all, had started off as a telegraph boy at $2.50 a week. Of course, he was only fifteen at the time, while the trumpeter, aging fast, had recently celebrated his nineteenth birthday. When he finally went up north again, it would be a one-way trip, and it would be time for the transfer of power to begin. From Joe "King" Oliver to Louis "Satchmo" Armstrong. As he later said:

> Knowin' that my tone was stronger than his [Oliver's], see, I would never play over [i.e., higher than] Joe. That's the respect I had for him, you know? But if he would have thought of it, he would have let me play the lead. You notice, all these records you hear more harmony . . . Joe's lead is overshadowed.

IN TIME, AND NOT MUCH of it, the twenties would come to be known as "The Jazz Age," with Satchmo on lead cornet and the libretto courtesy of

F. Scott Fitzgerald. Scott Joplin was dead, his previously popular ragtime was dying; some musical historians believe that his music's "ragged"— which is to say syncopated—melodies helped pave the way for the even more innovative sounds of jazz.

The word, like "profiteer," was another new coinage of 1920, at least in polite, white society, where it was roundly scorned and "widely held to be a springboard for drug taking and promiscuity." An article in the *Ladies Home Journal* asked: "Does Jazz Put the Sin in Syncopation?" The answer was in the righteous affirmative.

The derivation of the term is not certain. It may be the product of "a non-musical nineteenth century slang word, jasm, meaning energy, vigour or liveliness." Historian Ethan Mordden, however, believes the word descended from a particular kind of liveliness, that it came "from black patois (to jass: to copulate)." Mordden not only traced the etymology of the word but defined the music as well as anyone could. He wrote that jazz

> as popularly applied broadened out to include just about anything that one heard with a bass fiddle stalking below and a saxophone prancing above, the hot lick of musicians who hoisted "axes" (their word for their instruments). . . . They were soloists, these musicians, gadflies of tone living a code as hit or miss as that of the gangsters. Drugged, alcoholic, down and out when they weren't on the band—they respected only one truce, that of keeping to a steady tempo for the benefit of the dancers. No matter what the intention of a composer or lyricist—no matter how chaste or sophisticated—two seconds into any song they played, every song was jazz. That's how it was. . . . Jazz, it was said, made one lose control, but no: jazz was just something to hear while one lost the control that one was determined to lose anyway.

It was music for the lost generation, as Mordden explains, in that it broke all the rules—a mere two seconds into the tune and it became something different from what anyone had expected, unrelated to either the popular or classical music of the past. Jazz was a dirge with an upbeat. It seemed to stand outside of history, in music's parallel universe.

Yet even those who disdained the very notion of a lost generation, who much preferred jassing to whining, the shadows of the Great War be damned!—even they found the new music irresistible. They could not ignore what they perceived as the infectious, improvisational merriment of the sounds—the energy sometimes so frantic that it seemed the instruments would break into pieces. To them, as to the members of the lost generation, it was the perfect accompaniment to the era, but for an entirely different reason. The former wanted to drown their sorrows in the music; the latter wanted to blast the very notion of sorrow out of existence. Somehow, depending on your vantage point, jazz was capable of doing both.

BUT CHICAGO WOULD NOT REMAIN the capital of jazz for long. It might not even have still been the capital in 1920. The judgment, of course, is subjective, but the capital might in 1920 have been some 790 miles to the east, in Harlem, a city of almost 200,000 black men and women within the five largely white boroughs of New York City, population 5,621,000. Residents of the African-American enclave came from all over the world, running the gamut from high yellow to gleaming ebony. In 1920, the Harlem Renaissance is thought to have officially begun among them, and nothing like it had ever happened before. If the arts were exploding in the United States, Harlem was the epicenter, although geographically it was on the fringe, comprising the northern boundary of Manhattan.

The location had something to do with the musical outburst. John Kouwenhoven, a college professor and specialist in American popular culture, "trying to explain jazz, used an urban metaphor: the city's grid is comparable to jazz's basic 4/4 or 2/4 beat, and the skyscrapers are its solo improvisations . . . Louis Armstrong, Sidney Bechet, Jelly Roll Morton, and many others left Chicago for short or long periods of time to gig with New York bands and artists. . . . What better acoustic chamber could they have had than a city built *of* solid stone and *on* solid stone? (Chicago rests on mud . . .) Sounding much like [jazz musician and composer] Bix Beiderbecke, [New York architect] Raymond Hood pledged not 'to build the same building twice.'"

Marcus Garvey had something to do with it. It was in Harlem that he settled when first coming to the United States, and it was because of him that biographer Elton C. Fax could write about the first day of August 1920:

> Never before had that black community whirled with such excitement as, on the following day, it played host to a parade to end all parades. Marcus Mosiah Garvey, President of the Provisional Republic of Africa and President-General of the Universal Negro Improvement Association, had called his organization's first International Convention.
>
> Fifty thousand black delegates strutted along sun-drenched Lenox Avenue to the syncopated rhythms of twelve bands. Representing twenty-five lands, the marchers hailed from every state in the Union, from the West Indies, Central and South America, and Africa.

Further, believes historian Nathan Miller, it was part of Garvey's insistence on black pride that "Harlem was clean, it was prosperous, it was largely law-abiding. As a unique black city, it was shown off as an example of American democratic success." And, as a result, it attracted not just the top jazz musicians to its nightspots, but audiences both black and white to revel in their innovative performances.

And *Crisis* magazine had something to do with the Harlem Renaissance. Founded by W. E. B. Du Bois, who was also a founder of the National Association for the Advancement of Colored People, the magazine was the first significant forum of its kind. Historian Michael E. Parrish writes that "Du Bois encouraged Langston Hughes, Countee Cullen, Claude McKay, and countless other young black artists, who, lionized by wealthy white patrons, were said to represent the spirit of 'the New Negro,' a somewhat condescending phrase which suggested that African-Americans had never before displayed intellectual distinction."

BUT IT IS MUSIC THAT first comes to mind when one thinks of the Harlem Renaissance, the music that was played at places like Connie's Inn, Small's Paradise, or the Savoy, later to be memorialized in the song "Stompin' at the Savoy"—and the neighbors weren't happy about any of it. According to the *Amsterdam News*, "The idea of taking a residential community and making it the raging hell it is after dark is something that should arrest the attention of even ministers of the gospel." Years later, Edward Kennedy Ellington, known to all as "Duke," would concede the point that Harlem could get noisy late at night, but "there was another part of it that was wonderful. That was the part out of which came so much of the only true American art—jazz music."

The premier Harlem night spot was the Cotton Club, whose principal owner was Owney "The Killer" Madden, perhaps Prohibition's most vicious, soulless gun for hire. But also, somehow, one of its most tasteful impresarios of after-hours entertainment. First purchased in 1920 by the controversial black heavyweight boxing champion Jack Johnson and known then as the Club Deluxe, it passed into Madden's hands three years later. Under "The Killer," it quickly became "synonymous," said entertainer Cab Calloway, "with the greatest Negro entertainment of the twenties and thirties." For four years, beginning in 1927, after rising from the basement of a tiny midtown bistro in 1920, Ellington and his band were the house musicians at Chez Madden, and the Duke stood apart from the crowd before he even sat at the piano. He was "[e]legant, reserved without being stiff, articulate even in his evasions, well mannered to the point of ostentation, elitist despite his populist tendencies."

All of which meant that person and place were a perfect match. "This was no ordinary nightclub," writes Ellington biographer John Edward Hasse. "Printed programs announced the musical songs and sketches and identified the vocal and dance soloists. In time, the programs grew more high toned in their language. One from 1931 noted, 'Entr'acte: Dance to the strains of the incomparable Duke Ellington and His Record Artists.'"

The artists sat on a stage that was made to look like the veranda of a Southern plantation from a century or more earlier. There was even "a backdrop painted with weeping willows and slave quarters." The appropriateness was eerie. For although black faces filled the stage, white faces, and white faces only, comprised the audience at the Cotton Club. Madden and his partners allowed no African-Americans to enter, stationing "brutes at the door" to make sure of it. And Ellington, generally regarded as more a gentleman's gentleman than a black activist, was slow to anger about the policy when Madden's representatives first approached him. Says biographer Hasse:

> However Ellington felt about it, he must have decided that the advantages of working there outweighed the disadvantages. He was always a practical man who maintained his personal dignity and realized when to play the sly fox. After all, the Cotton Club promised a prestigious venue with steady work, good money, new kinds of experiences from which to learn, lots of opportunities for exposure to the press and other influential people, not to mention pretty young women who danced and sang in the show. How could he not accept [Madden's] offer?

But within months of accepting the offer, Ellington began to reach his full bloom as an artist, a man with gifts so unique as a composer and arranger that they are hard to categorize, and crowd appeal so great that he became the leading musical figure of the Harlem Renaissance. As a result, he was able in time to use "his influence to have the owners admit light-complexioned blacks, local black entertainers, and his own mother and father, after they moved to Harlem."

SOME OF THE WHITE CLIENTELE who initially made up the entire audience of the Cotton Club, and partial audiences of other clubs nearby, were Jewish investors who, in 1920, sensed the rise of black culture as it was beginning to stir, and as a result were most responsible for the refurbishing of Harlem, its rise from ghetto to hot spot. It was they, more than anyone else, to whom Garvey owed his gratitude for the neighborhoods he found so appealing. Most of the investors were surely more interested in the return on their money than in increasing prominence for black art, but in the end it didn't matter. In the end the effect was the same.

Most notable among Harlem's Jewish benefactors were members of the Spingarn family, among the greatest of American philanthropists at the time, and whose paterfamilias, the notoriously aloof Joel Elias Spingarn, served for a while as the chairman of the board of the NAACP.

After having lost his bid for a seat in the U.S. House of Representatives as a Republican four years earlier, Spingarn served in 1912 as a delegate to the Progressive Party convention. That was the year when the group was also known as the Bull Moose Party, named after their presidential candidate, Theodore Roosevelt, who claimed he was "feeling like a bull moose" despite having been denied the Republican nomination a month or so earlier. It was also a year in which Spingarn tried to add a statement condemning racial discrimination to the Progressive platform. He failed. A delegate again in 1916, and reading the zeitgeist more pragmatically, he didn't even try. Still, by himself, he succeeded nobly in battling racism.

The other major financier behind the cause of a thriving Harlem was Julius Rosenwald. The head of Sears, Roebuck and Company, his primary philanthropic interest was the establishment of schools for African-American children in the South, to which he donated millions of dollars of matching funds. Rosenwald also contributed more than $5 million to build Chicago's grand Museum of Science and Industry and spent five years as its president. As for his Harlem funding, the exact total is not known, but it too is in the millions.

The result of primarily Jewish funding was that Lenox and Seventh Avenues in Harlem became "the nightclub capital of the world." According to historian Lloyd Morris, "Long after the cascading lights of Times Square had flickered out, these boulevards were ablaze. Lines of taxis and private cars kept driving up to the glaring entrances of the nightclubs. Until nearly dawn the subway kiosks poured crowds on the sidewalks. The legend of Harlem by night—exhilarating and sensuous, throbbing to the beating of drums and the waling [sic] of saxophones, cosmopolitan in its peculiar sophistications—crossed the continent and the ocean."

AMONG THOSE OF SHALLOWER POCKETS than Spingarn and Rosenwald, but whose contributions still proved significant, were many who not only invested their money in Harlem but spent it there several nights a week. Seeking relief from days of unyielding stress on Wall Street, they found it where they had least expected: in the exotic presence of another race and the sultry jazz that always seemed to accompany the dark, elegant women gliding around them, sometimes making eye contact, sometimes not bothering. The men who accompanied them, or just looked longingly at them, were lean and handsome, attired like visiting dignitaries. It might almost have been another country, the night a short vacation in a culturally remote land.

Perhaps the majority of Harlem-frequenting whites were young jivesters and homosexuals, who felt more welcome among the openly gay artists of northern Manhattan, especially the elite writers, than they did anywhere else in New York. They might have to save their money for a night on the town, and it might take a few weeks to do so, but their pleasure in having a place like Harlem in which to dispense it made all the scrimping worthwhile.

If they were lucky, they might have seen Bessie Smith, who made her name in Harlem before she made it even bigger on the radio. Blessed with a voice as powerful as it was versatile, she was to female jazz singers what Louis Armstrong was to male vocalists—as he would occasionally put aside his horn and make that distinctly graveled voice of his into an instrument. The uniqueness of his sound on the trumpet and the sound of his vocal cords made an unparalleled combination.

But the packed audiences would also have been lucky to hear Mamie Smith, no relation. In 1920, most popular music was banal and unmemorable. Among the more successful tunes were "Daddy, You've Been a Mother to Me," "When the Moon Shines on the Moonshine," and "Who Ate Napoleons with Josephine When Bonaparte Was Away,"—and the lack of sophistication in the titles is a perfect complement to the melodies. All of these songs enjoyed brief spurts of popularity before descending to the oblivion that was their fate from the beginning.

But somehow, Mamie Smith, African-American through and through, became the first of her race to find a place on the very top of the charts. Starring in a musical revue in Harlem that summer, she found a spare afternoon to cut a record with her favorite background group, the Jazz Hounds. Their song, "Crazy Blues," is regarded as the first jazz record ever released, instrumental or vocal. It went on sale on August 20 and somehow broke through the morass of hokum melodies and bunkum lyrics to become the top-selling number of the entire year, with more than 100,000 copies eventually being purchased. Not only did the song *not* later pass into oblivion, but in 1994 it was inducted into the Grammy

Hall of Fame. A year later it was chosen to be permanently preserved in the National Recording Registry at the Library of Congress. That it achieved its stature in a year like 1920 was something of a miracle.

Mamie Smith, who would later star in a number of films, sang with restraint, but it was hard-won, and her tones were those of a woman who had been undeniably wronged.

> Now I can read his letters
> I sure can't read his mind
> I thought he's lovin' me
> He's leavin' all the time
> Now I see my poor love was blind.

> Now I got the crazy blues
> Since my baby went away
> I ain't got no time to lose
> I must find him today.

THE FEW PEOPLE WHO WANTED to see Paul Robeson perform in 1920 were not so lucky. He was acting then, not singing, and doing little of the former.

Robeson was one of the first blacks to attend law school at Columbia University, which stands on the southern edge of Harlem. A poor young man, he could afford the tuition only by playing professional football on the weekends: "for the Hammond (Indiana) Pros in 1920, the Akron Pros in 1920 and 1921, and the Milwaukee Badgers in 1922. He was paid between $50 and $200 per game. Although Robeson was one of the pioneer players of the National Football League, his career as a professional football player has been largely ignored by professional-football historians."

But a few months before the 1920 football season began, when the new Harlem YMCA opened, Robeson was asked to take part in the commemoration ceremony, starring in *Simon the Cyrenian*, by Ridgely Torrence, a white man strongly supportive of African-American art. "The play was about an Ethiopian who steps out of a crowd to help a tired and haggard Jesus Christ carry his cross up Calvary Hill to be crucified," writes Eugene H. Robinson, not a biographer of Robeson but a student of his work. "His role in this play was symbolic of his commitment to just causes and to oppressed people the world over, a dominant dimension of his life."

By the time the twenties ended, thanks in part to starring in one of many successful productions of Eugene O'Neill's *The Emperor Jones,* Robeson was on his way to becoming the leading black male performer of his generation, singer as well as actor. In the 1936 film version of *Show Boat,* the classic musical by Jerome Kern and Oscar Hammerstein II, Robeson played the dock worker Joe, who gave audiences of all races chills and heartache when he sang the show's most famously wrenching song, "Ol' Man River." Later, Robeson would record an inferior rendition of the number—in dance tempo, of all things—with Paul Whiteman's Orchestra, which might best be categorized as a group of semi-jazz musicians. For some reason, it was the Robeson version with Whiteman that was inducted into the Grammy Hall of Fame in 2006, two years after "Crazy Love" had arrived. But, under Whiteman's baton, Robeson sounds as if he is singing a soulful cha-cha, assuming there could ever be such a thing.

One of the most extraordinary public figures of the twentieth century, Paul Robeson was as controversial as he was talented. Openly a communist, he insisted that the reason for his affiliation was capitalism's treatment of the African-American. In 1942, he met privately but forcefully with Kenesaw Mountain Landis, the commissioner of major league baseball, a meeting "that ultimately led to Jackie Robinson's breaking down the barrier of Jim Crow and unleashing events that were to change the face of sports—and the nation."

A later meeting with President Truman did not go as well. Robeson demanded anti-lynching laws. Truman replied, in effect, that no one was in a position to make demands to the Chief Executive of the United States, no matter what the cause; and at that point a White House guard was summoned to show Robeson the door. He did not need the escort, departing with head held high, shoulders back, his belief that he was in the right unchallenged.

Robeson held to his politically incorrect positions on the Spanish Civil war, fascism, and imperialism—held to them, insisted on them, spoke out for them. He was not a shouter, not a posturer, and did not need to be; when he spoke, his presence alone was enough to command attention. In the McCarthy era, he would be blacklisted for his politics but remained uncowed, his dignity intact. He was the white man's most looming night-mare: a powerful, talented, and intelligent African-American who would not back down from anyone who stood in the way of his people's progress.

Later, during the most controversial war of the twentieth century, it was Muhammad Ali who became famous, and eventually imprisoned, for refusing military service by saying: "I ain't got no quarrel with them Viet Cong. No Viet Cong ever called me nigger." But thirteen years earlier, in 1954, several years before the Vietnam War began, with French participa-tion rather than American, Robeson had expressed the same sentiment more elegantly. Perhaps it was he who gave Ali the idea. "Shall Negro sharecroppers from Mississippi," Robeson asked, "be sent to shoot down brown-skinned peasants in Vietnam—to serve the interests of those who oppose Negro liberation at home and colonial freedom abroad?"

Even though he died in 1976, Robeson continues to be punished for his intransigence, his role in the history books continually diminished even though there has never been anyone like him in our nation: a superb athlete who played baseball and basketball in college as well as football; a glorious singer; a skilled actor in both light and serious roles, yet never accepting a role that made the black man a caricature; a trained lawyer; and a leading man in the fields of racial and political reform. At the height of American segregation, one of the country's few "Renaissance" men was black.

NO LESS ENDURING THAN THE music of the Harlem Renaissance has been the writing, in which such authors as Zora Neale Hurston, Arna Bontemps, Walter White, Claude McKay, Countee Cullen, and Langston Hughes, among others, did precisely what the white man and woman of letters were doing at the same time: remaking their literature. They produced work that was bolder, more personal, and more voluminous than it used to be. And, in their case, more distinctly African-American. But it was a white man, and an unlikely one at that, who played a major role, often unac-knowledged, in legitimizing the black literary sensibility of the twenties.

H. L. Mencken, who frequently gave off the scent of anti-Semitism while including many Jews among his closest friends, was similarly contradictory about African-Americans. Those biographers of Mencken who defend his attitude toward blacks, despite the many racist comments he uttered in his lifetime, adopt a believe-what-he-did-not-what-he-said attitude toward their subject—and what he did was serious, sleeves-rolled-up, suspenders-yanked-off-the-shoulders editing and advising. "Long before *Native Son* established Richard Wright as a Pulitzer prize-winning author," writes Mencken scholar Marion Elizabeth Rodgers, "he had discovered what members of the Harlem Renaissance, already in full swing by 1926, had recognized for themselves: that H. L. Mencken was a force in their own literary movement. That year, [novelist] Carl Van Vechten's best-selling *Nigger Heaven* paid Mencken homage by identifying him as the editor responsible for the success of black literature."

Like all gifted critics, Mencken knew what would happen before it started, because he knew where to look, what to feel; he could sense the growth and energy that would soon be apparent to all; and starting in 1920, when he was editing the fashionable magazine *The Smart Set*, Mencken began to spend more and more of his time encouraging African-American writers and social commentators. Among them was James Weldon Johnson. "Mencken had made a sharper impression on my mind than any American then writing," Johnson later said. "I had never been so fascinated at hearing anyone talk. He talked about literature, about Negro literature, the Negro problem, and Negro music." Johnson said that after his conversation, he felt "buoyed up . . . as though I had taken a mental cocktail."

Perhaps what is most remarkable about Mencken as an editor of African-American prose and poetry was the time he devoted to it, dedicating himself to authors who had never really been able to call themselves that before, men and women who had never previously been published. But a black writer, Mencken believed, had a sense of hope that had grown out of his centuries of sorrow, a view of himself of being integral to the world around him, even a part of it. The white author, according to Mencken, had neither. It was these qualities that he sought to encourage, the sentiment even more than the conventional notions of literary skill.

Mencken, however, had nothing to do with what might be called the magnum opus of the Harlem Renaissance, a collection of essays which in sum were a cultural history, called *The Gift of Black Folk*, by W. E. B. Du Bois, a sociologist and historian who himself might be called the magnum intellect of the Harlem Renaissance. Du Bois was the first African-American to earn a Ph.D. from Harvard, and his scholarship is evident through the more than 350 pages of his book. As is his passion for the black man's contribution to American culture. "The Negro is primarily an artist," he wrote, and then tried to explain, with admitted difficulty, near the book's end.

> Above and beyond all that we have mentioned, perhaps least tangible but just as true, is the peculiar spiritual quality which the Negro has injected into American life and civilization. It is hard to define or characterize it—a certain spiritual joyousness; a sensuous, tropical love of life, in vivid contrast to the cool and cautious New England reason; a slow and dreamful conception of the universe, a drawling and slurring of speech, an intense sensitiveness to spiritual values—all these things and others like them, tell of the imprint of Africa on Europe. There is no gainsaying or explaining away this tremendous influence of the contact of the north and south, of black and white, of Anglo Saxon and Negro.

ANOTHER WHITE MAN WITH A strong yet unlikely relationship to the artistic arousal of African-Americans was T. S. Eliot, or so cultural historian Ann Douglas believes, relating that

> English contemporaries [of Eliot] like Wyndham Lewis and Clive Bell saw [Eliot's 1922 modernist epic] *The Waste Land* as a form of "jazz," and the comparison bespeaks not only a loose use of the word but an important cultural connection. Eliot's hometown, St. Louis, with its large black population and rich Negro musical culture, was in many ways a Southern metropolis, and the young Eliot described his own accent as that of "a Southern boy with a nigger drawl." . . . He once signed himself (on a postcard to Ezra Pound) "Tar Baby." . . . Tom Eliot had dreamed of donning darker guises, of shaping his image by the blackface in the mirror, and he experimented with minstrel personae and language as he was perfecting

his craft in the years after the Great War. [He insisted] that his poetic instrument was not the lute, with its classical and romantic connotations, but the jazz-harmonica of African American music.

To me, this seems evidence of an aberrant wistfulness, if not even perversity, by Eliot the boy more than it does true kinship to the Harlem Renaissance by Eliot the man. In the seventeen years that he edited *The Criterion*, a British literary magazine he founded in 1922, never once did Eliot publish the work of a black American. Seldom, in fact, did he publish an article in support of the Harlem Renaissance or even acknowledge its influence in places outside New York. Mencken, on the other hand, often printed the works of black writers in *The Smart Set* and in a later journal that he co-founded, *American Mercury*.

And such esteemed white writers as Hart Crane, Waldo Frank, and Sherwood Anderson also shared Mencken's attitude. Not only did they support the artistic haven that Harlem had become; they were virtual students of it, especially of Jean Toomer, a male despite his name and one of Harlem's leading poets and novelists. What the three famed white American artists "hoped to get from their friendship with black moderns like Toomer," Douglas tells us, "was the Negro genius for religious feeling, the saving expressiveness that American Calvinism in their view had conspicuously lacked."

For instance, in Jean Toomer's "Conversion":

African guardian of souls,
Drunk with rum,
Feasting on strange cassava,
Yielding to new words and a weak palabra
Of a white-faced, sardonic god—
Grins, cries
Amen,
Shouts hosanna.

Langston Hughes, however, was the most exceptional of the Harlem literati, not to mention the most versatile—a novelist and newspaper columnist, a playwright, and an author of children's books, short stories, and works of nonfiction about the black experience in the United States. But, as if that were not enough, Hughes is best known, and most accomplished, as a poet. At the age of twenty-two, having dropped out of Columbia because he thought it racially prejudiced, he somehow landed a job as personal assistant to the eminent Carter G. Woodson. Hughes was thrilled. Like so many bright young black men, Hughes respected Woodson, admired his work ethic, looked up to his intellectual attainments, and was determined to equal them.

He began assisting Woodson as soon as he was able, less than a month later, with a burst of enthusiasm, a glow of pride.

A few days after that, he quit.

Woodson, although not visibly upset, was surprised. Hughes explained to him that although the work was edifying and Woodson himself an inspiration, the hours were too long, leaving him no time to develop his own writing skills. He told Woodson, with unwavering determination, that he had reached the point in his life at which he needed to concentrate on those skills to the exclusion of all else. Woodson had already seen the artist in Hughes, heard it when Hughes spoke, knew that it must find expression—and so he said he understood. Woodson wished the young man well; they parted with mutual good wishes.

Hughes immediately started looking for other work and had no trouble finding it. It did not, however, have quite the same cachet as the position he had left. In fact, what it had were dirty dishes, half-filled mugs of cold coffee, and napkins balled up and sticky. Within a week or two, Langston Hughes had found employment as a busboy, and he walked happily to and from a less-than-elegant restaurant for his daily duties.

His friends were stunned, disbelieving. *A busboy?* Hughes smiled at their consternation and tried to explain. A position as a busboy made fewer demands on his time. The restaurant was not open in the morning; he arose early and wrote until close to noon. The new job also made fewer demands on his mind: he could clear tables at the same time that he quietly recited lines of verse he would jot down on a notepad in the kitchen when he had a spare moment.

Hughes's earliest poems, not surprisingly, were heavily influenced by jazz. Note, not just the title or even the words, but the short, syncopated lines. "Jazz Band in a Parisian Cabaret," for instance, reads like song lyrics more than conventional poetry.

> Play that thing,
> Jazz band!
> Play it for the lords and ladies,
> For the dukes and counts,
> For the whores and gigolos,
> For the American millionaires,
>
> And the school teachers
> Out for a spree.
> Play it,
> Jazz band!
> You know that tune
> That laughs and cries at the same time.
> You know it.

Similarly, there was "Song for a Banjo Dance."

> Shake your brown feet, honey,
> Shake your brown feet, chile,
> Shake your brown feet, honey,
> Shake 'em swift and wil'—
>
> Get way back, honey,
> Do that rockin' step.
> Slide on over, darling,
> Now! Come out
> With your left.
> Shake your brown feet, honey.
> Shake 'em, honey chile.

Hughes's musically inspired poetry was a phase, his first; he was playing with tempo, not yet confident enough for serious content. Most of the latter came in such collections as *Scottsboro Limited*, *Montage of a Dream Deferred*, and the often inspiring *Let America Be America Again*.

> O, let America be America again—
> The land that never has been yet—
> And yet must be—the land where every man is free.
> The land that's mine—the poor man's, Indians, Negro's, ME—
> Who made America,
> Whose sweat and blood, whose faith and pain,
> Whose hand in the foundry, whose plow in the rain,
> Must bring back our mighty dream again.
> Sure, call me any ugly name you choose—
> The steel of freedom does not stain.
> From those who live like leeches on the people's lives,
> We must take back our land again,
> America! . . .
> Out of the wrack and ruin of our gangster death,
> The rape and rot of graft, and stealth, and lies,
> We, the people must redeem
> The lands, the mines, the plants, the rivers.
> The mountains and the endless plain.
> All, all the stretch of these great green states—
> And make America again!

Countee Cullen, on the other hand, never had a musical phase. A student of the classics, he began his career as a writer by emulating the English poets of centuries past and never stopped, although in time his own voice would emerge from the quiet din of his long-ago mentors. Cullen was Hughes's friend, but his opposite in style. Cullen writes below "On the Mediterranean Sea":

> That weaver of words, the poet who
> First named this sullen sea the blue,
> And left off painting there, he knew

How rash a man would be to try
Precise defining of such a dye
As lurks within this colored spume.
And for retelling little room
He willed to singers yet unborn
But destined later years, at morn,
High noon, twilight, or night to view. . . .

Hughes would never have produced such a piece.

Cullen also wrote a short poem about Sacco and Vanzetti, seeming to sympathize with them, to blame their fate on "a slumbering but awful God." But his shorter poem, another epitaph, this one "For an Anarchist," makes his position more difficult to understand.

What matters that I stormed and swore?
Not Samson with an ass's jaw,
Not through a forest of hair he wore,
Could break death's adamantine law.

THE HARLEM RENAISSANCE TOOK PLACE in academia as well, where its leader was the small, cerebral Alain Locke. A Harvard graduate, he became the first African-American Rhodes scholar, after which he joined the faculty at the all-black Howard University as an assistant professor of literature.

Like Du Bois, Locke would never have been found at a Jim Crow establishment like the Cotton Club. And like Du Bois, Locke would be unhappy with a landmark in American theatre, about which there was much gossip during rehearsals in 1920. Opening the following year, *Shuffle Along* was the first all-black musical revue to claim a Broadway stage. No matter that it ran for 504 performances, and no matter that it made stars out of Paul Robeson and Josephine Baker; both Du Bois and Locke thought *Shuffle Along* perpetuated the most humiliating of racial stereotypes, beginning with the title. It was, after all, written by a white man. Black theatre, Du Bois insisted, should be just that—black, entirely black, starting with the producer and playwright. And even though Noble Sissle and Eubie Blake, both African-Americans, were responsible for

Shuffle Along's music and lyrics, Du Bois believed that they, too, were conforming to stereotypes, giving no indication of the artistic growth of which his people were capable. Locke agreed.

The latter was "a pillar of the Harlem intellectual community, [who] urged African American composers to create 'jazz classics,' not the 'trashy type' of jazz played in clubs and cabarets. Hot jazz and blues would never be viewed as 'great Negro music,' he confidently predicted."

Shortly after taking up residence at Howard, Locke found that he had attracted a groupie in the student Langston Hughes, who had not yet worked for Woodson, not yet begun to bus tables. One summer, Hughes and Locke went to Europe, and the student ended up following the professor everywhere, learning all that he could from his polymathic idol. Locke enjoyed the adoration; it is not every man of his vocation who becomes a Valentino to a student. Historian and researcher David Levering Lewis informs us that

> Locke was as much in his element in Paris as on the Howard campus. He turned the Louvre and the Jeu de Paume into classrooms for Hughes. Seated in the Parc Monceau, his favorite, or strolling through the Luxembourg gardens, discoursing in French with hyper-literate Frenchmen and Francophone colonials, the little professor mesmerized his long-pursued companion with what seemed an incomparable display of learning, urbanity, and empathy. They had a "glorious time," and later in the summer met again in Venice.

When he wasn't enlightening Hughes, Locke was writing some of the most influential essays of the Harlem Renaissance. As historian Lewis notes, Locke "observed that European artists had already been rejuvenated at the African fountain. Pablo Picasso and Georges Braque found in African sculpture the insight that led them into cubism. And sculptors like Constantin Brâncuși and Wilhelm Lehmbruck were liberated through African sculpture to powerful restatements of human form. If they can, why can't we? Locke asked."

ERIC BURNS

It was a few years later, in 1920 or close to it, that a controversial phrase entered the African-American vocabulary: "the new Negro." It was he who was most responsible for the Harlem Renaissance. It was he whose example would inspire and thereby elevate the old Negro. And it was he who must, through his demeanor and accomplishments, lead to the new Caucasian, inspire him to accept the black man as an equal, not just artistically but in all ways.

Did Alain Locke coin the phrase? Probably not; at least, he never claimed to have done so. But he certainly made frequent use of it, as it suited his purposes to perfection. In his widely read essay "Enter the New Negro," Locke first offered a plaint for the scarcity of black culture—"The Negro mind reaches out as yet to nothing but American events, American ideas"—and then followed with a prescient warning about what might happen if the scarcity did not become a plenitude—"The only safeguard for mass relations in the future must be provided in the carefully maintained contacts of the enlightened minorities of both race groups."

The essay was all the talk among enlightened minorities of both races, who believed in carefully maintaining contacts. But they were, as Locke acknowledged, only minorities, and too small in number in 1920 to influence the violence and injustice that lay ahead for the races.

It was partway through a later, equally controversial essay that Locke found it appropriate to quote a few lines of poetry.

We have tomorrow
Bright before us
Like a flame.
Yesterday, a night-gone thing

A sun-down name.
And dawn today

Broad arch above the road we came.
We march!

Langston Hughes could not have been more proud.

AMONG OTHERS, THE NATION'S LEADING philosopher, William James, brother of the novelist Henry, kept an eye on Harlem in 1920, trying to understand the significance of events beyond the obvious. He succeeded to a remarkable extent. In fact, believes Ann Douglas, it might be said that James

> laid the philosophical basis for the American preference for popular culture over elite and self-consciously difficult art, for the choice of culture of politics that gave the Harlem Renaissance its point of origin. His notion of American culture of a plural and heterogeneous affair of simultaneous affects, collaboratively improvised out of what he called "the will to personate," was a viewpoint congenial to black aims and achievements; what the syncopated black ragtime music of the 1890s and 1900s was to Euro-American classical music, the quicksilver and irregular Jamesian discourse was to traditional Western thought.

IT WAS NOT THE GREAT migration of African-Americans from Southern cotton fields to Northern industry that first improved relations between blacks and whites in the United States. It was not the integration of baseball that deserves the credit. Nor was it the *Brown v. Board of Education* decision or Lyndon Johnson's Civil Rights Act a decade later. It was, rather, the black musicians and other artists and thinkers of the Harlem Renaissance and the white audiences who paid ever more attention to what was being sung and played and written that planted the seeds, admittedly slow to grow, for the civil-rights movement—all the way back in 1920. Art was the common denominator between the races: different kinds of art, surely, but causing the same basic impulses, the same tugs of humanity between black and white, the same responses to life at its most basic, the same pumping of juices from head to toe, the same responses to the primitive and the civilized alike. The music, the novels, the poems, the essays—they were the start of it all. The Harlem Renaissance is remembered by too few Americans today, but the feelings that radiated from it are still a monument that stands in the center of our cultural square.

All that is missing is the name of Paul Robeson carved into the base.

CHAPTER ſEVENTEEN

The Flapper

Thε ικονιc image of 1920, however, was a white woman, a vapid young thing with daringly short hair, daringly short skirts, and daringly bold and unladylike habits. Heavy on the lipstick and rouge, light on the self-restraint and traditional manners. And around her neck, perhaps, a long strand of fake pearls that she had tied into a loop, whirling the end of it around in circles like a child's toy as, fueled by bootleg alcohol, she whirled herself around the dance floor, frantic and loose-limbed and uninhibited in her contortions, exerting herself with "a hint of sexual frenzy that many an anxious elder found alarming"—and doing so long into the night.

In real life, she was a presence. As a symbol, she was a delusion. There could be no greater misrepresentation of the year, no greater irony when we think of the troubled, cold-hearted revolutionary period that had now begun, than what so many of us see in the mind's eye when the era is recalled to us.

HAVING WON THE RIGHT TO vote, a number of women believed that they had in the process won the right to redefine the very notion of femininity. Geoffrey Perrett summarizes:

> Before the First World War women were arrested for smoking cigarettes in public, for using profanity, for appearing on public beaches without stockings, for driving automobiles without a man beside them, for wearing outlandish attire (for example, shorts, slacks, men's hats), and for not wearing their corsets. Women accused of such offenses against public order and common decency were summoned before the courts, not only of small towns, but of big cities such as Chicago.
>
> In less than a decade these prosecutions stopped, simply because they seemed as absurd as they were futile.

Also absurd, at least according to some who observed the behavior of women in 1920, were the lengths to which some of them went to pursue a redefining of their societal roles.

"The girl who jumped on to a table at a Harlem nightclub," writes Lucy Moore, "and started swinging her arms wildly above her head as the [music] played was a type of woman America had never seen before. The word 'flapper' described a chick desperately flapping her wings as she tried to fly, although she had not yet grown adult feathers." According to the Oxford English Dictionary, it also described "a young woman, esp. with an implication of flightiness or lack of decorum."

What Moore does not tell us is that the word seems to be of late nineteenth-century British origin and referred to a prostitute.

There was no more obvious, or popular, means for a flapper to lose her decorum publicly than to do the Charleston, one of the most popular dances of the time. In his book *From Harding to Hiroshima*, Barrington Boardman describes the moves.

> Originating with Southern blacks, this fast fox-trot had four hundred different steps, and instructions for the basic moves were as follows: "You have to learn to toe in . . . then stand on

the balls of your feet, pigeon-toed . . . your body swings from side to side . . . the knees knock when they come together . . . make it snappy." Most adults considered the dance overly physical and lacking in grace, and it would be banned by many colleges.

THE OTHER TWO MOST POPULAR dances of the decade, just starting to catch on in 1920, were the Black Bottom, "which involved hopping forward and backward and slapping the rump," and whose name alone was enough to bring a chuckle in Harlem and to be considered a breach of etiquette elsewhere; and, second, the Varsity Drag, more of an upper-class Caucasian specialty. Sometimes a young woman might find herself spinning so crazily to the latter that, although she could not actually flap her wings, she *could* flap her skirt—in some cases part way up the thigh!

> Everyone!
> Down on your heels
> Up on your toes
> Stay after school
> Learn how it goes
> Everybody does the varsity drag! . . .
>
> Babe:
> It's hotter than hot!
> Newer than new!
> Meaner than mean!
> Bluer than blue
> Gets as much applause as waving the flag!

It was madness, claimed the many who were offended by the new American woman, freedom run amok—and not the kind of actions truly representative of the era, nor the kind of actions representative of most of the era's young women, who comported themselves just like their mothers and older sisters did. It was true: flappers were a minority of the female population. But in their eye-popping aberrations, they hoped to catch the eye of a wealthy young man watching from the back of the speakeasy. Or, if not that, perhaps they would catch the lens of a photographer who, even back then, could not resist one of journalism's fundamental principles: blowing the atypical out of proportion to attract readers and viewers. Unfortunately, too many historians, relying on these photographs and accompanying news reports as firsthand sources, began the long, gradual process of distorting the truth of the year. The extraordinary became the norm, the norm too dull to be newsworthy.

Many of these footloose women were loose in other ways as well. They had already been drinking with men; now they went further. The title character in Willa Cather's *A Lost Lady*, Marian Forrester, could hardly believe it, expressing her bewilderment to a young male admirer:

> "And tell me, Niel, do women really smoke after dinner now with the men, nice women? I shouldn't like it. It's all very well for actresses, but women can't be attractive if they do everything men do."
>
> "I think just now it's the fashion for women to make them-selves comfortable before anything else."
>
> Mrs. Forrester glanced at him as if he had said something shocking. . . . "Don't men like women to be different from themselves? They used to."

It had nothing to do with what men wanted: at issue was what *women* wanted. And as Perrett previously pointed out, they were no longer being arrested for public displays of puffery. In fact, "There was a huge increase in the number of female cigarette smokers," so much so that cigarette manufacturers were turning out *sixteen times* as many of their products in 1920 as they had in 1900. The reason, overwhelmingly, was the newly enfranchised voter.

After writing the preceding in *The Smoke of the Gods: A Social History of Tobacco*, I cited the work of psychoanalyst A. A. Brill, who came to a conclusion that he summarized as follows: "More women now do the same work as men do [the result of their having taken over previously male-dominated jobs during the war]. Many women bear no children; those who do bear have fewer children. Feminine traits are masked. Cigarettes, which are equated with men, become torches of freedom. Then, perhaps catching himself, realizing that he sounded insufficiently Freudian for the era, he shifted gears. 'Smoking,' he said, 'is a sublimation of oral eroticism; holding a cigarette in the mouth excites the oral zone.'"

In her book *Cigarette Wars*, Cassandra Tate not only agrees with Brill, but is more explicit:

> Particularly when smoked by women, cigarettes seemed to unleash a disquieting sexuality. Although there is an element of sensuousness in the use of any kind of tobacco (the mouth and hands being intimately involved whether it is chewed, snuffed, or smoked in pipes, cigars, or cigarettes), the effect seems more pronounced with cigarettes. Perhaps this has something to do with the frequency with which cigarettes are brought to the mouth, with the smoke being deeply inhaled, suggesting a titillating degree of intimacy.

MRS. FORRESTER, WHO LIVED IN the relative isolation of a small town in the Midwest, would have been even more shocked had she seen how some young women in New York were attiring themselves. Author Bill Bryson writes: "The amount of fabric in the average dress, it was calculated, fell from almost twenty yards before the war to a wispy seven after." It hardly seems possible. Especially when one can also read, from journalist Frederick Lewis Allen, that by the time the decade had reached its later years, "young women had reduced the yardage of their garments by one-half." If both surmises are true, which is unlikely, the onset of the Great Depression very nearly coincided with the invention of the G-string.

Nonetheless, it *is* true that a minority of women now dressed, at least for evenings in Harlem nightclubs and other such recreations, with "breathtaking skimpiness." In this way and others, from overly rouged cheeks to flesh-colored stockings, which from a distance seemed to be no stockings at all, they were advertising more access to themselves than they had ever done before: permitting hugs, kisses, even the ultimate in access: sexual intercourse without sanction of marriage.

Were such displays of redefined femininity inevitable? Probably. Women had worn the yoke of the male ever since the first human beings had organized themselves into communities. Were the displays inevitable in the United States in 1920? Just as probably, and not solely because of the Nineteenth Amendment. Margaret Sanger might not have opened her first birth-control clinic yet, but her public insistence on a woman's right to make all decisions related to her body had echoed throughout their intended audience for more than half a decade now. If a woman wanted to take cigarette smoke into her body, it was her right. If she wanted to clothe her body scantily, it was her right. If she wanted either to give birth or protect herself from such a possibility, she was yet again within her rights. Or so she believed, and so she behaved, for the first time ever, despite opposition in varying degrees to these freedoms, opposition that exists to the present time.

It was not what the Misses Stanton, Mott, Stone, and Anthony had had in mind when they labored so hard, so long ago, for female equality.

AND, AS IT TURNED OUT, the Roaring Twenties was not the decade that anyone had in mind when he or she looked ahead after the Great War, nor the period that future generations imagine when they look back through the distorted lens of popular culture. The flappers are a kind of footnote in this book because that is precisely what they were in their time, a time more desperate than carefree, more unjust than equitable, more punishing than leisurely, more revolutionary than placid, more worrisome than confident, more threatening than assured.

But it was also a time of excitement, excess, and enthusiasm, sudden leaps in the national blood pressure, fanaticism over distractions in an era in which so much happened from which Americans needed distraction. That the Red Sox had made a mistake in selling Babe Ruth to the Yankees was evident several months after the transaction, as he accumulated statistics in 1920 that read like fantasies or misprints; his 54 home runs, for example, were more than fourteen of the other fifteen major league *teams* amassed that year and broke the existing record (his own record, by the way) by 25. Ruth also drove in 137 runs, batted an eye-popping .376, and single-handedly saved a sport that had been mired in the ignominy of the so-called Black Sox scandal only the year before. The Curse of the Bambino, which would supposedly prevent Boston from winning the World Series again for 86 years, was under way.

But Ruth was not alone in fevering the popular culture. Jack Dempsey beat the bruising Frenchman Georges Carpentier in the first million-dollar heavyweight prize fight; the Book-of-the-Month Club was founded and became an immediate success; crossword puzzles turned into a national rage, as did the Chinese table game of mah jongg, in which the players manipulated 144 tiles instead of 52 playing cards. Americans were fascinated by pointlessness: flagpole sitters sat as still as Buddhas on their elevated platforms; marathon dancers were just barely moving after dragging themselves across the dance floor as long as they could, in some cases for several days with minimal breaks; and six-day bicycle races also became an inexplicable attraction for both rider and viewer.

Said the Broadway star Billie Burke, "The Roaring Twenties were very pleasant if you did not stop to think." Most people didn't stop to think. And still don't, as they look back.

If they did, they would see not just the pervasiveness of hardship throughout the decade, but the horrible prelude it proved to be—for at its opposite end, there was a different kind of explosion on Wall Street. The stock market crashed, and much of the United States crashed along with it. The value of investments dropped like never before, never since; the term "Depression" described not just the ruination of financial accounts, but the attitude of an entire nation, so many people so painfully victimized by a lack of income and, with it, a lack of opportunity. The New Deal helped, but it took another Great War, after yet another decade, to jump-start economic growth again. Ten years, it might have been, from Prohibition to stock-market crash, but they held a century's worth of turmoil and jubilation, irrationality and intrigue, optimism and injustice.

It all began in 1920.

EPILOGUE

L UIGI GALLEANI, WROTE PAUL AVRICH in 1990, "has fallen into oblivion. Today he is virtually unknown in the United States outside a small circle of scholars and a number of personal associates and disciples, whose ranks are rapidly dwindling. No biography in English has been devoted to him, nor is he so much as mentioned in most general histories of anarchism or in the comprehensive survey of American anarchism by William Reichert."

Yet, in his time, Galleani was the anarchist whose influence both A. Mitchell Palmer and William J. Flynn feared above that of all others. He had established such a track record of terrorism before arriving in the United States that the nations in which he settled seemed to feel more comfortable deporting him than imprisoning him. Behind bars, after all, he was an incentive for his fellow anarchists to attempt to free him, or, if that did not work, to seek reprisal through acts of violence. Deportation meant he was somebody else's problem.

For organizing a demonstration of students in Switzerland in 1887, Galleani was dispatched to France, which later forwarded him home again to Italy, which seemed stuck with him. The Italian courts found him guilty of conspiracy and sentenced him to five years in prison. But he escaped and fled to London. It was from there that he booked passage to the United States, arriving as a forty-year-old in 1901.

He wasted no time in trying to advance his cause. When silk workers in Paterson, New Jersey, went on strike, Galleani set out immediately for the factory town to speak on their behalf. By all accounts, he was fiery, eloquent, dramatic; the crowd that had gathered to hear him grew in both size and intensity as he raised his animus against capitalism to a crescendo. It was at this point, with the Paterson police believing that the mob was threatening to storm the factory and wreak vengeance against those who had continued to work inside, that they opened fire on the insurgents. One of the bullets struck Galleani in the face, but he survived with no more permanent damage than slight scarring. Arrested for inciting the riot, he managed yet another escape, this time fleeing to Canada, his life on the run continuing, but the pace picking up now as law enforcers in packs closed in.

Eventually he sneaked back into the United States and, taking up residence in the quarrying community of Barre, Vermont, became the editor of the largest Italian-language anarchist newspaper in the country, *Cronaca Sovversia (Subversive Chronicle)*. The Great War was raging at the time and America had finally become a combatant; aliens were not eligible to serve but nonetheless had to register. Galleani was livid, and historian Paul Avrich paraphrases the article that Galleani wrote about it for his paper. "Once you register, the authorities will have you on their rolls; they will know where to find you should they want you. Compulsory registration, he argued, violated the Thirteenth Amendment to the Constitution, which prohibits 'involuntary servitude.' You need not collaborate with the warmongers, he declared. If you refuse to register in the thousands, the authorities will be hard put to arrest you."

Before authorities shut down *Cronaca Sovversia* in 1918, fifteen years after its first issue, Galleani had published even more incendiary material, including several ads for a booklet that contained instructions for making nitroglycerine.

But it was as an orator, not a publisher, that he made his greatest mark. "You heard Galleani speak," said Carlo Buda, an anarchist who had done so, "and you were ready to shoot the first policeman you saw!" And from another: "I have never heard an orator more powerful than Luigi Galleani. . . . His voice is full of warmth, his glance alive and penetrating, his gestures of exceptional vigor and flawless distinction."

The spoken word mattered to radicals like these men. "Attending lectures was another popular activity among the Italian anarchists," Avrich tells us, "and especially the lectures of Galleani, whom they prized above all other speakers."

In September 1919, Galleani came out of hiding briefly to demonstrate his vocal gifts to fellow subversives in Taunton, Massachusetts. So inspired were they by his words that four of them immediately began work on a bomb, which they planned to drive to the American Woolen Company's mill in the nearby town of Franklin. Workers there were striking, and the Galleanisti, as they were known, wanted to show their support. They did, in a manner of speaking, but not according to plan. The bomb exploded, all right, but in transit, not in the mill. All four anarchists were killed. Their support was noted and the strike kept on.

Police tracked Galleani from Taunton and this time caught him. But rather that having him stand trial on any of numerous charges that merited a hearing, U.S. officials inexplicably joined in the game of "hot potato" that Europeans had been playing with him. Galleani and eight of his cohorts were expelled from the United States and returned to Italy, where he served fourteen months in prison for sedition. Never again did he depart from his homeland.

His followers in the United States, however, did not need his presence to remain fervid about his principles. In Italy, after being released from prison, he continued his seditious activity, continued to write, urging on the working man, making his case for violence, his language becoming no less fiery with age or distance. His pamphlets and copies of his speeches were smuggled into America by the anarchists who continued to pass through the gates of Ellis Island, and the words were as often as possible converted into propaganda of the deed—the letter bombs, for example, that were mailed to prominent American citizens in 1919, the impetus for the first of the Palmer raids.

Also, with time, American authorities came to believe that the attack on Wall Street on September 16, 1920, the attack that killed more than forty Americans and wounded at least 140 others, was also the work of the

Galleanisti. In fact, they were certain that one man was responsible for both making the bomb and positioning the wagon in front of the Morgan Bank, and although they could not prove it, they were no less certain of the man's identity.

Other than that he was Carlo Buda's brother, little is known of Mario Buda. He subscribed to *Cronaca Sovversia*, often made donations to it, admired Galleani as if he were a messiah. Whenever he could, he attended Galleani's lectures, arriving mesmerized, departing with a vow to take action. A short, compact man, by mid-adulthood his hairline had receded from the tip of his forehead to the crown of his head. His cheeks were lined, slightly sunken; and a mustache spread a short distance across his upper lip. It is a description that fits many, although not all, of the eyewitness accounts of the man who fled from the wagon minutes before it erupted in flame.

Prior to that, the BOI had been keeping a close eye on Buda. Apparently, though, not close enough. Some investigators believed that he played a role of some sort in the South Braintree robbery for which Sacco and Vanzetti were arrested and later both sanctified and executed. Others went so far as to suspect that Buda, Sacco, and Vanzetti were the leaders of the 1919 bombing wave.

Sacco and Vanzetti were indicted for the payroll robbery on September 11, 1920, and, according to the scenarios linking the three men, Buda, fearing that he might soon be joining his friends behind bars, went into hiding. But he was not seeking shelter so much as a private place to plot his revenge. He could not allow his two friends to be incarcerated or, should it come to that, executed without a sign of protest. "After selecting a target," writes Susan Gage, "he made his way to New York, where he assembled the horse, wagon, and bomb materials. After depositing his load on Wall Street the morning of September sixteenth, he left for Providence, acquired a passport, and fled to Naples," where he would live more than four decades longer than those he was alleged to have murdered. Like Galleani, with whom he surely visited from time to time, he never returned to American shores.

Avrich admits that Buda's identity has not been proven and, at this late stage, never will be. Strangely, incomprehensibly, his name is not recorded anywhere in the Bureau of Investigation's files on the bombing.

But, says Avrich, Buda must be considered the leading suspect. The Wall Street bombing "fits what we know of him and his movements. I have it, moreover, from a reliable source and believe it to be true."

Gage identifies that source as Charles Poggi, a New York waiter and earlier Italian immigrant. Although apparently not a Galleanisti himself, Poggi knew many of them, considered some of them *paisani*, and once told Avrich that Buda's nephew openly bragged about "my uncle's bomb." At this stage, it seems more reasonable to accept Avrich's conclusion than to reject it. There are no holes in his story, and no alternative conclusions that seem nearly as convincing.

MISSING FROM A PROMINENT ROLE in the investigation, which went on for twenty years, was Attorney General A. Mitchell Palmer. By the end of 1920, with the job continuing to wear on him, he still had not fully regained his health, and his reputation was in decline because of his raids and the subsequent harassment of innocents simply because of their foreign birth. His title notwithstanding, he was gradually being forced to the outside of American law enforcement's elite. He had also been left outside the field of potential Republican presidential nominees, with few besides himself taking his candidacy seriously. Soon, the Harding administration would be voted into office, and Palmer would be replaced as attorney general by Harry M. Daugherty.

As for the BOI, behind-the-scenes control was rapidly passing to Palmer's young lieutenant, J. Edgar Hoover, who was just as likely as his nominal boss to harass innocents, but was much more sly and even destructive in his methods. Hoover would wield his control over the agency that replaced the BOI, the Federal Bureau of Investigation, for half a century, always serving the cause of law and order, but not always paying attention to justice.

The same, of course, could be said of Palmer and his methods of reacting to immigrants in 1920. He had always believed that foreigners were behind the Wall Street bombing, and as time went on he narrowed the field to anarchists and then to Italian anarchists. Although his scorch-the-earth methods cannot be condoned, it seems that—after so much time has passed, and with the case file still open somewhere on a dusty shelf at FBI headquarters—his conclusion was the right one after all. However irresponsible his behavior, however passionate his prejudices, A. Mitchell Palmer was one of the few people who knew the truth about the most ominous event in this year that so few people understood at the time and even fewer seem to understand now.

ACKNOWLEDGMENT/

For the past ten years, which is six books out of a total production of ten, Deborah Celia of the Westport, Connecticut Public Library, has been my researcher. Now she has quit on me. Just walked out, turned her back, closed the door behind her. Her cover story is that, after a long and admirable career at the library, she has decided to retire—and I admit it might have a few grains of truth to it. But no matter; I insist on taking her departure personally.

Information-gathering is not as easy as it seems. It sometimes requires creativity as much as diligence; information is not always stashed away where one might think. Debbie, however, has consistently outwitted the stashers, refusing to be thwarted by even the most arcane of filing systems. I have come to believe that facts she cannot find are facts that don't exist, that events she cannot track down are events that didn't occur. God, I'll miss you, Debbie. Then again, you're still going to have a computer with you in Florida, aren't you? Perhaps it isn't over between us yet. I was thinking that maybe you could leave me your phone number, and . . . well, perhaps it would be better if we talked about this privately.

The Westport Public Library, however, has been, and continues to be, much more than a one-woman show. Under the directorship of Maxine

Bleiweis, who manages to be bubbly despite her ceaseless labors, it has become a gem of New England learning and conviviality, an institution like no other of its size in the country. My thanks go to staffers Susan Madeo, who procured hard-to-find volumes for me, and to those at the reference desk, especially Caryn Friedman, Margie Frielich-Den, and Sylvia Schulman, for assistance with this and other books of mine.

Then again, Sylvia has retired, too.

Is it something I said?

I also express my gratitude to the Woman's Christian Temperance Union, KDKA Radio in Pittsburgh, and Planned Parenthood for providing materials accessible nowhere else, never before published. I would like to have offered thanks to the NAACP office in either New York or Washington, but neither had the courtesy to return my numerous phone calls, and thus I could not bring the esteemed Carter G. Woodson as fully to life as I would have liked.

Speaking of bibliographies, Yale University's Beverly Gage did not set out to do me a favor when she wrote *The Day Wall Street Exploded: A Story of America in Its First Age of Terrorism*, but her book was, more than any other volume upon which I relied for *1920*, indispensable. Hers is the definitive book on what may be fairly described as the definitive event of my own volume.

And I must express similar appreciation to Doris Weatherford, who wrote so comprehensively in *A History of the American Suffragist Movement*.

Phil Gaskill was the book's copy editor, and I thank him for his diligence, which resulted in several fewer errors in the finished product. Thus, any errors that remain are entirely Phil's fault, for not having spotted those, too. (Once, just once, I wanted to see an author eschew humility and immaturely blame someone else for mistakes that are entirely his fault. I have taken it upon myself to do so—but not sincerely.)

In a similar vein, I must express my appreciation to Bob Van Der Linden, the chairman of the National Air and Space Museum at the Smithsonian Institution in Washington. Bob provided me with a brief, but much needed, education on aviation in 1920.

Editor and associate publisher Jessica Case, who makes more contributions to her books than anyone else with whom I have ever worked, is a wonder. I believe she offered eight suggestions to improve the manuscript. I considered them diligently. She was right in all eight cases. Then she went on to supervise matters as diverse as secondary rights and publicity, in the latter case with the tireless efforts of Iris Blasi.

My long-time agent, Timothy Seldes, suffered a stroke several years ago, and sold his business, the better to take care of himself. I hope you are taking care of yourself well, Tim, and that you know you are always on my mind as I work.

But, *mirabile dictu*, along comes Linda Konnor. My new agent, Linda does not usually represent volumes of this kind. For deciding to represent this one, and for steering me to Pegasus books, which are distributed by Norton, I will be forever appreciative.

1920: The Year That Made the Decade Roar is my tenth book. I mean no offense to others who performed similar tasks, but the cover design for the book you hold in your hands is my favorite of them all. Thank you, Andrew Smith. And thank you, Maria Fernandez, for the interior design of the volume.

And thank you, Toby Burns. Thank you *so* much, Toby Burns. My son and I were having a steak dinner in Manhattan one night when he asked me the title of my forthcoming book. *"The Year That Made the Decade Roar,"* I said, *"A Surprising History of America in 1920."* He took a few more bites of steak, not looking at me. Then: "Nah," he said, "that's too clunky. How about just . . ." and he spoke the title by which the book has ever after been known. My agent and editor were both so pleased with Toby's suggestion, which I e-mailed them at nine the next morning, that by nine-thirty they had changed my title to his on all of their various working copies.

I also think that, in this "acknowledgments" section, I should acknowledge something about myself. My last name might consist of but a single syllable ending in a consonant, but I am half-Italian, the half that counts. I have spent more time in Italy than in any other country except my own, and while there have listened to men and women speak their native tongue as if it were music. Which, to my ears it is. I do not understand a word they say; I simply listen to the concert of their sounds. My favorite place as a child was the kitchen of my maternal grandmother, Henrietta

Yacovoni, and I was raised on homemade pasta with homemade sauce and homemade bread to wipe the bowls. The scent of her kitchen filled the house and brightened the spirits.

The point of this seeming digression? The fact that so many villains, and suspected villains, in my book are Italians is just that: fact. If I were going to demonstrate bias against any nationality in the preceding, it certainly would not have been against my own *paisani*. But certain numbers of them behaved ignobly in the matters previously considered, and I have had no choice but to report their misbehavior.

And a final note, which I admit is more of a digression than the previous one but irresistible to me nonetheless. Eubie Blake, who with Noble Sissle wrote the music and lyrics for *Shuffle Along*, accomplished far more than that in his career. He was responsible for such standards as the rousing "I'm Just Wild About Harry" and the touching "Memories of You"; and was honored by having those and many more of his tunes collected in the 1978 Broadway musical *Eubie!*. Further, he was presented with at least seven honorary doctorates and the Presidential Medal of Freedom.

And I knew him. Or, more properly, met him. In 1983, as an NBC News correspondent, I was assigned to cover the festivities for his hundredth birthday. My reports appeared on the *Today* show and *NBC Nightly News with Tom Brokaw*. My recollections of the event are dim, but I remember that Blake was fragile—happy, mostly coherent, but fragile. We spent several hours together as my crew set up its gear and we chatted off the record; as the interview was conducted on the record; and as the crew wrapped up and stowed its gear and Eubie and I went back to more informal chatter. The conversation never waned.

I mention this because it is an extraordinary feeling to produce a historical volume set almost a century ago and find myself writing about someone who is not only part of the book but was, for a brief time, part of my life—a man who, in fact, I "knew." I am left with a feeling of sweet eeriness, as if I had been part of 1920 myself.

Such a remarkable year it was!

BIBLIOGRAPHY

Original Documents, Pamphlets, Periodicals
Boston Herald (BH)
Boston Post (BP)
Brooklyn Daily Eagle (BDE)
Collier's Weekly (CW)
Declaration of Sentiments and Resolutions (DSR)
Journal of Economic History, Cambridge University (JEH)
KDKA "History of Broadcasting and KDKA Radio, found in files at Carnegie Library in Pittsburgh (KDKA)
KDKA 65th anniversary CD (KDKA-CD)
League of Nations Covenant (LNC)
Louisville Courier-Journal (LC-J)
The Magazine of Wall Street (MWS)
NAACP brochure about Carter Woodson (NAACP)
New York Times (NYT)
New York Times Magazine (NYTM)
New York World (NYW)
The New Yorker (NY)
Pittsburgh Sun (PS)
Report of the Labor Research Association, prepared by Robert W. Dunn (RLRA)
Saturday Evening Post (SEP)
Wall Street Journal (WSJ)
Woman's Christian Temperance Union educational materials, unpaginated (WCTU)

(Websites are listed under specific references in "Notes" section, which follows.)

Books

Abels, Jules. *In the Time of Silent Cal: A Retrospective History of the 1920's.* New York: Putnam, 1969.

Allen, Frederick Lewis. *The Big Change: America Transforms Itself, 1900–1950.* New York: Harper, 1952.

———. *Only Yesterday: An Informal History of the Nineteen-Twenties.* New York: Harper & Brothers, 1957.

Altman, Billy. *Laughter's Gentle Soul: The Life of Robert Benchley.* New York: W.W. Norton, 1997.

Angle, Paul M. *Crossroads: A Distinguished Historian's Fascinating Account of a Fateful Year in American History.* Chicago: Rand McNally, 1963.

Archer, Jules. *They Had a Dream: The Civil Rights Struggle from Frederick Douglass to Marcus Garvey to Martin Luther King and Malcolm X.* New York: Viking, 1993.

Asinof, Eliot. *1919: American's Loss of Innocence.* New York: Donald J. Fine, 1990.

Avrich, Paul. *Anarchist Portraits.* Princeton, New Jersey: Princeton University Press, 1988.

———. *Sacco and Vanzetti: The Anarchist Background.* Princeton, New Jersey: Princeton University Press, 1996.

Barnouw, Erik. *A History of Broadcasting in the United States, Volume I—to 1933.* New York: Oxford University Press, 1966.

Barr, Andrew. *Drink: A Social History of America.* New York: Carroll & Graf, 1999.

Behr, Edward. *Prohibition: Thirteen Years That Changed America.* New York: Arcade, 1995.

Berg, A. Scott. *Lindbergh.* New York: G.P. Putnam's Sons, 1998.

Bergreen, Laurence. *Louis Armstrong: An Extravagant Life.* New York: Broadway Books, 1997.

Blum, John Morton. *Woodrow Wilson and the Politics of Morality.* Boston: Little, Brown, 1956.

Boardman, Barrington. *Isaac Asimov Presents From Harding to Hiroshima: An Anecdotal History of the United States from 1923-1945.* New York: Dembner, 1988.

Boorstin, Daniel. *The Americans: The National Experience.* Norwalk, Connecticut: Easton Press, 1992.

Bruccoli, Matthew J. *Scott and Ernest: The Fitzgerald-Hemingway Friendship.* New York: Random House, 1978.

Bryson, Bill. *One Summer: America, 1927.* New York: Doubleday, 2013.

Burns, Eric. *The Smoke of the Gods: A Social History of Tobacco.* Philadelphia: Temple University Press, 2007.

———. *The Spirits of America: A Social History of Alcohol.* Philadelphia: Temple University Press, 2004.

Calloway, Cab, and Bryant Rollins. *Of Minnie the Moocher and Me.* New York: Thomas Y. Crowell, 1976.

Cannato, Vincent J. *American Passage: The History of Ellis Island*. New York: Harper, 2009.

Cantor, Norman F. *The American Century: Varieties of Culture in Modern Times*. New York: HarperCollins, 1997.

Carswell, Catherine. *The Savage Pilgrimage: A Narrative of D.H. Lawrence*. Cambridge, England: Cambridge University Press, 1981.

Carter, Paul A. *Another Part of the Twenties*. New York: Columbia University Press, 1977.

Cashman, Sean Dennis. *Prohibition: The Lie of the Land*. New York: Free Press, 1981.

Chernow, Ron. *Titan: The Life of John D. Rockefeller, Sr.* New York: Random House, 1998.

Chesler, Ellen. *Woman of Valor: Margaret Sanger and the Birth Control Movement in America*. New York: Simon & Schuster, 1992.

Clarke, Donald. *The Rise and Fall of Popular Music*. New York: St. Martin's Press, 1995.

Coben, Stanley. *A. Mitchell Palmer: Politician*. New York: Columbia University Press, 1963.

Coffey, Thomas M. *The Long Thirst: Prohibition in America: 1920–1933*. New York: W.W. Norton, 1975.

Collier, Peter, and David Horowitz. *The Fords: An American Epic*. New York: Summit Books, 1987.

Cooper, John Milton, Jr. *Pivotal Decades: The United States, 1900–1920*. New York: W.W. Norton, 1990.

———. *The Warrior and the Priest: Woodrow Wilson and Theodore Roosevelt*. Cambridge, Massachusetts: Belknap Press of Harvard University Press, 1983.

Daniels, Jonathan. *The Time Between the Wars: From the Jazz Age and the Depression to Pearl Harbor*. Garden City, New York: Doubleday, 1966.

Dash, Mike. *The First Family: Terror, Extortion, Murder, and the Birth of the American Mafia*. New York: Random House, 2009.

Davis, Kenneth C. *Don't Know Much About History: Everything You Need to Know About American History but Never Learned*. New York: Crown, 1990.

Douglas, Ann. *Terrible Honesty: Mongrel Manhattan in the 1920s*. New York: Farrar, Straus and Giroux, 1995.

Douglas, Emily Taft. *Margaret Sanger: Pioneer of the Future*. New York: Holt, Rinehart and Winston, 1970.

Du Bois, W.E.B. *The Gift of Black Folk*. Millwood, New York: Kraus-Thompson Organization, 1992.

Dunn, Donald H. *Ponzi! The Boston Swindler*. New York: McGraw Hill, 1975.

Eliot, T.S. *The Complete Poems and Plays*. London: Faber, 2004.

Ellington, Edward Kennedy. *Music Is My Mistress*. Garden City, New York: Doubleday, 1973.

Fax, Elton C. *Garvey: The Story of a Pioneer Black Nationalist*. New York: Dodd, Mead, 1972.

Ferrell, Robert H. *The Strange Deaths of President Harding.* Columbia, Missouri: University of Missouri Press, 1996.

Fitzgerald, F. Scott. *The Great Gatsby.* Norwalk, Connecticut: Easton Press, 1987.

———. *The Last Tycoon.* New York: Charles Scribner's Sons, 1969. (Foreword by Edmund Wilson.)

———. *This Side of Paradise.* Norwalk, Connecticut: Easton Press, 1987.

Flexner, Eleanor. *Century of Struggle: The Women's Rights Movement in the United States.* Cambridge, Massachusetts: The Belknap Press of Harvard University Press, 1959.

Flexner, Eleanor, and Ellen Fitzpatrick. *Century of Struggle: The Woman's Rights Movement in the United States,* expanded edition. Cambridge, Massachusetts: The Belknap Press of Harvard University Press, 1996.

Fox, Stephen. *Blood and Power: Organized Crime in Twentieth-Century America.* New York: Morrow, 1989.

Frewin, Leslie. *The Late Mrs. Dorothy Parker: The First Complete Biography of America's Wittiest Woman.* New York: Macmillan, 1985.

Fuess, Claude M. *Calvin Coolidge: The Man From Vermont.* Fuess Press, 2007.

Furnas, J. C. *Great Times: An Informal Social History of the United States, 1914–1929.* New York: G.P. Putnam's Sons, 1974.

———. *The Life and Times of the Late Demon Rum.* London: W.H. Allen, 1965.

Fussell, Paul. *The Great War and Modern Memory.* London: Oxford University Press, 1975.

Gelb, Arthur, and Barbara Gelb. *O'Neill: Life with Monte Cristo.* New York: Applause, 2000.

Gill, Brendan. *Here at The New Yorker.* New York: Random House, 1975.

Gioia, Ted. *The History of Jazz.* New York: Oxford University Press, 1997.

Goggin, Jacqueline. *Carter G. Woodson: A Life in Black History.* Baton Rouge: Louisiana State University Press, 1993.

Goodall, Howard. *The Story of Music: From Babylon to the Beatles: How Music Has Shaped Civilization.* New York: Pegasus, 2014.

Gordon, Avery F., and Janice Radway. *Ghostly Matters: Haunting and the Sociological Imagination.* Minneapolis: University of Minnesota Press, 1997.

Gordon, Lois, and Alan Gordon. *American Chronicle: Six Decades in American Life, 1920–1980.* New York: Atheneum, 1987.

Gordon, Lyndall. *T. S. Eliot: An Imperfect Life.* New York: W.W. Norton, 1998.

Grant, Colin. *Negro With a Hat: The Rise and Fall of Marcus Garvey.* Oxford, England: Oxford University Press, 2008.

Gray, Madeline. *Margaret Sanger: A Biography of the Champion of Birth Control.* New York: Richard Marek, 1979.

Green, James R. *The World of the Worker: Labor in Twentieth-Century America.* New York: Hill and Wang, 1980.

Greenberg, David. *Calvin Coolidge.* New York: Times Books, 2009.

Gurko, Miriam. *The Ladies of Seneca Falls.* Norwalk, Connecticut: Easton Press, 1990.

Hardy, Thomas. *Tess of the D'Urbervilles.* Norwalk, Connecticut: Easton Press, 1984.

Harris, Stephen L. *Harlem's Hell Fighters: The African American 369th Infantry in World War I.* Washington, D.C.: Brassey's, 2003.

Hart, Moss. *Act One: An Autobiography.* New York: Random House, 1959.

Hasse, John Edward. *Beyond Category: The Life and Genius of Duke Ellington.* New York: Simon & Schuster, 1993.

Hemingway, Ernest. *The Sun Also Rises.* Norwalk, Connecticut: Easton Press, 1990.

Holbrook, Stewart H. *Dreamers of the American Dream.* Garden City, New York: Doubleday, 1957.

Hoover, Herbert. *The Memoirs of Herbert Hoover: The Cabinet and the Presidency: 1920–1933.* New York: MacMillan, 1952.

Horton, James Oliver. *Landmarks of African American History.* New York: Oxford University Press, 2005.

Huggins, Nathan Irvin. *Harlem Renaissance.* New York: Oxford University Press, 2007.

Jackson, Major, ed. *Countee Cullen: Collected Poems.* New York: Library of America, 2013.

Jenkins, Alan. *The Twenties.* New York: Universe Books, 1974.

Josephson, Matthew. *The Robber Barons: The Great American Capitalists, 1861–1901.* Norwalk, Connecticut: Easton Press, 1987.

Kangel, Robert. *The One Best Way: Frederick Winslow Taylor and the Enigma of Efficiency.* New York: Viking, 1997.

Keats, John. *You Might As Well Live: The Life and Times of Dorothy Parker.* New York: Simon and Schuster, 1970.

Klein, Maury. *Rainbow's End: The Crash of 1929.* New York: Oxford University Press, 2001.

Kobler, John. *Ardent Spirits: The Rise and Fall of Prohibition.* New York: G.P. Putnam's Sons, 1973.

Krass, Peter. *Carnegie.* Hoboken, New Jersey: John Wiley & Sons, 2003.

Kyvig, David. *Repealing National Prohibition.* Chicago: University of Chicago Press, 1979.

Lacey, Robert. *Ford: The Men and the Machine.* Boston: Little, Brown, 1986.

Lathem, Edward Connery, ed. *The Poetry of Robert Frost: The Collected Poems.* New York: Henry Holt, 1969.

Lawrence, D. H. *The Rainbow.* New York: The Modern Library, 1943.

———. *Women in Love.* New York: Viking, 1977.

Lee, Henry. *How Dry We Were: Prohibition Revisited.* Englewood Cliffs, New Jersey: Prentice-Hall, 1963.

Lender, Mark Edward, and James Kirby Martin. *Drinking in America: A History.* New York: Free Press, 1982.

Levin, Phyllis Lee. *Edith and Woodrow: The Wilson White House*. New York: Scribner, 2001.

Lewis, David Levering. *When Harlem Was in Vogue*. New York: Penguin, 1997. (Reprint edition.)

Lewis, Sinclair. *Main Street*. Norwalk, Connecticut: Easton Press, 1965.

Lewis, Tom. *Empire of the Air: The Men Who Made Radio*. New York: HarperCollins, 1991.

Lynes, Russell. *The Lively Audience: A Social History of the Visual and Performing Arts in America, 1890–1950*. New York: Harper & Row, 1985.

McAuliffe, Mary. *Twilight of the Belle Epoque: The Paris of Picasso, Stravinsky, Proust, Renault, Marie Curie, Gertrude Stein, and Their Friends through the Great War*. Lanham, Maryland: Rowman & Littlefield, 2014.

McCague, James. *Moguls and Iron Men: The Story of the First Transcontinental Railroad*. Norwalk, Connecticut: Easton Press, 1990.

McCullough, David. *The Path Between the Seas: The Creation of the Panama Canal, 1870–1914*. New York: Simon and Schuster, 1977.

McFarland, Philip. *Mark Twain and the Colonel: Samuel L. Clemens, Theodore Roosevelt, and the Arrival of a New Century*. Lanham, Maryland: Rowman & Littlefield, 2012.

Mellow, James R. *Invented Lives: F. Scott & Zelda Fitzgerald*. Boston: Houghton Mifflin, 1984.

Meredith, Scott. *George S. Kaufman and His Friends*. Garden City, New York: Doubleday, 1974.

Miller, Donald L. *Supreme City: How Jazz Age Manhattan Gave Birth to Modern America*. New York: Simon & Schuster, 2014.

Miller, Kristie. *Ellen and Edith: Woodrow Wilson's First Ladies*. Lawrence, Kansas: University Press of Kansas, 2010.

Miller, Nathan. *New World Coming: The 1920s and the Making of Modern America*. New York: Scribner, 2003.

Moore, Lucy. *Anything Goes: A Biography of the Roaring Twenties*. New York: Overlook Press, 2010.

Mordden, Ethan. *That Jazz! An Idiosyncratic Social History of the American Twenties*. New York: Putnam, 1978.

Morgan, Janet. *Agatha Christie: A Biography*. New York: Knopf, 1985.

Morris, Joe Alex. *What A Year!* New York: Harper Brothers, 1956.

Morris, Lloyd. *Incredible New York: High Life and Low Life from 1850 to 1950*. Syracuse, New York: Syracuse University Press, 1996.

Murray, Robert K. *The Harding Era: Warren G. Harding and His Administration*. Minneapolis, Minnesota: University of Minnesota Press, 1969.

Nasaw, David. *Andrew Carnegie*. New York: Penguin Press, 2006.

Nelson, Peter N. *A More Unbending Battle: The Harlem Hellfighters's Struggle for Freedom in WWI and Equality at Home*. New York: Basic Civitas Books, 2009.

Niven, Penelope. *Thornton Wilder: A Life*. New York: Harper, 2012.

O'Neill, Eugene. *The Collected Plays of Eugene O'Neill: Volume One*. New York: Modern Library, 1974.

Parrish, Michael E. *Anxious Decades: America in Prosperity and Depression, 1920–1941*. New York: Norton, 1992.

Perrett, Geoffrey. *America in the Twenties: A History*. New York: Simon and Schuster, 1982.

Powers, Richard Gid. *Secrecy and Power: The Life of J. Edgar Hoover*. New York: Free Press, 1987.

Raine, Craig. *T. S. Eliot*. Oxford, England: Oxford University Press, 2006.

Rampersad, Arnold, and David Roessel, eds. *The Collected Poems of Langston Hughes*. New York: Knopf, 1994.

Reed, John. *Ten Days That Shook the World*. New York: Penguin, 1977.

Roberts, Sam. *Grand Central: How a Train Station Transformed America*. New York: Grand Central Publishing, 2013.

Sann, Paul. *American Panorama*. New York: Crow, 1980.

Savage, Lon. *Thunder in the Mountains: The West Virginia Mine War, 1920–21*. Pittsburgh, Pennsylvania: University of Pittsburgh Press, 1990.

Schoener, Allon, ed. *Harlem On My Mind: Cultural Capital of Black America*. New York: New Press, 2007.

Segall, Grant. *John D. Rockefeller: Anointed with Oil*. Oxford, England: Oxford University Press, 2001.

Seldes, Gilbert. *The Stammering Century*. Gloucester, Massachusetts: Peter Smith, 1972.

Smith, Gene. *When the Cheering Stopped: The last years of Woodrow Wilson*. New York: William Morrow, 1964.

Smith, Page. *Redeeming the Time: A People's History of the 1920s and the New Deal, Volume 8*. New York: McGraw-Hill, 1987.

Stansell, Christine. *American Moderns: Bohemian New York and the Creation of a New Century*. New York: Metropolitan Books, 2000.

Stevens, Doris, ed. by Carol O'Hare. *Jailed for Freedom: American Women Win the Vote*. Troutdale, Oregon: NewSage Press, 1995.

Stewart, Jeffrey, ed. *Paul Robeson: Artist and Citizen*. New Brunswick, New Jersey: Rutgers University Press, 1998.

Sullivan, Mark. *Our Times: The United States, 1914–1918: V, Over Here*. New York: Charles Scribner's Sons, 1933.

———. *Our Times: The United States, 1900–1925: I, The Turn of the Century*. New York: Charles Scribner's Sons, 1926.

————. *Our Times: The United States, 1900–1920: VI, The Twenties*. New York: Charles Scribner's Sons, 1935.

Summers, Anthony. *Official and Confidential: The Secret Life of J. Edgar Hoover*. New York: G.P. Putnam's Sons, 1993.

Teachout, Terry. *Pops: A Life of Louis Armstrong*. Boston: Houghton Mifflin Harcourt, 2009.

Teichmann, Howard. *George S. Kaufman: An Intimate Portrait*. New York, Atheneum, 1972.

————. *Smart Aleck: The Wit, World and Life of Alexander Woollcott*. New York: William Morrow, 1976.

Tejada, Susan. *In Search of Sacco and Vanzetti: Double Lives, Troubled Times, and the Massachusetts Murder Case that Shook the World*. Boston: Northeastern University Press, 2012.

Time-Life Books, editors. *This Fabulous Century: 1920–1930, Volume III*. New York: Time-Life Books, 1969.

Tindall, George Brown. *America: A Narrative History: Volume I*. New York: W.W. Norton, 1984.

Trani, Eugene P., and David L. Wilson. *The Presidency of Warren G. Harding*. Lawrence, Kansas: The Regents Press of Kansas, 1977.

Tumulty, Joseph P. *Woodrow Wilson As I Know Him*. Garden City, New York: Doubleday, Page & Company, 1921.

Vaill, Amanda. *Everybody Was Young: Gerald and Sara Murphy, a Lost Generation Love Story*. Boston: Houghton Mifflin, 1998.

Van Drehle, David. *Triangle: The Fire That Changed America*. New York: Grove Press, 2003.

Wade, Wyn Craig. *The Fiery Cross: The Ku Klux Klan in America*. New York: Simon and Schuster, 1987.

Walworth, Arthur. *Woodrow Wilson I: American Prophet*. New York: Longmans, Green, 1958.

————. *Woodrow Wilson II: World Prophet*. New York: Longmans, Green, 1958.

Weatherford, Doris. *A History of the American Suffragist Movement*. Santa Barbara, California: ABC-CLIO, 1998.

Weinberg, Meyer. *A Short History of Capitalism*. [S.I.]: New History Press, 2002.

Wharton, Edith. *The Age of Innocence*. Norwalk, Connecticut: Easton Press, 1973.

White, William Allen. *The Autobiography of William Allen White*. New York: Macmillan, 1966.

————. *A Puritan in Babylon: The Story of Calvin Coolidge*. New York: Macmillan, 1958.

Wickes, George. *Americans in Paris: 1903–1939*. Garden City, New York: Doubleday, 1969.

Wilkerson, Isabel. *The Warmth of Other Suns: The Epic Story of American's Great Migration*. New York: Random House, 2010.

Winchester, Simon. *The Men Who United the States: America's Explorers, Inventors, Eccentrics, Mavericks, and the Creation of One Nation, Indivisible*. New York: Harper, 2013.

Yagoda, Ben. *About Town: The New Yorker and the World It Made*. New York: Scribner, 2000.

Yardley, Jonathan. *Ring: A Biography of Ring Lardner*. New York: Random House, 1977.

Zuckoff, Mitchell. *Ponzi's Scheme: The True Story of a Financial Legend*. New York: Random House.

NOTE*S*

Introduction
xi: "a punishing, postwar recession," Miller, Donald L., p. 115.

xii: "When will hate be exhausted?", quoted in McAuliffe, p. 309.

xii: "shallow, depraved, and corrupt," Bryson, p. 68.

xii: "some kind of radical depletion," quoted in Niven, p. 166.

xii: "Neither race had won," Fussell, p. 13.

xiv: "Prohibition is better," and "Why don't they pass," www.brainyquote.com/quotes/keywords/prohibition.html.

Chapter One: "Two Sheets of Flame"
3: "was very short and stocky," Bryson, p. 282.

5: "technology of haste," Boorstin, p. 102.

5: "with little regard to safety," ibid., p. 103.

6: "a national disgrace," and "made of dirt," Winchester, p. 282.

6: "By the final decade," McFarland, p. 31.

7: "a small 'mobilization army,'" www.history.army.mil/books/AMH-V2/AMH%20V2/chapter2.htm.

9: "For millions of people," McCullough, p. 614.

9: "Wall Street seemed to be," Gage, p. 18.

9: "Sales and re-sales," *WSJ*, July 4, 1919.

10: "the sidewalks were as usual thronged," Sullivan, *United States*, p. 176.

10:    "aggregation of ingenuity," and "powered the unprecedented," McFarland, p. 231.

11:    "While in Juneau Tuesday," *NYT*, July 16, 1920.

11:    "little correspondence," and, "inflated rises," Bryson, p. 208.

12:    "Fluctuations in sugar," *MWS*, p. 13.

13:    "the explosion darkened the area," Brooks, p. 1.

13:    "That was the loudest noise," quoted in Gage, p. 31.

13:    "I was sitting at my desk," quoted in ibid., p. 32.

13:    "was at the southeast corner," quoted in ibid., pp. 31–2.

13:    "'he felt a concussion," Nasaw, *Patriarch*, p. 69.

13:    "was lifted completely," ibid., p. 31.

14:    "Survivors on the street," Brooks, p. 5.

14:    "was hurled down the steps," Gage, p. 32.

14:    "For several blocks," Sullivan, p. 177.

14:    "A nearby automobile," *NYP*, "Wall Street's Unsolved Bombing Mystery," Richard Bryk, March 26, 2001. Posted in *Breaking News, Posts*.

14:    "as nine-tenths of a billion dollars," Brooks, p. 9.

Chapter Two: Homeland Security

20:    "The joint session," quoted in Reed, pp. 270–271.

21:    "were found to be carrying," and "neither man had been arrested," Bryson, 275.

22:    "one of the most notorious anarchists," quoted in Gage, p. 207.

22:    "licking the altars," quoted in Bryson, p. 280.

23:    "With his neatly trimmed beard," Gage, p. 208.

23:    "hatred of capitalism," Avrich, *Portraits*, p. 167.

24:    "[o]ne of the most difficult," Avrich, *Sacco and Vanzetti*, p. 209.

24:    "Mrs. Martin's linen closet," Wade, p. 33.

25:    "in caves in the bowels," quoted in ibid., p. 43.

27:    "blaze of revolution," and "like a prairie fire," quoted in ibid., p. 165.

27:    "announced that a plot," Daniels, p. 46.

27:    "as if something," quoted in Bryson, p. 278.

27:    "Alice [Roosevelt] Longworth," ibid., p. 46.

27:    "a terrific explosion," Murray, *Red Scare*, p. 78.

28:    "This was a big loss," Bryson, p. 279.

28:    "The more I think of it," quoted in Coben, p. 71.

29:    "initiated the first," Gage, p. 120.

29:    "most spectacular," Moore, p. 227.

30:    "2,000 REDS ARRESTED," *NYW*, January 3, 1920, p. 1.

30:    "Meetings wide open," *NYT*, January 3, 1920, p. 1.

30:    "I was sent up," quoted in Coben, pp. 228–9.

30:    "some six thousand to ten thousand," Bryson, p. 281.

31: "There is no time," *WP*, January 4, 1920, p. 4.

31: "The January raids," Murray, *Red Scare*, p. 217.

31: "halted the advance," ibid., p. 217.

32: "only 762 were ordered deported," Cannato, pp. 326–7.

32: "By then," ibid., p. 326.

32: "many domestic radicals," Murray, *Red Scare*, p. 240.

32: "complete collapse," and "The Attorney-General," quoted in Coben, p. 222.

33: "one-legged, one-armed," *NYW*, November 25, 1919.

33: "perpetual joke," ibid.

33: "The passport regulations," *NYT*, July 18, 1920.

Chapter Three: The Long, Black Night of the Spirits
40: "I came unexpectedly," quoted in Kobler, p. 119.

40: "east to Wheeling," Burns, *Spirits*, p. 105.

41: "Sometimes bartenders baptized," ibid., p. 106.

42: "organized mother love," *WCTU*.

42: "Tremble, King Alcohol," and "Young Man," *WCTU*.

43: "locomotive in trousers," quoted in Asinof, p. 227.

44: "One day a laborer," Burns, *Spirits*, p. 154.

45: "informed that there are," quoted in Behr, p. 69.

45: "pleaded, they wheedled," Mordden, p. 142.

45: "actually purchased," Burns, *Spirits*, p. 159.

46: "I do it the way," Mordden, p. 142.

46: "controlled six Congresses," quoted in Steuart, p. 11.

46: "demanding that a worldwide prohibition," Burns, *Spirits*, p. 158.

48: "[t]he air became thick," ibid., pp. 190–1.

49: "He blended two parts," Perrett, p. 176.

50: "Last Sunday I manufactured," quoted in Mordden, p. 147.

50: "Mother's in the kitchen," Kobler, p. 238.

51: "In southern Florida," Perrett, p. 175.

51: "To get started," adapted and condensed from Burns, *Spirits*, pp. 195–6.

52: "Appointments varied, of course," Burns, *Spirits*, p. 199.

53: "The headwaiters," Miller, Donald L., p. 124.

53: "Door fitters were in especial demand," Lee, pp. 55–6.

54: "never saw corpses," quoted in Furnas, *Great Times*, p. 353.

54: "speak softly shop," quoted in Cashman, p. 43.

54: "Hush! Don't 'ee sing so loud," Hardy, p. 26.

54: "Robert Benchley," Mordden, p. 134.

54: "[f]ederal officials believed," Burns, *Spirits*, p. 197.

55: "People made jokes," Burns, *Spirits*, p. 199.

55:   "it took money," *This Fabulous Century*, p. 160.
55:   "New York speakeasy owners," Cashman, p. 44.
56:   "[O]rganized crime afflicted," Fox, p. 11.
56:   "Nothing like it," Dash, p. 268.
57:   "a tightening of the throat," Bryson, p. 160.

Chapter Four: Resolutions and Sentiments
59:   "There is but one way," quoted in Parrish, pp. 138–9.
59:   "a reward for what women," Cantor, p. 151.
60:   "a large property owner," Gurko, pp. 23–4.
60:   "The governor, in response," Tindall, Volume I, pp. 92–3.
60:   "In some colonies," Gurko, p. 24.
61:   "When, in the course of human events," and following quotes from the Declaration of Sentiments and Resolutions, *DSR*, unpaginated.
63:   "It was argued," Gurko, p. 101.
65:   "The precedent was so unusual," ibid., p. 72.
66:   "protested her disenfranchisement," ibid.
66:   "With my own teeth," quoted in Gordon and Radway, pp. 157–8.
66:   "Ever the innovator," Weatherford, p. 165.
66:   "[T]all and slender," ibid., p. 113.
67:   "to take the responsibility," ibid., p. 250.
67:   "had the incredible experience," ibid., p. 251.
67:   "The women who had voted," ibid., p. 254.
67:   "Knowing that she would be tried," Seldes, p. 280.
68:   "white and frail," ibid., p. 179.
68:   "To think I have had," quoted in http://www.biography.com/people/susan-b-anthony-194905.
68:   "Both the organized women's movement," Cooper, Jr., p. 63.

Chapter Five: Civil Wrongs
70:   "We were *all* poor," and "churchpeople, thieves," and "a woman hollered," quoted in Bergreen, p. 15.
70:   "Chastized as the devil's music," Gioia, p. 31.
70:   "Does Jazz Put the Sin," quoted in Bryson, p. 69.
70:   "Those Baptist rhythms," Gioia, p. 31.
70:   "[Buddy] Bolden," ibid., p. 31.
71:   "the mournful energy," Moore, p. 45.
71:   "entered just a fraction," Bergreen, p. 205.
72:   "transformed whatever piece," ibid.
72:   "put a new piece together," quoted in Bergreen, p. 128.

73:   "He really did perform," Teachout, p. 15.

74:   "The black population in Northern cities," Green, p. 98.

75:   "The French allied forces," Horton, p. 161.

75:   "About 2 A.M.," http://www.northcarolinaroom.wordpress.com/2012/02/23/
      the-battle-of-henry-johnson.

76:   "I am of the opinion," *SEP*, August 24, 1918.

77:   "In Chicago," Weinberg, p. 213.

78:   "learned about the colonization," Archer, p. 85.

78:   "But when Marcus Garvey," Grant, p. 184.

79:   "I am President-General," quoted in ibid., pp. 77–8.

79:   "eventually claimed a circulation," Archer, p 94.

80:   "did what no black person," Grant, p. 320.

80:   "Have this day," quoted in ibid., p. 333.

80:   "Garvey intends to reorganise," quoted in ibid., p. 334.

81:   "to encourage black," http://www.bbc.co.uk/history/historic_figures/garvey_
      marcus.shtml.

81:   "Today I made myself," quoted in http://www.afropoets.net/marcusgarvey2.html.

82:   "Garvey is a West Indian Negro," quoted in ibid., p. 98.

83:   "Mr. Garvey immediately," Grant, pp. 371–2.

84:   "Garvey's and the Black Star Line's," Grant, pp. 373–4.

84:   "spectacular antics," quoted in Smith, Page, pp. 213–14.

85:   "learning to accept insult," quoted in *NAACP*, p. 2.

85:   "was not the mere gathering," ibid.

86:   "is merely the logical result," *Current Biography, 1944*, p. 742.

86:   "Father of Black History," quoted in Goggin, p. 181.

87:   "a key to our freedom," quoted in ibid., Goggin, p. 209.

87:   "Dr. Woodson often said," *NAACP*, p. 2.

Chapter Six: The Robber Barons and Their Serfs

91:   "with the regularity," Bain, p. 288.

92:   "Between a third and two-fifths," Kyvig, *Daily Life*, p. 12.

93:   "As the historian Paul Johnson," quoted in Roberts, p. 92.

93:   "the bitch-goddess SUCCESS," quoted in www.goodreads.com/quotes
      168833-the-moral-flabbiness-born-of-the-worship-of-the-bitch-goddess-SUC-
      CESS.

94:   "association of poverty," quoted in Drabelle, p. 187.

95:   "There is no right," quoted in Abels, p. 19.

97:   "We work in *his* mine," quoted in Perrett, p. 46.

97:   "forced striking miners," Savage, p. 12.

98:   "the Hatfields had tied," Savage, p 10.

98: "had been only a boy," ibid., p. 11.

98: "rather handsome young man," ibid., p. 12.

99: "The report circulated," ibid., p. 21.

100: "cutting telephone and telegraph wires," ibid. 47.

101: "The demand for coal," ibid., p. 48.

102: "between the men," quoted in McFarland, p. 413.

103: "In 1920," photo sent to author by Matewan city officials.

Chapter Seven: The Beginning of Ponzi's Dream

104: "a decidedly working-class neighborhood," Zuckoff, p. 19.

105: "that relatives weary of paying," Dunn, p. 9.

105: "dreamed aloud about," Zuckoff, p. 20.

106: "I ship stuff," and "a crate o' tomatoes," quoted Dunn, p. 9.

107: "with his growing skills," ibid., p. 9.

108: "I have no figures," quoted in ibid., p. 32.

108: "Ponzi was given a job," Zuckoff, p. 47.

109: "thin, graying, tiny," ibid., p. 31.

109: "He sold groceries," Dunn, p. 10.

111: "That night, doctors removed," pp. 53–4.

112: "Always have a goal," quoted in ibid., pp. 30–31.

112: "In April 1906," Zuckoff, p. 93.

112: "could be purchased," http://www.images.businessweek.com/ss/09/0311_madoff/3.htm.

112: "more mundane and obscure," Zuckoff, p. 93.

113: "The coupon had cost," ibid., p. 95.

114: "Sixty-six coupons," ibid., pp. 95–6.

114: "A confident tone of voice," Dunn, p. 2.

116: "salesmanship and psychology," quoted in ibid., p. 112.

118: "For every $10," Parrish, p. 221.

119: "Securities Exchange Company," quoted in Zuckoff, p. 133.

120: "DOUBLES THE MONEY," *BP*, July 24, 1920.

121: "Ponzi literally couldn't," Bryson, pp. 337–8.

Chapter Eight: The Ignoble Experiment

126: "a Hogarthian degradation," quoted in Miller, Donald L., p. 122.

127: The statistics on crime during Prohibition are provided by http://www.albany.edu/~wm731882/organized_crime1_final.html.

127: "Most often, the cutting," Burns, *Spirits*, p. 218.

128: "It did not quarrel with," ibid., p. 218.

128: "The person who drinks," quoted in Barr, p. 241.

128: "seemed a notice," Holbrook, p. 105.

129: "They should have permitted," quoted in Bryson, p. 173.

129: "Bootleggers claimed," Burns, *Spirits*, p. 219.

129: "a no-frills mixture," ibid., p. 220.

130: "a distillation of alcohol," ibid., p. 220.

130: "She just liked to drink," ibid., p. 220.

130: "people wet their whistles," ibid., p. 220."

130: "The experienced drinker," Morris, p. 36.

130: "Farm hands in the Midwest," Burns, *Spirits*, p. 221.

131: "I call it legalized murder," quoted in Mordden, p. 135.

131: "The victim of 'jake paralysis,'" Shepherd, *CW*, July 26, 1930.

132: "so vicious a poison," Burns, *Spirits*, 223.

132: "Recipes were invented," Birmingham, pp. 241–2.

133: "In 1925," ibid., p. 223.

133: "In 1927," Mordden, p. 135.

134: "During the period," Kyvig, *Repealing*, p. 24.

134: "reviewed the literature," Lender and Martin, p. 139.

135: Table of figures, and "Obviously, drinking decline," Abels, p. 87.

135: "In 1943," Lender and Martin, p. 138.

135: "seemed more clear-headed," Burns, *Spirits*, p. 280.

137: "There is less drinking," quoted in ibid., p. 282.

Chapter Nine: Planning Parenthood

138: "if any of the Republican members," quoted in Weatherford, p. 241.

139: "confidence that the [Ohio] legislature," quoted in ibid., p. 241.

139: "Many women also went," ibid., p. 241.

139: "devotion to states' rights," ibid., p. 242.

139: "that they filed suits," ibid., p. 240.

140: "conscience struck," Weatherford, p. 243.

140: "Vote for suffrage," quoted in Flexner and Fitzpatrick.

141: "Women screamed frantically," *NYT*, August 19, 1920.

141: "a point of personal privilege," and, "I changed my vote," quoted in Weatherford, p. 243.

141: "Unable, despite threats and bribery," Flexner, pp. 323–4.

142: "had no experience," Weatherford, p. 196.

143: "Carrie Chapman Catt summed it up," ibid., p. 244.

143: "Never in the history of politics," quoted in ibid., p. 242.

145: "fine, clean and honest," Gray, p. 23.

145: "Then she faced her worst test," Douglas, Emily Taft, p. 9.

146: "Have Jake sleep on the roof," quoted in Miller, Nathan, p. 264.

146: "Her standard lecture," Chesler, pp. 218–9.
146: "'What Every Girl Should Know,'" Gray, p. 43.
147: "indicative of a higher," Chesler, p. 66.
147: "insisted that existing," ibid., p. 66.
147: "The editors printed," Miller, Nathan, p. 266.
147: "The marriage bed," quoted in Gray, p. 74.
147: *The Western Watchman*, quoted in ibid., p. 75.
148: "In Defense of Assassination," ibid., p. 75.
149: "In court, however," ibid., p. 76.
149: "Don't wait to see," and "If there is," and "By taking the above," *FL*, Project Gutenberg eBook, March 26, 2010, [eBook #31790], unpaginated.
150: "where a new system," Furnas, p. 94.
151: "a brilliant pamphlet," Chesler, p. 145.
151: "However small this operation," ibid., p. 146.
151: "No other class," ibid., p. 146.
151: "The little woman," *BDE*, October 26, 1916.
152: "to do away with the Jews," *NYT*, January 5, 1917.
152: "die, if need be," quoted in Chesler, p. 153.
152: "[T]he national wire services," ibid., pp. 153–4.
153: "Regardless of the outcome," quoted in Cooper, Jr., *Pivotal Decade*, p. 207.
154: "beyond verbal instruction," ibid., p. 157.
155: "to rest and be alone," ibid., p. 158.
156: "made a curious refrain," ibid., p. 159.
157: "sought to prevent," Miller, Nathan, p. 269.
158: "[t]o purify the breeding stock," quoted in Bryson, p. 365.
158: "the surest, the simplest," quoted in ibid., p. 362.
159: "The real hope of the world," quoted in Parrish, p. 135.

Chapter Ten: The End of Ponzi's Scheme
160: "was tiny, at four foot eleven," Zuckoff, p. 79.
161: "By July 4," ibid., p. 221.
162: "recognized internationally," quoted in Zuckoff, p. 184.
163: "QUESTIONS THE MOTIVE," *BP*, July 26, 1920, p. 1.
163: "If Mr. Rockefeller," quoted in Zuckoff, p. 294.
163: "'immoral' because it would be," quoted in Dunn, p. 228.
164: "PUBLIC NOTICE," quoted in *BP*, July 27, p. 1.
165: "*EXTRA* COUPON PLAN," quoted in ibid., July 30, 1920, p. 1.
166: "DECLARES PONZI IS NOW HOPELESSLY INSOLVENT, quoted in ibid., August 2, 1920, p. 1.
167: "fabulous sum," Zuckoff, p. 228.

168: "The clerk persisted," ibid., p. 288.
168: "There are no second acts in American life," Fitzgerald, *Last Tycoon*, p. 189.
168: "A few days after," ibid., pp. 293–4.
169: "The deportation scene," Dunn, pp. 251–2.
170: "When he was down," quoted in Zuckoff, p. 310.
170: "corresponded with some regularity," ibid., p. 311.
171: "Perhaps I made a mess," quoted in ibid., p. 311.
172: "by running a small rooming house," ibid., p. 310.
172: "I hit the American people," ibid., p. 313.
172: "I am doing fairly well," quoted in ibid., p. 313.
173: "It was false hope," ibid., p. 313.
173: "a swindle in which," *The Random House Dictionary of the English Language, Second Edition, Unabridged.* New York: Random House, 1987.
174: "Ponzi was a great equalizer," *NYT*, December 15, 2008.

Chapter Eleven: The Closed Door in the White House
176: "they talked like master," Walworth, Volume I, p. 9.
176: "There were readings," ibid., p. 10.
177: "First, he wanted," Cooper, Jr., *Warrior*, p. 107.
179: "It seemed the whole," Smith, Gene, pp. 37–8.
180: "THE HIGH CONTRACTING PARTIES," *LNC*.
181: "narrow, selfish, provincial purposes," quoted in Walworth, Volume II, p. 269.
182: "I have fighting blood," quoted in ibid.
184: "Omnipotence," *LC-J*, December 9, 1916.
184: "We have petticoat government!" quoted in Miller, Kristie, p. 193.
184: "So began my stewardship," quoted in Levin, p. 344.
185: "It has been written," ibid., pp. 515–16.
185: "was petulant, irascible," Blum, p. 191.
186: "a completely discounted factor," Smith, Gene, p. 102.
186: "What this country needs," quoted in ibid., p. 102.
186: "Mme. President," quoted in ibid., p. 214.
188: "The only decision that was mine," quoted in Levin, p. 344.
188: "senators of both parties united," *NYT*, March 20, 1920,
188: "Edith withheld the news," Miller, Kristie p. 216.
189: "has been criticized," ibid., pp. 216–7.
189: "Mr. Wilson died," quoted in Smith.

Chapter Twelve: On the Air
193: "a central need," Barnouw, p. 48.
193: "Experimental stations opened in New York," Perrett, p. 229.

194: "AIR CONCERT 'PICKED UP,'" *PS*, September 29, 1920.

194: "If a retail store," quoted in Abels, p. 195.

195: "On the roof," Barnouw, p. 69.

196: "Will anyone hearing this broadcast," *KDKA*, p. 4.

196: "while . . . crowds stood," ibid., p. 4.

196: "And so it seems, ladies and gentlemen," *KDKA-CD*.

196: "many of whom," Lewis, Tom, p. 153.

196: "To increase audience," *KDKA*, p. 3.

198: "The first regularly broadcast church services," ibid., p. 2.

198: "the electronic equivalent," and "middle-class consumers," quoted in Miller, Donald L., p. 302.

Chapter Thirteen: The Ohio Gangsters

200: "In the end," Murray, p. 120.

201: "When one surveys," and other Harding Inaugural excerpts from http://www.bartleby.com/124/pres46.html.

201: "He writes the worst English," quoted in *NYTM*, "The Language Thing," Maureen Dowd, July 29, 1990.

202: "did not provide moral leadership," Trani and Wilson, pp. 191–2.

202: "had another side," Hoover, p. 48.

203: "Forbes nonetheless had earlier once," ibid., p. 429.

204: "worthless," quoted in Wish, p. 352.

204: "Forbes was indeed selling," Dean, p. 140.

204: "and even hardware," Murray, p. 460.

205: "You yellow rat!", quoted in Trani and Wilson, p. 182.

206: "Years later," Dean, p. 141.

207: "In an ironic twist," ibid., p. 141.

208: "Given the fact," Dean, p. 142.

209: "without doubt," Murray, p. 106.

209: "definitely knew about," ibid., p. 484.

210: "a gay crowd," quoted in Kramer, 434.

211: "Mystery had surrounded Smith's death," Dean, p. 144.

211: "Although Jess Smith's suicide," Murray, p. 437.

212: "illegally transferring," ibid., p. 159.

212: "maintained that he had been unaware," Trani and Wilson, p. 181.

213: "If anybody does not like," Murray, p. 482.

214: "was regarded as above suspicion," Trani and Wilson, p. 106.

215: "When the hearings commenced," Dean, p. 157.

215: "a decade of financial difficulties," Wish, p. 357.

217: "My God, this is a hell of a job," quoted in White, *Autobiography*, p. 619.

218: "the most beautiful woman," Dean, p. 26.

219: "I believe I can swing it," White, *Puritan*, p. 241.

220: "Some will say," *CDS*, Volume XLIV, Number 65, December 11, 1923.

Chapter Fourteen: The Investigation

227: "sent off to Barren Island," Gage, p. 199.

227: "Are the authorities," *NYW*, September 22, 1920.

228: "the murder hour," quoted in Brooks, p. 12.

229: "Remember, we will not tolerate," quoted in Gage, p. 171.

230: "The Anarchist Fighters," quoted in ibid., p. 172.

230: "Carusso, Abato, Ferro," Brooks, p. 15.

230: "fit nobody's picture," Gage, p. 175.

230: "neither a Sicilian," Brooks, p. 16.

231: "In the week before," Gage, p. 176.

231: "a passenger in a Hudson Tube train," Brooks, p. 16.

231: "I know when," quoted in ibid., p. 17.

232: "Lunacy Commission," quoted in Gage, p. 176.

232: "millionaires who ought to be killed," Brooks, p. 17.

232: "a lopsided gray cap," ibid., p. 18.

233: "With just a handful," Gage, p. 172.

233: "A chauffeur named," ibid., p. 197.

234: "Dupont Powder Company," and "Danger," quoted in Gage, p. 198.

234: "She told police," ibid., p. 198.

234: "It was revealed," *NYT*, September 17, 1920.

235: "[Palmer] suggested," ibid., p. 183.

236: "For a decade and more," Brooks, p. 19.

237: "notorious for its Italian criminals," quoted in Gage, p. 226.

Chapter Fifteen: Uproar in the Arts

240: "satirized Gopher Prairie," Miller, p. 64.

240: "The days of pioneering," and "a bulwark of sound religion," Lewis, p. 1.

241: "owed much of its success," Furnas, p. 83.

241: "inventing stereotypes," ibid., pp. 83–4.

242: "What is the greatest thing," quoted in Miller, p. 65.

242: "Home is the place where," quoted in Lathem, ed., "The Death of the Hired Man," p. 38.

242: "pointed at the fuzzy brown head," and "'Yump, probably be changes,'" Lewis, p. 367.

243: "This is a hell," and "How about some of that champagne," Hemingway, p. 61.

243: "For a true writer," http://www.nobelprize.org/nobel_prizes/literature/laure-ates/1954/hemingway-speech.html.

244: "Women—of whom he had expected," Fitzgerald, *Paradise*, p. 238.

245: "she wrote to him," Milford, p. 56.

245: "And she added," quoted in ibid., p. 56.

246: "practiced in front," ibid., pp. 142–3.

246: "There was no automatic," ibid., p. 383.

246: "So we beat on," Fitzgerald, *Gatsby*, p. 159.

247: "Here was a new generation," Fitzgerald, *Paradise*, p. 255.

249: "sham, spurious," Lawrence, *Rainbow*, p. 410.

249: "organised fighting," and "tumbling into the bottomless pit," ibid., p. 308.

249: "[s]he hated religion," ibid., pp. 270.

249: "The two men had," Lawrence, *Women*, p. 193.

250: "I do not claim," quoted in Pilley, W. Charles. *John Bull*, September 17, 1921.

250: "I should like to know," *LHS*, December 2, 1913.

250: "I believe the nearest," quoted in Mackenzie, pp. 167–8.

251: "savage enough pilgrimage," Carswell, book title, various references.

252: "his extravagance of personality," Morgan, p. 78.

252: "desolate, tranquil," and, "was dreary, yes," Hack, p. 65.

253: "wanted to hug someone," ibid., p. 74.

253: "The intense interest," Christie, *Mysterious Affair*, p. 193.

254: "curiously colourless," Morgan, p. 25.

255: "Apart from replying," Christie, *Autobiography*, p. 511.

256: "Hercule Poirot, a Belgian detective," *NYT*, August 6, 1975.

257: "a thin-skinned sensitive," quoted in www.googlebooks.com/?id=CnnX6jlFuf ec&pg=PA67&dq=a+thin-skinned+sensitive,+a+dithering+compass.

258: "You [Americans] will be having," quoted in Douglas, Ann, p. 181.

258: "Let us go then," Eliot, p. 13.

261: "Smoke of a brick-red dust," quoted in www.americanpoems.com/poets/ carlsandburg/12898.

263: "a curious restaurant," Manchester, p. 34.

264: "was a heavy drinker," Smith, Page, pp. 1007–8.

264: "he worked briefly," ibid., p. 1008.

264: "was based on a story," ibid., p. 1008.

264: "Only when the eye," quoted in Gelb and Gelb, pp. 261–2.

265: "overthrown by his own fear," Perrett, p. 275.

265: "striking and dramatic study," Smith, p. 1008.

265: "a simon pure uncompromising American tragedy," Gelb and Gelb, p. 634.

265: "had little plot," Perrett, p. 274.

265: "Supposing I was to tell you," O'Neill, p. 85.

266: "slut," O'Neill, 128.

266: "In its time," Gelb and Gelb, p. 638.

266: "so full of meat," quoted in ibid., p. 639.

266: "hid behind a pillar," Perrett, p. 274.

266: "I have an innate feeling," quoted in Gelb and Gelb, p. 638.

267: "Vicious Circle," quoted in Frewin, p. 36.

267: "illuminating not only the world of theatre," Hart, p. 35.

268: "nearly all famous," ibid., p. 152.

268: "[*New Yorker* art critic Murdock] Pemberton," Yagoda, p. 31.

269: "Every girl," quoted on algonquinroundtable.org/quotes.html.

269: "I know I'm drinking," and "That woman speaks, and "I like to have a martini," and "Men seldom make passes," quoted on brunerbiz.com/humour/Algonquin-round-table-quotes/high_#4.

269: "You can lead a horticulture," quoted in www.phrases.org.uk/meanings/4181000.html.

269: "I know a man," and "We wish you," quoted in Altman, p. 168.

269: "For an entire decade," Meister, p. 190.

271: "The Algonquin Round Table," quoted in Teichman, *Kaufman*, p. 64.

272: "These things don't last forever," quoted in enwikipedia.org/wiki/AlgonquinRound Table/#Decline_of_the_Round_Table.

272: "These were no giants," quoted in ibid.

273: "Americans had more steel," quoted in www.manythings.org/voa/history/173.htm.

Chapter Sixteen: The "Jass" Age

274: "Fate was a very serious musician," quoted in Bergreen, p. 144.

275: "Best dance music," quoted in Teachout, p. 53.

275: "Knowin' that my tone," quoted in ibid., p. 73.

276: "widely held to be," Bryson, p. 69.

276: "'Does Jazz Put the Sin," quoted in ibid., p. 69.

276: "a non-musical nineteenth-century slang," Goodall, p. 245.

276: "from black patois," and "as popularly applied," Mordden, p. 153.

277: "trying to explain jazz," Douglas, Ann, p. 451.

278: "Never before had that black community," Fax, p. 1.

278: "Harlem was clean," Miller, Nathan, p. 220.

278: "Du Bois encouraged Langston Hughes," Parrish, p. 220.

279: "The idea of taking a residential community," quoted in Schoener, ed., p. 79.

279: "there was another part of it," Hasse, p. 114.

279: "synonymous with the greatest Negro entertainment," ibid., p. 132.

279: "[e]legant, reserved without being stiff," quoted in Miller, Donald L., p. 504.

279: "This was no ordinary night club," Hasse, p. 102.

279: "a backdrop painted with weeping willows," Calloway, p. 88.

279: "brutes at the door," quoted in Miller, Donald L., p. 515.

280: "However Ellington felt about it," Hasse, pp. 100–101.

280: "his influence to have the owners," Miller, Donald L., p. 515.

281: "feeling like a bull moose," quoted in Morris, *Colonel*, p. 215.

281: "the nightclub capital of the world," Miller, Donald L., p. 516.

281: "Long after the cascading lights," Morris, Lloyd, p. 333.

283: "Now I can read his letters," www.songlyrics.com/mamie-smith/crazy-blues-lyrics/.

283: "for the Hammond (Indiana) pros," Stewart, Ed., pp. 44–45.

283: "The play was about an Ethiopian," Stewart, ed., p. 190.

284: "that ultimately led," ibid., p. 205.

285: "I ain't got no quarrel," and "Shall Negro sharecroppers," quoted in www.iancfriedman.com/?=284.

286: "Long before *Native Son*," Rodgers, p. 310.

286: "Mencken had made," quoted in ibid., pp. 179–180.

286: "buoyed up," quoted in ibid., p. 180.

287: "The Negro is primarily an artist," Du Bois, p. 287.

287: "Above and beyond," ibid., p. 320.

287: "English contemporaries [of Eliot]," ibid., p. 112.

288: "hoped to get from their friendship," ibid., p. 94.

288: "African guardian of souls," http://www.poemhunter.com/poem/conversion.

290: "Play that thing," quoted in Rampersad and Roessel, eds., p. 60.

290: "Shake your brown feet, honey," quoted in ibid., p. 29.

291: "O, let America be," quoted in http://allpoetry.com/poem/8495513-Let_America_Be_America_Again-by-Langston_Hughes.

291: "On the Mediterranean Sea," Jackson, ed., p. 103.

292: "slumbering but awful God," ibid., p. 144.

292: "What matters that I stormed," ibid., p. 36.

293: "a pillar of the Harlem intellectual community," Miller, Donald L., p. 517.

293: "Locke was as much in his element," Lewis, pp. 87–8.

293: "observed that European artists," Huggins, p. 80.

294: "The Negro mind," quoted in ibid., p. 116.

294: "The only safeguard," quoted in ibid., p. 115.

294: "We have tomorrow," quoted in ibid., p. 118.

295: "laid the philosophical basis," Douglas, Ann, p. 116.

Chapter Seventeen: The Flapper

296: "a hint of sexual frenzy," Bryson, p. 69.

297: "Before the First World War," Perrett, p. 157.

297: "The girl who jumped," Moore, p. 69.

297: "Originating with Southern blacks," Boardman, p. 16.

298: "which involved hopping forward," Bryson, p. 69.

298: "Everyone! Down on your heels," quoted in www.allmusicals.com/lyrics/goodnews.varsitydrag/htm.

299: "And tell me, Niel," Cather, pp. 111–112.

299: "There was a huge increase," Burns, *Smoke*, p. 175.

299: "More women now do the same work," ibid., p. 175.

300: "Particularly when smoked by women," Tate, p. 24.

300: "The amount of fabric," Bryson, p. 69.

300: "breathtaking skimpiness," Bryson, p. 69.

302: "The Roaring Twenties," quoted in Miller, Donald L., p. 529.

Epilogue

303: "has fallen into oblivion," Avrich, *Portraits*, p. 167.

304: "Once you register," Avrich, *Sacco and Vanzetti*, p. 59.

304: "You heard Galleani speak," quoted in enwikipedia.org/wiki/Luigi_Galleani.

305: "I have never heard," Avrich, *Sacco and Vanzetti*, p. 49.

305: "Attending lectures," Avrich, *Portraits*, p. 173.

306: "After selecting a target," Gage, p. 326.

307: "fits what we know of him," ibid., p. 326.

307: "my uncle's bomb," ibid., p. 326.

INDEX

INDEX

Schmedeman, Albert G., 189
Schultz, Dutch, 126
Scott, Robert T., 32–33, 235
Securities Exchange Company (SEC), 114–120, 125, 162–167
segregation, 74, 77, 81, 285
Seldes, Gilbert, 67
Seneca Falls Convention, 60–63, 143
Shepard, William C., 131
Show Boat, 284
Shuffle Along, 292–293
Simon the Cyrenian, 283
Sinclair, Harry F., 214–217
Sissle, Noble, 292
slavery, 64–66, 71
Smart Set, The, 286, 288
Smith, Bessie, 282
Smith, Gene, 179
Smith, Jesse W., 202, 207–212, 220
Smith, Mamie, 282–283
Smith, Page, 84, 264
Smoke and Steel, 261
Smoke of the Gods: A Social History of Tobacco, 299
smoking, xii, 297–301
socialists, xv, 19–20, 146–147, 156, 191, 227–228, 235–236, 240
Sons of the American Revolution, 228–229
Spanish-American War, 6–7
speakeasies, 22, 52–55, 91, 126, 132, 203, 298. *See also* entertainment
Spingarn, Joel Elias, 280–281
Spirits of America: A Social History of Alcohol, 44, 46, 52, 128, 132
sports, 39, 70–71, 198, 283–285, 295
St. Cyr, Johnny, 70
Stanton, Elizabeth Cady, 63–64, 68, 301
Stanton, Henry Brewster, 64
steel industry, 7–8, 11, 93
Stein, Gertrude, xii, 247
sterilization laws, 157
Steuart, Justin, 46
Stewart, Michael E., 21

stock market, 11, 115
stock market crash, 302
Stone, Lucy, 65–66, 68, 301
Strange Death of President Harding, The, 220
Strange Interlude, 262–263
Straton, John Roach, 129
strikes, 88–89, 94–97, 102
suffrage movement, 58–66, 138–143, 179
Sullivan, Mark, 10, 14
Sun Also Rises, The, 243
Swift, Gustavus, 45
Swig, Simon, 166–167
Swope, Herbert Bayard, 267

T

Taft, William Howard, 178
Tate, Cassandra, 299–300
Taylor, Deems, 241
Teachout, Terry, 73
Teapot Dome, 213–217
"technology of haste," 4–5
television, xvi–xvii, 198
Tell Me a Story, 254
Ten Days That Shook the World, 20
terrorism, xiii, xvii, 3–4, 9–24, 225–237, 302–308. *See also* Wall Street bombing
Tess of the d'Urbervilles, 54
Testerman, C. C., 98–100, 103
That Jazz, 133
Thayer, Webster, 22
Thirteenth Amendment, 64, 304
This Side of Paradise, 244–245, 247
Thomson, Virgil, 73
Thorpe, Herbert A., 148
Time-Life, 55
Tindall, George Brown, 60
Toohey, John Peter, 268
Toomer, Jean, 288
Torrence, Ridgely, 283
Trader's Guide, 113
Trani, Eugene P., 201, 214
Treaty of Versailles, xi, xviii, 7, 46, 179–180
Triangle Shirtwaist Factory fire, 92